M000289230

RX FOR DEER HUNTING SUCCESS

Time-Tested Tactics from The Deer Doctor

Peter J. Fiduccia

Skyhorse Publishing

Copyright © 2016 by Peter J. Fiduccia

All rights reserved. No part of this book may be reproduced in any manner without the express written consent of the publisher, except in the case of brief excerpts in critical reviews or articles. All inquiries should be addressed to Skyhorse Publishing, 307 West 36th Street, 11th Floor, New York, NY 10018.

Skyhorse Publishing books may be purchased in bulk at special discounts for sales promotion, corporate gifts, fund-raising, or educational purposes. Special editions can also be created to specifications. For details, contact the Special Sales Department, Skyhorse Publishing, 307 West 36th Street, 11th Floor, New York, NY 10018 or info@skyhorsepublishing.com.

Skyhorse® and Skyhorse Publishing® are registered trademarks of Skyhorse Publishing, Inc.®, a Delaware corporation.

Visit our website at www.skyhorsepublishing.com.

10 9 8 7 6 5 4 3 2 1

Library of Congress Cataloging-in-Publication Data is available on file.

Cover design by Tom Lau
Cover photo credit: Peter Fiduccia

Print ISBN: 978-1-5107-0500-5
Ebook ISBN: 978-1-5107-0501-2

Printed in China

Contents

POINTS TO PONDER

TIPS TO LURE BUCKS

Foreword

In his poem "The Idea of Order at Key West," Wallace Stevens evokes a young woman singing as she walks along the shoreline. As daylight fades and the wind freshens, those listening to the young woman's voice slowly come to understand that her song, as opposed to the turmoil of the threatening sea, lends certitude to their world. Stevens's narrator suggests that the woman has the ability to see and hear beyond the natural world and make sense out of nature's chaos—chaos that quails the ungifted. He explains:

> She was the single artificer of the world
> In which she sang. And when she sang, the sea,
> Whatever self it had, became the self
> That was her song, for she was the maker. Then we,
> As we beheld her striding there alone,
> Knew that there never was a world for her
> Except the one she sang and, singing, made.

What, you may ask, does any of this have to do with deer hunting? I would answer little to nothing, but it has EVERYTHING to do with Peter Fiduccia and his artistry. Like any good researcher, Fiduccia meticulously annotates his observations. Like any prudent analyst, Fiduccia painstakingly codifies his findings. And like any gifted teacher, Fiduccia deftly disseminates his hard-won knowledge to his students. But what sets Fiduccia apart is his artistry. Fiduccia, like Stevens's singer, is an artist, and as Stevens suggests, he sees and hears more than the rest of us. By hearing and seeing more, he has the ability to find order in what may seem chaos to the common mind.

Likewise, in his short story "Sonny's Blues," James Baldwin's narrator comments on the challenges and rewards of the artist—in this case a musician. What he says applies to artists of all stripes and to all those, like Fiduccia, who hear what the rest of us cannot.

> All I know about music is that not many people ever really hear it . . . But the man who creates the music is hearing something else, is dealing with the roar rising from the void and imposing order on it as it hits the air. What is evoked in him, then, is of another order, more terrible because it has no words, and triumphant, too, for that same reason. And his triumph, when he triumphs, is ours.

Fiduccia's triumph, then, is ours, too. His gift is to hear and see beyond the abilities of the less gifted. In terms of understanding the natural world—the world of the whitetail deer—where others react to the chaos with confusion and wonder, Fiduccia senses order. Where others see random actions, Fiduccia perceives patterns. Where others merely surmise and hope for the best results, Fiduccia moves with confidence born of research, experience, and perceptive intuition.

Joseph Campbell, author of the Jungian-based classic of comparative mythology *Hero with a Thousand Faces*, makes a distinction between a celebrity and a mythic hero. In Campbell's view, a celebrity—think here of most popular hunting show hosts and guests—is one who sucks in light and seeks attention: "Look at me! Look at me!" A hero, in contrast, emits light. He or she spreads illumination and shares gifts for the common good. Such is Peter Fiduccia. Each time I pick up one of Fiduccia's books or see him on YouTube, a DVD, or television, in the back of my mind I hear the strains of Aaron Copland's "Fanfare for the Common Man" start to play. He is the expert for the hoi polloi, the common man, the antidote to the "professionals" who demonstrate through their actions and attitudes that the rarified hunting experiences they recount are only for the chosen and anointed. Fiduccia is the professional for the rest of us, as he is the one who concludes in print:

> Believe me, if you hunted in the areas where most of these TV hosts hunt, you would be killing the same kinds of trophy animals. I challenge any other show hosts to hunt the pressured areas of the Northeast or New England. I'll bet none of them would go home with the kind of bucks you see them kill week after week on their shows.

He even tells you—whether or not you believe it—that "I am not a better deer hunter than you. In fact none of the so-called pros are. The only difference in everyday hunters and us is that we get more opportunities to hunt in prime areas."

Like that other mythic frontiersman from New York, Natty Bumppo, protagonist of James Fenimore Cooper's *The Leatherstocking Tales*, variously known as Leatherstocking, Hawkeye, Long Rifle, Pathfinder, and, most tellingly, Deerslayer, Peter Fiduccia merits attention for his encyclopedic knowledge, the sagacity he imparts, and the ethos of stewardship through which he delivers his insights.

Perhaps the most eloquent deer hunting story in American literature is William Faulkner's "The Old People," the precursor to his classic "The Bear." In that story, Faulkner, a deer hunter in the Delta area of his beloved Mississippi, encapsulates both the beauty of the hunt and the moral imperative incumbent upon the hunter when he describes the old hunter, Sam Fathers, instructing young Isaac McCaslin.

> At first there was nothing. There was the faint, cold, steady rain, the gray and constant light of the late November dawn . . . Then the buck was there. He did not come into sight; he was just there, looking not like a ghost but as if all the light were condensed in him and he were the source of it, not only moving in it but disseminating it, already running . . . the antlers even in that dim light looking like a small rocking-chair balanced on his head. "Now," Sam Fathers said, "shoot quick and slow."

In that simple directive, "shoot quick and slow," Faulkner captures the urgency of the hunt and the requisite obligations of the hunter. Perhaps not quite so lyrically expressed, but just as poignantly, Peter Fiduccia's works do the same for the twenty-first century reader. Fiduccia, like Faulkner, is essential reading.

—*Dabney Gray*, PhD
Associate Professor English
Stillman College
Tuscaloosa, AL

Acknowledgments

I grew up in Brooklyn, New York, where guys and gals graduated life with Ph.Ds in street smarts and common sense. Brooklyn sports included stick ball, Johnny-on-the-Pony, blackball (a rock hard, tiny black ball used for playing handball), and softball. Softball was ironically played in a school yard on a concrete field. Sliding into a base was optional, but somewhat expected. Although it was a tough neighborhood, I loved every second of living there, and growing up "Brooklyn" was the land that ultimately made me the person I am today.

In 1961, I was in my first year at Fort Hamilton High School. "The Fort," as we affectionately referred to it, is located on Shore Road in Bay Ridge. It is only a few hundred yards from a bay known as The Narrows. It is the tidal strait that forms the principal channel through which the Hudson River empties in to the Atlantic Ocean. The Narrows have long been considered to be the maritime gateway to New York City, and historically has been one of the most important entrances into the harbors of the Ports of New York and New Jersey.

I graduated from The Fort in 1964, the year the construction on the Verrazano Bridge was completed. From the windows in the school, the Verrazano's monumental 693 foot high double towers added a spectacular Birdseye view of the Bridge and The Narrows that connected Brooklyn to Staten Island. In the early sixties Staten Island was so rural that much of it was dotted with farms. It also had a lot of undeveloped areas where pheasants and other wildlife thrived, including a small population of white-tailed deer. Since that time, the white-tailed deer herd of Staten Island has swelled to considerable proportions. Today, Staten Island is known for harboring record class Boone & Crockett bucks. Because Staten Island is one of New York City's five boroughs, however, no hunting of any kind is permitted, as per a law which bans hunting within city limits.

During my three years at The Fort, I spent many Saturdays wandering through Staten Island's rural areas scouting for deer and studying other critters, instead of working more diligently on my school projects. Staten Island's deer herd was primarily responsible for causing me to spend too much time daydreaming during my classes about where my next scouting trip would take place. At the time, I never would have imagined that I would eventually end up working full-time living as an outdoor journalist, as well as being given the epithet, "The Deer Doctor" by twelve-time All Star 3rd baseman and Hall of Famer, Wade Boggs).

From the time I was about sixteen years old, once a week I would stop in a local sporting goods store (for discretionary reasons I'll call the store Nick's Sporting Goods). To my mom's displeasure, I would end up spending most of the part-time wages I earned working at Louie's Meat Market shopping Nick's Sporting Goods. My patronage to Nick's was unfailing. As an avid bass angler, I spent a lot of time fishing the two large bodies of water in New York City's Central Park. It seemed that every week I added yet another Arbogast bass lure to my ever bulging Arbogast bass lure collection. Even though I hadn't gone deer hunting yet each month I would buy a gun-cleaning kit, a Hot-Seat, or some other hunting related item to add to my assemblage of hunting products. Even today, I can still smell the pungent odors of new leather boots, gun cleaning solutions, wool clothing, and other familiar pleasant odors of that store. They remain firmly implanted in the nerve cells in my olfactory bulb.

Arriving at Nick's Sporting Goods one day, I was startlingly greeted by a sign heavily scotched taped to the inside of the front door: *"Closed for good, ran off with my brother's wife. We won't be back!"* Fifty-three years later, I still get agitated each time I recall reading that blasted sign. Because I could not accept the fact the "Nick" chose his brother's wife over his dutiful responsibility to keep his sports store open, I desperately hoped that his brother quickly found him and the tall, blonde, and blue-eyed Norwegian Viking damsel that he absconded with. I mused to myself, if "Nick" survived that encounter, he would certainly have to come back and reopen his store. I thought it was a flawless assumption, but my reasoning would prove to be surprisingly incorrect. I suppose life has its tribulations and miseries.

Actually, at the time, rumor had it that his brother wasn't in the least bit interested in locating double-crossing Nick or his betraying Viking wife. So the store remained closed during the several remaining years I lived in Brooklyn. Friends who still live in the area have told me the sporting goods store has been a Chinese restaurant for the last thirty years. The details of this anecdote are true to the best of my recollection. The fictitious name of the sporting goods store I used was included on *purpose*. I suspect you can guess why.

On a more serious note, I didn't realize it then, but I had no conscious attraction or deep understanding about why I had a desire to stalk deer. All I knew was that I was drawn to the hunt like a moth is drawn to fire. And so, my destiny was unknowingly already aligned the white-tailed deer without me realizing it at that time. When I contemplate how deer hunting was in 1961, and how it is now, I can assure you that deer hunting information and tactics were nothing close to what they are today. Deer hunting was much more basic in the 1950s and 1960s. At that time, hunters bought a hunting license, a set of red and black plaid wool trousers and jacket, a pair of leather boots, gloves, a hat, a firearm, perhaps a scope and binoculars, ammo and a compass. They then set off into the woods to sit on a stump for a few hours, simply waiting for a buck to amble by. When a buck didn't happen to go past their deer stand, it was customary for a group of hunters to get together and put on a deer drive.

Only a scant few hunters—really only those who were fur trappers—even used deer scents back then. A majority of hunters knew little, if anything at all, about mock scrapes or rubs. Nor did hunters understand how bucks used their tarsal glands. To the best of my recollection the use of a grunt call was nearly nonexistent in the mid-sixties. Hunters could have never imagined back then that the primary grunt had sub-sounds of the primary grunt vocalization, and that each sub-sound that was communicated meant something different to other deer. That kind of detailed anatomical, biological, and behavioral information would need two more decades to reach to the masses of deer hunters nationwide.

Going back fifty-five to sixty-five years ago (the 1950s and 1960s), hunters in deer camps didn't gather around the fireplace and discuss subjects like; moon phase theory; overhead and underfoot. Back then if a hunter talked about hunting funnels, inside corners, the three phases of the rut, stalking the edges, rattling, creating mock rubs and scrapes, food-plots, and other cutting edge strategies (all topics that are commonly discussed and understood by a majority of today's hunters), his hunting companions would not have *understood* or *even believed* a single word he said. Not that it would have mattered to them much, as they would have tossed him out of the cabin door long before he was finished talking. He would have surely been thought of as an alien from Mars in any deer camp of that era.

In comparison, today deer hunters are armed to the teeth with information about deer biology, anatomy, behavior, and tactics. The web is full of chatrooms discussing every possible interpretation, analysis, or view on all types of deer hunting strategies. They have the latest technology in Two-Way Radios, flashlights, GPS devices, and other electronic gear. Hunters purchase camo clothes, rubber boots, deer calls, rattling antlers, deer scents, portable treestands, decoys, scent eliminators, and countless other deer hunting goods. These items are no longer viewed by hunters as simply products. Instead they are justifiably seen as hunting *tools* to provide them with top-notch deer hunting strategies.

As I sit here writing this, fifty-three years after my first deer hunting encounter, I find my bond to the white-tailed deer more firm than ever before. I'm astonished that the connection between this grand animal and me has truly come to pass for a boy from Brooklyn in the way that it has. With each new book I pen, my goal is to extend myself as an author in the candid hope of becoming better at my craft. As with past books I have written, I enjoyed composing my latest whitetail book, *Rx to Whitetail Hunting Success*, and I hope you will enjoy reading it and that you will garner some useful information from it as well.

In the acknowledgements section I get to thank all the folks who have helped in over the years in my writings, and in my other media ventures. The people that I owe the *most gratitude* to however, is you, my loyal and appreciated readers. You have allowed me to take an incredible and unimaginable journey over the last three plus decades. And so, within this space I want to formally acknowledge and express my genuine gratefulness to you all. I am humbled by your support. I assure you it hasn't gone unnoticed or unappreciated by me.

There are also other people that I want to salute here to whom I owe accolades and my gratitude. I hope I didn't miss someone, but if I did, please accept my apologies.

- **Leo and Ralph Somma:** You are both my *treasured* companions. I think of you both as my brothers rather than my cousins. It is hard to describe how much I value our bond.
- **Joseph and Lucy Fiduccia:** Every day I miss you both more than the day before.
- **Ed Rodriguez:** Even though your incredible demanding schedule as the CFO of Creation Entertainment only allows us to see each other a couple of times a year (mostly during the Las Vegas Star Trek Convention), you are my *best friend* and an incredibly loyal, generous, and cherished buddy.

- **Ted Rose:** You are a kind and generous person and a terrific whitetail photographer. Thank you for your support, and for the privilege to use your images within my writings.
- **Jay Cassell:** You are the personification of the words loyal, dependable, and trustworthy. You are also my most trusted advisors and my most guarded of friends.
- **Chuck Adams:** Thanks for your support and your valued friendship over the last three decades.
- **Tod Alberto:** Thank you for your continued support I sincerely appreciate it.
- **And:** Tony Lyons, Art Aldrich, Ed Best, many thanks to you all.

Chapter 1

Revealed: Why Older Bucks Don't Breed Most Does

It was November 15, 2014, the opening day of New York State's firearms season. I spent most of the morning hunting a stand called Porqupine on the north side of our land. During the five hours I was in the blind, I saw sixteen does and three young antlered bucks. Each buck accompanied a different group of does. While watching a raggedy six-point buck chasing one of the adult does back and forth through the woods fifty yards from my blind, I thought to myself, *I hope this guy doesn't get lucky and end up breeding that doe!* As Lady Luck would have it, the buck finally wore the doe down, mounted her, and did his business. As they scampered off into a tangle of brush, I found myself thinking how many misconceptions there are about which bucks actually get to breed during the three phases of the rut.

I was deep in thought about that when I glanced at my watch. "Wow, it's 11 a.m.," I mumbled to myself. It was time to change stands. After eating a quick lunch, I headed up to a blind called Big View that overlooks more than twenty-five acres of fields, many of which are planted in a variety of food plots. Over the summer, we had video-taped nine adult bucks sporting good headgear as they regularly fed in the food plots throughout the season. Two of the bucks that I nicknamed "The Boys" had terrific sets of antlers, and I was more than reasonably sure they were at least four and a half years old. All the other antlered bucks were probably two and a half to three and a half years old; all of them had eight-point racks.

Photo Credit: Ted Rose.

By 2 p.m. I had seen more rutting activity by younger bucks. One was a large four-pointer who refused to let any of the does eat peacefully as they came into the food plots. He chased several does for more than thirty minutes before one adult doe who had enough of his immature harassment turned, got up on her two back legs, and kicked the living snot out of the poor young buck's head. As it turns out, it didn't frighten the buck in the least. In fact, it emboldened him. He slammed into her ribcage with his antlers, and as she recovered from the shock, he tried to mount her.

I was so engrossed in observing the action that I nearly missed an eight-point buck watching the whole thing take place from the edge of our refuge. He was one of the smaller eight-points we had seen during the summer but not one of the nine bucks we were interested in hunting. When I looked back at the four-point buck, he was again trying to mount the doe. This time, she accepted his advances. I'm not sure she liked him, but she had enough of his harassment and just wanted him out of her way so she could settle down and eat. The eight-point witnessed what took place without making a single attempt to chase off the four-pointer or to try and service the doe himself.

Therein lie the facts about which bucks get to breed does during the rut. Despite what many hunters believe or assume, not all female deer are bred by the so-called "dominant" buck or other adult bucks with impressive antlers. At my deer hunting seminars, I regularly hear comments—mostly by hunters practicing quality deer management—along the lines of, "Sometimes I pass on taking an adult buck with exceptional antlers so he can pass on his genes." The truth is that such speculations and deer management practices are off base and rarely accurate.

There is no doubt that a majority of female deer in any given herd are bred by

Research suggests that older bucks, particularly those past their prime, may not service as many does as once believed. Photo Credit: Ted Rose.

adult bucks and not younger bucks, especially males between one and a half and two years old. Countless research studies have confirmed that. However, could this mean only large-antlered bucks get to pass on their genetics and yearlings don't? The real question is whether mature bucks actually service as many female deer as is generally assumed by hunters. Studies on this subject do suggest that adult bucks with run-of-the-mill (mediocre) sets of antlers will breed more does than was once believed. In other words, average-antlered bucks sire more fawns than trophy-class antlered bucks.

In my research on this subject, it appears that most biologists agree that when it comes to Mother Nature's rule of natural selection, average is the norm and the trump card. As described in Dictionary.com, natural selection is "A process fundamental to evolution as described by Charles Darwin. By **natural selection,** any characteristic of an individual that allows it to survive to produce more offspring will eventually appear in every individual of the species, simply because those members will have more offspring."

While I may not have been an A student at Fort Hamilton High School in Bay Ridge, Brooklyn, I did well in the sciences. I recall enjoying reading about the rule of natural selection and how it made perfect sense to me. Natural selection is the steady progression by which biological traits become more or less common in any given species as a consequence of inherited genes or traits. Simply, natural selection is the key mechanism of evolution.

If you need more evidence, all you have to do is take a close look at the human species. It is definitely

Charles Darwin.

In 1858, Charles Darwin and Alfred Russell Wallace published a new evolutionary theory, which was explained, in detail, in Darwin's On the Origin of Species (1859). Darwin based his theory on the idea of natural selection. Photo Credit: Canstock Photo Inc./ RonRowan.

more common to see average-looking couples who will bear ordinary-looking off-spring than couples like Brad Pitt and Angelina Jolie would bring forth. Do you need further convincing? There was a program on The Discovery Channel that documented when men looked at pictures of a group of women and asked to select the most appealing face, they repeatedly chose the most ordinary face as the most attractive. Understanding the meaning of natural selection helps one understand why it is feasible to believe more female deer are bred by bucks with less-than–eye-popping antlers than once believed. Average reigns within the animal kingdom, and antlered bucks sire more offspring than trophy-class antlered bucks do.

Following this logic a step further, it seems reasonable to say that hunters who practice selective removal by passing a quality antlered buck to let that buck pass on his genetics may indeed be making a miscalculation. Should they be steadfast in pursuing a selective management program, however, they should be prepared at least to accept the findings of many research studies. Such papers basically state that to improve a herd's genetics, managers must concentrate intensely on perfecting their selective removal program because exceptional breeding success is particularly random.

Female deer, particularly adult does like the one seen here, will very often select bucks with average size antlers to breed with. Photo Credit: Canstock Photo Inc./RonRowan.

In reading an article about the annual Southeast Deer Study Group meeting in Mobile, Alabama, that took place more than a decade ago, I read that researcher Randy W. DeYoung stated, "The most successful breeders are usually nothing special to look at." DeYoung and his other research team members had studied a herd of whitetail deer on a three-thousand-acre piece of property. The land was fenced, but DeYoung referred to the fence as "a strong suggestion rather than an actual barrier."

The age class of the bucks on the property was skewed toward younger deer with yearlings making up about 45 percent of the males. Bucks that were three and a half years old or older made up about 30 percent of the male population. From 1992 to 2001, the herd's buck-to-doe ratios ranged from an amazing one to one to an equally impressive one to two and a half.

Over the time the study took place, researchers collected blood samples, muscle tissue, and antler tissue to acquire a dossier of DNA markers. The samples were gathered by three methods: from shed antlers, from deer killed by hunters, and from trapped deer. Live deer were tagged, antlers were given identifications, and pictures and video were taken to help researchers recognize and age different bucks. In the end, when the researchers were finished cataloging the DNA samples and comparing them with new DNA samples from year to year, they were able to categorically identify which bucks did the breeding during the fall rut. They sampled 441 different deer and knew the exact age of 265 of them. They recorded DNA from 145 deer, 53 of which were bucks. Of the DNA-identified bucks, the research team knew the precise age of 35 individual bucks. At that time of the study (2001), the 35 bucks had sired 91 fawns.

By now you're wondering which bucks did the breeding? The study determined that reproductive success was highest for the adult bucks. About 65 percent of the breeding was done by bucks that were three and a half years old even though they only accounted for 30 percent of the buck population in the study. Yearling bucks sired 12 percent of the fawns even though they accounted for 44 percent of the bucks within the study. I would speculate that is a figure most hunters would more than likely be surprised by, given the fact most think yearling four-points, spikes, and other small-antlered bucks don't do any or very little of the breeding.

According to DeYoung, "By far, the bucks' median (average) age for reproduction was two and one-half years." When the successful breeding bucks' data was compared to bucks likely to be sires, the team of researchers documented that only 20 percent of all the bucks within the study were actually breeding during any given year. More astonishingly, even if a buck was successful in breeding a doe, and some bucks in the study did produce multiple fawns, the data recorded that on average, most bucks didn't reproduce more than one fawn in their lifetimes.

DeYoung reported that buck number 141 sired thirteen fawns from 1994 to 2000. "This guy wasn't much to look at for antlers, but he must have been a heck of a dancer. He was the ultimate. He never sired many fawns in a single year, but he was consistently successful."

The most surprising data to come out of the research was that the most imposing bucks within the study herd actually never reproduced. DeYoung stated about one buck, "He carried a very high-scoring rack, but we found no evidence he ever sired a fawn." Another big-antlered buck did have some breeding success. DeYoung reported buck number 166 had a gross Boone & Crockett score of 160 inches when it was found dead. The buck had sired nine fawns in three years.

The well-known and highly respected Valerius Geist, Professor Emeritus of Environmental Science, Faculty of Environmental Design, University of Calgary, felt that some of the older adult bucks opt out of breeding. His theory is based on his belief that when older mature bucks try to breed, they are severely beaten up by more fit and aggressive bucks.

When Professor Geist did a study on mule deer herds that were not hunted, he discovered some huge bucks would not challenge other bucks for breeding rights. Some

impressive bucks would actually seek cover and hide from bucks that were potential foes. These bucks remained in the area, however. Professor Geist felt that they hung around in hopes that a breeding opportunity would develop that they could capitalize on.

Like Professor Geist, I have seen this type of older buck behavior with whitetails. I have videotaped bucks with average antlers breeding a doe within sight and close range of an adult buck whose antlers were significantly larger. Whether those older bucks remain docile

Research done by Professor Valerius Geist discovered that adult mule deer bucks that were living in nonhunted herds often did not take to task lesser antlered bucks for breeding rights. Photo Credit: Depositphotos.

because they are too old to fight or because they are timid by personality—or a combination of both elements—is yet to be determined. But the behavior certainly exists.

Interestingly, Professor Geist discovered when older bucks avoid getting into fights, they preserve their energy during the rut. Over my 50 years of deer hunting, I too have noticed some older bucks will avoid physical confrontation. Once the breeding season has passed, they are in reasonably good physical condition and have a shorter period of recovery from injuries and weight loss. This, in turn, means they will be better prepared to survive a harsh winter and emerge in the spring in prime condition to grow yet another set of impressive antlers.

On the flip side, Mother Nature is not always kind to aggressive breeding bucks. She has them pay a hefty toll for being one of a herd's breeders. They enter the worst time of year, winter, in poor physical condition. They are most often riddled with injuries, suffering from pain, malnourished, and weak. They enter a serious recovery mode to make it through the winter. Should they survive, they will start spring in such poor condition that there isn't much nourishment left in their bodies to grow a quality set of antlers. But like any high school teenager, they feel as if they are made of steel and go into the next rut as aggressively as they did the prior breeding season—ready to fight for the right to sire with does.

By now it should be obvious that buck breeding success within any given herd is arbitrary and haphazard. With that said, however, I guarantee I'll still have trouble in my future whitetail seminars convincing hunters and landowners that the largest antlered and oldest bucks don't do all the breeding of female deer.

Nothing about whitetails is ever written in stone. No doubt new insights, studies, research, and papers will continue to try to sort out this issue even further. For me, my lab is our farm. From fifty-one years of studying, hunting, reading, and videotaping whitetail deer, I have inherently come to learn about their biology, behavior, and anatomy. On this subject I stand fast on the fact that not all big-bodied, large-antlered adult bucks breed the majority of does—just like not all large-antlered bucks only make big rubs.

Much older bucks like the one shown here like the buck shown here, are generally assumed to breed a majority of the does. However, research has brought to light contradictory investigative information. Photo Credit: Ted Rose.

Chapter 2

Mother Nature Sets Rut Dates—Not the Moon

When it comes to proliferation of her animals, Mother Nature's law is to leave as little to chance as possible. This rule applies to all living organisms. In order to pass on their genetic markers, each species' breeding behaviors, biology, pregnancy gestation period, and birth of the offspring is carefully preordained by Mother Nature. Whitetail deer are known as seasonal short-day breeders. Basically, that boils down to the fact that the timing of the birth of fawns is vital for the species' propagation and existence.

In every book and magazine article I have written since 1991, I have discussed the rut and its timing, biology, and behavior ad nauseam. I do so in hopes of enlightening hunters to the fact that the rut's timing is incredibly reliable. I also try to dispel the many age-old rumors regarding the rut.

Some of my pet peeves about the rut are the falsehoods circulated by well-meaning but misinformed hunters and, worse yet, vendors who like to sell their products. A few of the more frustrating claims include that cold weather is

During the peak rut it doesn't matter what phase the moon is in—bucks will seek out receptive does. Photo Credit: Ted Rose.

Photo Credit: Depositphotos.

the key factor in initiating the rut, the moon plays a major role in the timing of the rut, or the breeding cycle of the rut can be different in a northern part of a state than it is in the southern part of the same state. As I have said countless times, if you believe any or all of the above, please call me. I have a bridge to sell you—an expensive bridge, in fact.

The fact is, these environmental prompts are not reliable cues for Mother Nature, and therefore they are not adaptive in nature, although some whitetail authorities insist these things—moon phase, temperature, cloud cover, and so on—adjust the timing of the reproductive cycle, or rut, of the whitetail deer. There are no scientific research studies or legitimate documentation by scientists, biologists, or other experts in the field that support such claims.

In my last book, *Whitetail Tactics—Cutting Edge Strategies That Work*, published by Skyhorse Publishing, I included a chapter titled "Anatomy of the Rut: Real World Timing." It provided not only information about the rut and elements about its genesis but also included two charts that provided state-by-state and province-by-province peak days and weeks of the primary rut. This information was included to help hunters estimate when they could expect prime rutting behaviors of bucks and does.

This chapter expands on that analysis. It is based on research about the correlation between when the whitetail's rut starts throughout different latitudes in North America and the crucial link of each related to fawn birth, survival, and physical development. This information is essential to any hunter who not only wants to be a more informed deer stalker but also wants to capitalize on knowing more about the rut and understanding why it is so reliable.

Does give birth to fawns in spring in order to provide their offspring with the greatest opportunity for survival. Photo Credit: Canstock Photo Inc.

Because of the importance of the whitetail's breeding and birthing schedule, reliable cues are essential to trigger the onset of reproductive activity, or the rut. What Mother Nature relies on is decreasing daylight, more accurately referred to as a photoperiod. Photoperiodism is the proportion of daylight to darkness. This is a fail-safe natural trigger of the rut. In the fall, declining daylight to increasing darkness is going to take place no matter what (barring, of course, some supernatural catastrophe). In other words, nature has to depend on an unwavering cue card that is sure to set off the genesis of the rut year-in and year-out.

Therefore, regardless of the deer's environment, the whitetail doe's anatomy is tailored to become impregnated at an appropriate time in the fall so the fawns will be born during spring when their survival is more likely. The pregnancy usually lasts about six and a half to seven months, or 195 to 210 days, with the average being about 200 days.

Hopefully by now it is clear that there is no adaptive logic to support any other theories—moon phase and so on—about the rut. If it weren't for the foolproof prompt of photoperiodism, breeding and birthing would fluctuate dramatically from year to year and from one area to the other. Fluctuations this wild in the rut would result with does giving birth to fawns in absurdly early or ridiculously late times of the year. Both those early and late dates would result in low rates of fawn survival.

According to Charles Darwin, of whom I am fond of quoting, the "law of natural selection" must step in to reduce poorly timed breeding seasons for whitetails. By the law of evolution, wildly swinging whitetail breeding dates or other unreasonable cues have proven to be negative evolutionary traits, and therefore those whitetails are dropped from the genetic pool because offspring born early or late most often perish. Using the words law and evolution together can often cause confusion, as the words law and theory have very different meanings. In science, however, their meanings are similar. A theory is an explanation backed by "a considerable body of evidence," while a law is a set of regularities expressed in a "mathematical statement." A law explains what will happen under certain circumstances, while a theory explains how it happens. When I wrote about the importance of latitude and longitude being a major triggering factor for the onset of the rut, I stated that the breeding cycle of the whitetail has a small window of occurrence in the northern-most ranges to a longer window of occurrence in the southern parts of its range. As mentioned in that chapter, deer living north of 36° latitude breed from mid-October to mid-December with the peak of the primary rut taking place in mid-November.

Please write those time frames down in stone if you live anywhere in North America above the 36° latitude mark; places north of the 36° latitude cover a tremendous portion of the United States and Canada. In this case, fawns are born during late May

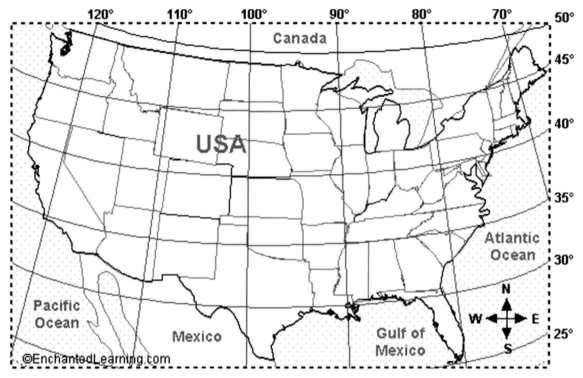

Photo Credit: Enchantedlearning.com.

and early June. If you do the math backward counting the days, you will confirm when the peak of the rut takes place.

As noted above, southern breeding of whitetails generally has a more generous window of breeding activity (please note I use the word generally because the statement isn't written in stone). In the latitudes between 28° and 36°, a majority of the herd will breed in late September and as late as March. That doesn't mean that some southern deer don't breed in November, because they do. Most, however, breed from December to January.

Traumatic Elements

There are many stressful factors that can stall, diminish, or even cancel all or part of a white-tailed deer's breeding cycle. Some breeding cycles can even be drawn out, but an extended rut is one of the worst possible scenarios, as it not only leads to high fawn birthing fatalities, but it also takes a heavy toll on the adult bucks and

One of the primary factors that is often responsible for delaying or ending the breeding season and/or having a doe miss her cycle is deep snow depth. Photo Credit: Canstockphotos

does. Other factors include lack of quality foods, excessive accumulation of deep snow, prolonged ice coverage, high herd population numbers, heavy predation, and so on. These factors can all lead to a delay in the peak of the rut, sometimes causing it to be off by a week or more.

Well-Balanced Herds

Deer herds that are nutritionally healthy are well balanced. They have stable buck-to-doe ratios that enhance the social order within the herd. A well-managed social order among female deer within a herd helps maintain calm and stability during fawning. Veteran does generally breed earlier than does breeding for the first time, which explains the importance of the first rut, commonly referred to as the early-to-mid-October pre-rut, when some of the oldest does breed. This social behavior helps to disperse females raising fawns over a wider area within their given range, thereby reducing stress within the female deer population. The more experienced older does have their fawns first, followed by younger females that develop their own fawning grounds in neighboring areas. In a behavior similar to dispersal, female deer that are giving birth for a second time move up to a quarter-mile away to have their fawns. This behavior helps expand the new fawning ground areas traditionally not used by other older does within the herd.

Interestingly, bucks play a role here, too. When it comes to bucks being aggressive during the rut, they often pick fights within their age class and antler size. To make the rut well ordered, a buck's age also plays an important role by keeping the breeding season less combative and more orderly. While DNA studies verify that some adult bucks (not the oldest) tend to do some mating, several research studies have proposed that breeding females often prefer to mate with bucks close to their own age.

In heavily hunted areas where the average adult buck may be younger than elsewhere, mature does will often evade the romantic overtures of younger bucks. Unfortunately, this could be a factor that not only delays mating but also creates a frenzied rut by young bucks that spend their entire day and night chasing does. Obviously, this could lead to a lot of stress and weight loss by female deer at a time when winter is approaching and they will need every ounce of strength they have.

I have also read that noted professor and researcher Karl V. Miller hypothesizes that prime glandular scent pheromones left at rubs and scrapes by mature bucks within a given herd excite does and bring them into their estrus cycles earlier than normal. These factors and a host of other similar elements can lead to a tumultuous rut that generates feverish competition among does to secure fawning grounds, which can lead to increased fawn mortality.

Conclusion

The overriding factor about the onset of the whitetail's breeding season is clearly regulated by photoperiodism, an evolutionary adaptation that provides for does fawning during the preeminent time of spring. Given the extreme importance of the timing of the breeding season, birthing dates that are late or early can be directly related to poor herd structure. It is not the moon phase, a warm spell, or any of the other ill-founded theories given about when, where, and why the rut will take place. Instead, all the stress-related factors I mentioned are scientifically proven reasons for altering the dates of the whitetail's breeding cycle. To prevent an untimely rut, then, a herd must be kept in good nutrition, as proper herd populations reduce stress levels. Luckily, most deer herds in North America fall within good parameters, as evidenced by the continued success of the whitetail deer throughout the United States and Canada.

Because of the general good health of deer, you can bet the farm on when the rut will take place. Each of the three phases of the whitetail's breeding season—pre-, primary, and late ruts—north of 36° latitude will occur this year, next year, and for years to come reliably from mid-October to mid-December. The pre-rut will take place in mid-October, the primary rut will happen in November (the 13 to the 17, give or take a few days), and the late rut will occur mid-December. Plan your hunts and tactics accordingly—the reliability is assured.

Photoperiodism is the sole trigger of the white-tailed deer's breeding season. Photo Credit: Depositphotos.

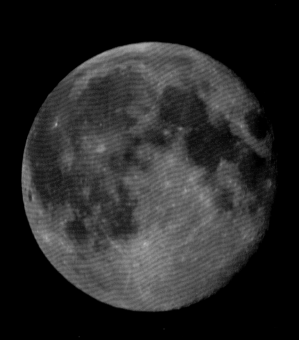

Chapter 3

Scientific Research Debunks Moon Phase Theories

There is no doubt that there is a continuing stream of information about the benefits of hunting by moon positions, or phases, and how they affect deer behavior. Some of the moon phase theories regarding deer include general movement, high and low activity levels, the breeding season, and the most controversial position of all, the moon's influence on the exact timing of the breeding season, or rut.

Each year you'll see magazine articles that tout how hunters can chart the powerful influence of the moon on ocean tides and tie various phases of the moon to help forecast the primary times to hunt deer. It is said certain natural forces of the moon act as triggers that influence deer behavior.

Over the past two decades, researchers have studied the reaction of deer and other wildlife to changes

This image is of a Waxing Gibbous moon phase. The debate is whether or not different moon phases can ensure a hunter's success. Photo Credit: Canstock Photo Inc.

Photo Credit: Canstock Photo Inc.

in the position of the moon and sun and have presented thought-provoking observations about hunting deer in relation to various phases of the moon.

So, can keeping track of the different phases of the moon really provide an advantage to ensure a deer hunter's success? That is an enigma yet to be determined with any authenticity by the scientific community. With that said, though, there are some observers who steadfastly fix a definite correlation between why deer and other animals move less during daylight hours and increase their movements at dusk. Their observations note that deer activity is greater when the moon is full, therefore hunting during the daylight hours after a full moon "can yield excellent results." Furthermore, according to those who support moon phase tactics, any hunter who is keenly aware of the different phases of the moon will be in an enhanced position as to when he or she can expect to see an increase in deer movement or activity.

Moon Phase Deer Hunting

Today, many hunters are still convinced that to be successful they need to watch the moon phases to accurately predict deer activity. I offer this thought: Hunters are apt to predict deer movement and activity much more accurately by simply understanding weather movement or front patterns. For me, the most disconcerting propaganda spewed by moon phase devotees is their resolute assertion that the moon doesn't only have an impact on deer activity; its various phases have a direct effect on deer breeding activity. Their assertion is that a female deer's reproductive cycle is influenced by the different phases of the moon, and their period peaks in the three or four days surrounding the second full moon after the autumnal equinox.

I'm particularly annoyed by this particular moon phase claim. Therefore, I respectfully put forth the following rebuttal. Admittedly, a lot of research is still being done to demonstrate that the deer's rutting activity is governed by a phase of the moon. To date, however, the research has not been accompanied by any valid

The latest research regarding moon phase as it relates to a doe's reproductive cycle has not been supported by documentation. Photo Credit: Canstock Photo Inc.

documentation that has been universally accepted by the scientific community. The scientific fact is straightforward. The mating season of deer is solely governed by the onset of photoperiodism—not the moon phase. Count on it being the primary genesis of initiating the rut. By now you must realize that I don't place a lot of confidence in the moon dictating the precise dates of activity levels in the whitetail rut. While it is possible that a particular moon cycle might happen to coincide with an active rut one year more than another, basing my hunting strategies and my valuable hunting time to align with different cycles of the moon is beyond what I'm willing to support, at least to the level that a few other whitetail authorities endorse.

I concede that the gravitational pull of the moon is strong and that its pull affects many natural wonders in our world. There is no doubt in my mind about that. Some years ago, researchers from the University of Georgia's School of Forest Resources examined if the moon's lunar phases affect the timing of the whitetail deer's breeding season and their behavior. The researchers wanted to find out if deer hunters should concentrate their hunting strategies during a full, new, or partial moon. They also wanted to discern if any of the moon's cycles, or phases, actually make a difference related to activity, breeding, or signaling when a doe has her estrus period.

David Osborn, Dr. Karl Miller, and Robert Warren, UGA wildlife research biologists, used breeding date data from a variety of state wildlife agencies to determine if the moon phases had any effect on whitetail doe estrus cycles and, therefore, the rutting activities and behavior of bucks. Breeding dates were gathered from captive deer in four states and more than two thousand free-ranging does in seven others. This information was compiled during a period that stretched nineteen years. It was then compared to lunar cycles throughout the birth date ranges of deer.

"We would expect annual breeding dates for a population to be similar if the calendar date and therefore the same length of daylight, was the driving influence," explained Osborn. "We would expect annual breeding to be less similar if moon phase is the driving influence because a particular moon phase might vary as much as twenty-eight days across a year."

Matt Knox, Virginia's deer project leader, said, "It's really impossible to choose a specific date because of a variety of outside factors. I'd say that November 15 is a pretty consistent date for the peak, but it's going to vary a few days on either side." These results confirm what I wrote about these specific dates thirty years ago in my first book, *Whitetail Strategies—A No-Nonsense Approach to Successful Deer Hunting*, in 1995.

Dr. Warren of the University of Georgia said, "The timing of the rut is influenced by various factors, but moon phase doesn't appear to be one of them." Dr. Warren went on to state, "weather, food availability, human activity, and a variety of other factors all play a role in the timing of the rut, but breeding activity typically happens within a relatively predictable period, no matter what the moon phase happens to be. It is controlled far more by the length of daylight than anything else."

Deer biologist Gary Levigne, who works with Maine's Department of Inland Fish and Game, contributed to the UGA study, and he echoed the theory that the "timing of the rut is based almost entirely on photoperiodism."

I was most impressed with an article I read in *Deer and Deer Hunting* magazine in March 2014 entitled "Eclipsing the Moon Theory." The piece was written by Jeremy Flinn, a Master of Science from Mississippi State University; Dr. Steve Demarais, Professor at MSU and Co-Director of the MSU Deer Lab; and Dr. Bronson Strickland, Associate Professor at MSU and Co-Director of the MSU Deer Lab. I strongly recommend you get this issue of *Deer and Deer Hunting* and read this well-composed editorial.

The article basically begins by informing the reader, "Many hunters believe these [moon phase] theories so much they plan their hunting trips around the moon phase or positioning. In fact, millions of dollars are spent every year on moon-influenced products, such as calendars, books, and even trail cameras with moon phase stamping on photos. There's a lot of marketing hype, but has scientific evidence ever supported these claims?"

The article goes on to discuss deer activity, the rut, and moon phases.

I will include a few summation and conclusion comments from the article that strengthen my long-held ideas on this subject.

Each deer season, countless hunters plan their hunt around a phase of the moon or its positioning, despite the hard-core scientific evidence claiming "No studies support the theory that moon phases affects deer activity and/or deer movement."

One caption in the piece read, "No studies support the theory that the moon affects deer activity or movement. The rut will remain relatively consistent from year to year." A sidebar within the article went on to say: "Moon theory advocates examine several pieces of the moon. From moon phase to illumination, the trouble with the moon theory doesn't necessarily lie with the moon, however. One factor that has generated questions is cloud cover. How can the percentage at which the moon is illuminated affect deer activity and movement if the moon is not visible?

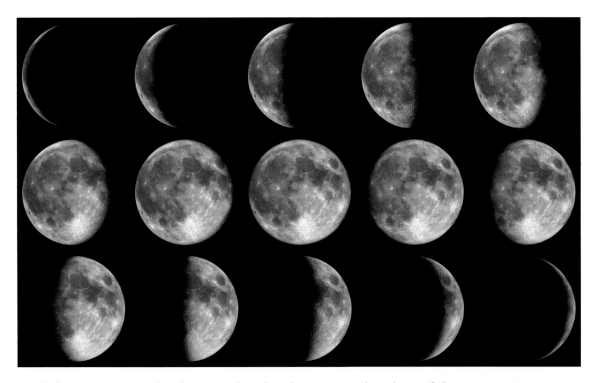

Each deer season, countless hunters plan their hunts around a phase of the moon or its positioning, despite the hard-core scientific evidence claiming, "No studies support the theory that moon phases affects deer activity and/or deer movement." Photo Credit: Canstock Photo Inc.

It is possible that, as with photoperiod, deer unconsciously process the change in illumination through the optic nerve without cloud cover, but that's not always the situation. In some years, the entire rut may occur under cloudy skies. So if the deer can't physically see the moon, how could it still affect activity and movement? It's our opinion it does not. If hunters want to plan their time in the stand on factors, they should look at weather conditions, hunting pressure, changing food sources, and the time of year."

In the conclusion, the authors stated: "The bottom line is no studies support the theory that the moon affects deer activity or movement. Weather, hunting pressure and time of year will likely be the most driving factors for deer activity. Photoperiod, nutrition, genetics and adult buck-to-doe ratio are driving forces of the breeding season. No matter what you believe we'll leave you with two facts. First, whitetails are crepuscular, meaning they are most active at dusk and dawn. Second, no matter where you are in the whitetail's range, there are likely three weeks of fall during which you can't go

Interestingly, moon theories have not been submitted by the scientific community, but rather by a few well-known outdoor writers. Photo Credit: Canstock Photo Inc.

wrong, and these will remain relatively consistent from one year to the next regardless of the moon phase or position."

Moon Overhead and Underfoot

Not too long ago, the moon overhead and underfoot theory came to light not by scientists, biologists, or academics but rather by an outdoor writer, Jeff Murray. His proposed hypothesis was based on reviewing precursors including Solunar Table Charts and game activity tables, as well as the assembly of some "hearsay" information. The overhead or underfoot moon position theory is based on the idea that the moon's gravitational pull is more powerful when it is directly overhead or underfoot and the strongest when overhead. This phenomenon is what causes high and low tides. There is also some limited scientific testimony advocating that it may have some impact on the behavior of all animals.

Almost the entire scientific community has rejected the overhead/underfoot moon theory. Photo Credit: Canstock Photo Inc.

Therefore, the theory went on to purport that the moon's gravitational pull must also stimulate deer to initiate higher degrees of movement or travel than normal. There was a study conducted in Texas that provided some negligible support to the overhead or underfoot moon position theory. The researchers placed radio collars on twenty-five bucks over a three-year period. They discovered that buck activity closely matched the typical activity model: peak activity taking place at dawn and dusk during the first and last quarters of the moon. The study was seen by Jeff Murray, the original theorist, as supposedly supporting his affirmation about the overhead or underfoot conjecture because the moon is peaking underfoot or overhead at dawn and dusk during its first and last quarters.

Some research on this suggests that maximum activity occurs when there is a full moon or a new moon. It is also said that all animal movements are at their weakest levels when there is a quarter-moon or a three-quarter moon. This is allegedly because the moon's and sun's gravitational forces are most powerful when they are directly above or directly below our head, hence the terms overhead and underfoot.

As usual, however, an overwhelming number of academics within scientific communities dismissed the overhead and underfoot theory. They also rejected most other moon phase theories related to increased deer movement and specifically the idea that a phase of the moon establishes the dates for the onset of the rut. Two well-known moon phase researchers, Dr. James Kroll and Ben Koerth, concluded, "Moon phase does not appear to predictably affect deer activity."

My conclusion about the moon phase is that a majority of hunters, me included, are left with more unresolvable questions than authenticated answers from moon theorists, such as Jeff Murray and Charles Alsheimer. Both men are noted hunters and outdoor communicators and I respect them both. However, I am in disagreement regarding their feelings on this particular subject. Although I am not a scientist, I do subscribe to the axiom scientists often use before claiming a theory is scientifically acceptable. I am paraphrasing here, but a theory must provide hard-core factual evidence that is undisputable proof. To date, none of the advocates of any moon phase theories can claim they have done that.

Recently, many hypotheses—supposedly proven by science—that were included in textbooks and taught in schools for decades as substantiated facts about the galaxy, universe, religion, math, history, and even nature, have been proven incorrect. So in the end, I suppose it could be fair to say it's prudent to withhold final judgment about what the most vocal lunar theorists claim about moon phase theories. Nevertheless, it is hard for me to ignore scientific academics on the matter of the moon phase and its effect on deer and deer hunting. Until one of the moon phase theorists demonstrate to the hunting community hard-core scientific proof about their lunar theorist claims, I will remain a nonsupporter of moon phase theories.

Besides being a skeptic, however, I'm also prone to hedge some of my bets. Even when I am predominantly sure that I am correct, I don't slam the door behind me, instead I leave it cracked open ever so slightly. Therefore, the tendency not to burn bridges behind me applies to my non-beliefs in the various moon phase theories, especially when it comes to moon phases related to deer hunting.

I have talked and written about Earth's perihelion and aphelion to the sun and the moon's apogee and perigee to Earth for over twenty years. Perihelion is the point in the orbit of a planet, this case Earth, where it is nearest to its star (our sun). The opposite is true of aphelion, which is the point in the orbit where the celestial body and/or object is at it farthest point from its star. I have theorized that when the Earth is in its closet perihelion to the sun, the whitetail's rut may be sluggish. My hypothesis is not based on any hard-core science, but rather sort of a common-sense guess on my part.

The difference in distance between Earth's nearest point to the Sun (January) and its farthest point (July) is about 3.1 million miles. Earth is about 91.4 million miles from the sun at perihelion, and about 94.5 million miles at aphelion. When Earth achieves perihelion with the sun, it is winter in the northern hemispheres. My notion is that because Earth is known to have an elliptical orbit (as science tells us all celestial bodies in our solar system have), my presumption is that its perihelion to the sun can vary, albeit ever so slightly, year to year. Some years Earth may be a tad bit closer to the sun than 91.4 million miles. At a time the Earth *is* a touch closer, winter temperatures ought to be a faintly warmer. Even slightly warmer temperatures during the rut can result in bucks being lethargic during the day and more sexually active during the cooler temperatures at night. The rut is still happening, only there is less activity during daylight hours. Please note that I did not say there was no activity during the daytime.

Earth's moon around the planet is also elliptical with one side of the moon being closer to Earth than its far side. The side of the moon closest to Earth is called the perigee and the far side is referred to as the apogee. Astrophysicists tell us the moon's distance from Earth is approximately 238,000 miles. But again, because all celestial bodies in our solar system have elliptical orbits, the real distance of each full moon varies throughout the year from what astrophysicists say is 225,804 miles during the Moon's perigee, and 251,968 miles at its apogee. Therefore, who's to say those exact mileage distances can't vary even in an infinitesimal manner? In times when the moon is perigee (closest to Earth) the moonlight from each full moon should be theoretically brighter on a clear night, and even on a cloudy night. The moonlight that each full moon emits will solely depend on that particular full moon's location in the sky.

Of course, the moon doesn't really emit any moonlight at all. Moonlight is actually a result of sunlight reflecting off the moon. Therefore, there is another variable to ponder. When Earth is at its aphelion (farthest point) with the sun, theoretically that should result in the Earth receiving fainter moonlight. Each full moon during an aphelion period then should result in dimmer moonlight of each full moon compared to full moons providing brighter moonlight evenings when Earth is at its perihelion with the sun. This brings up yet another conjecture: are the full moons that are giving off weaker moonlight having yet another effect on deer movement? Well lunar experts, what do you say?

All this brings me back to burning bridges down and slamming doors closed tightly. Over my five decades of hunting deer, I can't argue with the facts that my records (and memory) document that, at times, I have witnessed that there is more deer-feeding activity during a full moonlit night that is generally followed by lethargic movement patterns the next day. There, I've said it—there *might* be some ever so slight relationship to a moon phase and deer feeding and general movement patterns after all. With that admission stated, however, I reiterate there is still *no* scientific evidence to support neither my guesswork nor anyone else's theories on moon phases and their relationships to deer movement, feeding patterns, timing of the rut, and particularly, influencing when female deer come into their estrus cycles.

With all that said, what should you do? My advice is the same as it has been since I first addressed this subject decades ago. A day afield hunting deer beats the heck out of a day of staying at home. I strongly recommend that hunters forget worrying about what effects the moon's cycle or phase plays in their deer hunting and all the hype that goes along with it. As I wrote in several of my other books, "Take this advice to the deer hunting bank because the information I just shared with you is as good as gold: Hunt the calendar, the weather, not moon phases."

This chart will assist in recognizing the different names applied to the moon's phases. Photo Credit: Canstock Photo Inc.

Moon Phrases and Terms

Moon Rise: A minor period that occurs for a short time around the time the moon rises.

Moon Overhead: Describes a period of the moon that begins approximately six hours after the moon rise period. Moon Overhead is referred to as a major period, and it comes into existence immediately after the moon is directly overhead.

Moon Set: A short period of about six hours that occurs directly after Moon Overhead when the moon actually sets.

Moon Underfoot: This term occurs about six hours after moon set. It denotes when the moon is said to be on the other side of the earth directly underfoot. This phase is also known as a major period.

Major Period: Every day of the month the moon has four peak activity times, often referred to as the two major and the two minor times. Major feeding periods are two hours long. If a Solunar Chart or table denotes a major time will occur at 5:30 a.m., you would want to be settled into your stand location no later than 4:30 a.m. and remain there until at least 6:30 a.m.

Minor Period: Minor feeding periods are only about one hour long, meaning if a minor period is occurring at 6:15 p.m., it would require you to be at a location no later than 5:45 p.m. and remain until 6:45 p.m. However, there are certain days of the month that are far better than the rest. These are known as peak activity periods, and there are generally two in every month. The best animal activity of the entire month will be seen during these periods. According to some Solunar Chart descriptions, it is said that these peak activity periods align precisely with a new or full moon.

The above photo will help identify the different designations applied to moon phases. Photo Credit: Canstock Photo Inc.

Moon Phases

There are eight phases that the moon undergoes. When it is said that the moon is waxing or on the rise, it refers to a moon that is getting larger; a full moon that is declining is referred to as a waning moon. Other lunar terms to describe our moon are new moon, half-moon, and full moon.

- A new moon is when the moon cannot be seen because it is directly between the earth and sun and does not catch the sun's light.
- A waxing crescent moon is when the moon looks like a crescent, and the crescent increases, or waxes, in size from one night to the next.
- The first quarter moon, or half-moon, is when half of the lit portion is visible after the waxing crescent phase.
- A waxing gibbous moon takes place when more than half of the lit portion is seen and the shape increases, or waxes, in size nightly.
- The waxing gibbous phase happens between the first quarter and full moon phases.
- A full moon is when the entire moon is lit. The full moon phase occurs when the moon is on the opposite side of the earth from the sun.

- A waning gibbous moon occurs when more than half of the lit portion can be seen and the shape decreases, or wanes, in size nightly. The waning gibbous phase takes place between the full moon and last quarter phases.
- The last quarter moon, or half-moon, is when half of the lit portion of the moon is visible after the waning gibbous phase.
- A waning crescent moon is when the moon looks like a crescent, and the crescent decreases, or wanes, in size from one night to the next.

Chapter 4

Interesting Whitetail Insights

This chapter is included by popular demand. In *Whitetail Strategies—The Ultimate Guide*, my third volume in the *Whitetail Strategies* book series, I included a chapter titled "Little Known Deer Facts." I was surprised when it turned out to be one of the most popular chapters of all the deer books I have penned. I received countless e-mails professing how so many of you found the information in that chapter "enlightening," "informative," "highly interesting," "clarifying," and even "welcomed."

With that in mind, this chapter is filled with more new statistics, truths, mind-provoking, and myth-busting information about deer and deer hunting. I sincerely hope anyone reading this book enjoys the chapter as much as others did in *Whitetail Strategies—The Ultimate Guide*. Feel free to e-mail to let me know how you enjoyed it—or not! You can reach me at peter@fiduccia.com.

Adaptive Behavioral Strategies: These are ongoing behaviors—not instincts—that deer and other wildlife alter in order to develop better survival tactics. There was a time when deer fed more throughout the day. As time went on, they received more hunting pressure from humans and other predators. This forced deer to adjust their feeding patterns to dawn and dusk, when human predation is less. In heavily hunted areas, adaptive behavioral tactics by deer are also responsible for making adult bucks limit daytime feeding to just short periods at dawn, midday, and dusk. Deer have learned that by keeping

Photo Credit: Ted Rose.

This image was taken by Kate Fiduccia, Director of Operations for New York Custom Processing, LLC. The beef at NYCP is professionally aged by hanging it at industry-suggested temperatures consistently ranging from 34 degrees F to 38 degrees F. "To properly age venison, it, too, should be hung in a cooler with consistently cool temperatures," notes Kate Fiduccia. Photo Credit: New York Custom Processing, LLC.

a majority of their movement under darkness, their chances of survival are much greater.

Aging Game Meat: The proper and safest way to age meat is to not allow it to hang for long periods of time in varying temperatures. For game meat to be most favorable, it must be kept at consistent temperatures no more or less than 34 to 38 degrees Fahrenheit. Deer meat freezes when hung in colder temperatures, which halts bacteria growth. When hung in temperatures of more than 38 degrees Fahrenheit, the bacteria process will speed up exponentially and cause the meat to spoil. The best choice to age deer meat for hunters who don't have access to a walk-in refrigerator is to hang the deer carcass overnight to help remove all the body heat, then butcher the deer the following day. The meat can then be stored in a home refrigerator at the proper temperatures for about five days. This will help to properly tenderize or age the meat and greatly increase its flavor.

Albino Deer: A true albino deer will have all white hair, pink eyes and nose, and gray hooves. Albinism is caused by recessive genes. Both the buck and doe must carry and pass on these characteristics, which cause the fawn to not produce the pigments required to have the usual brown colorations known to deer. Oddly, the pink eyes are not caused by color but rather are due to the blood in the eye vessels being visible. As in all albinos, including humans, albino deer commonly have a hearing deficiency.

Allen's Rule: This rule asserts that among warm-blooded animals, the extremities, such as the ears, legs, and tails, are shorter in the coldest part of their range than in the warmest part. Allen's Rule came to be accepted by observation and research

During the period when a buck's antlers are in velvet, they are very cautious of causing injuries to their antlers. Photo Credit: Canstock Photo Inc.

of the Coues whitetail deer in southern Arizona, which have much larger ears and tails in relation to their body size than northern deer.

Antler Minerals: Antlers are made up mostly of calcium and phosphorus and small amounts of magnesium ash. The minerals are replaced in the skeleton after the antlers are fully grown.

Antlers in Velvet: Velvet is actually a modification of the deer's regular skin that has a number of unique physical characteristics. The velvet consists of an outer layer of coarse collagen fibers and an inner layer of finer collagen fibers. Because of these fibers, which are composed of protein, it is almost impossible to strip velvet from an antler crosswise. The velvet must be stripped off longitudinally, or in the same direction that it was grown.

Average Buck Weight: A healthy adult whitetail buck living within a bountiful range has an average live body weight of about 165 pounds. Biologists state that after field dressing a buck, its weight will be reduced by about thirty to forty pounds. Exceptionally heavy bucks will lose twice that or more after they are field dressed. For instance, the largest free-range buck was officially recorded on government scales in Ontario, Canada, in 1977. The buck field dressed at an amazing 431 pounds and was said to have a live weight of approximately 510 pounds! A buck taken in Minnesota had a recorded field dressed weight of 402 pounds with an estimated live weight of 511 pounds and was claimed to be the largest buck ever taken. Two bucks taken in Wisconsin had field dressed weights of 491 and 481 pounds, respectively. All these bucks could be classified as super-heavyweight champs of the whitetail world!

By aggressively rubbing their back legs together over the penial area, bucks will often use self-gratification to release sexual tension and to reduce exasperation. Photo Credit: Ted Rose.

Average Height: The average deer stands approximately thirty-eight inches at the shoulder.

Bergmann's Rule: This rule states that animals of the same species will be larger in body size the farther north or south of the equator that they are found.

Buck Drooling: Another lesser-known behavior of male deer is that they drool during the rut. The more mature a buck is, the more he will drool. During the peak of the primary rut, it is not unusual to witness an adult buck with long strings of drool hanging down from his lips. The more sexually excited the male becomes, the more he drools. Some biologists say that an adult buck can drool as much as a quart or more of saliva in a twenty-four-hour period. The drool is often left at primary scrape sites, tree rubs, overhanging branches, and licking sticks to advertise what buck left it there and his current state of rutting status.

Buck Masturbation: Males in most species of animals masturbate, and whitetail bucks are no exception to that rule. They gratify themselves to help reduce frustration—and thereby the tension that could lead to serious injury or death from fights within the male hierarchy. Cervidae, or deer, are totally capable of breeding as soon as their velvet is shed in autumn to the end of March. Since female deer generally copulate with male deer for only up to thirty hours per year, masturbation plays a big role in the world of the Cervidae.

Bullet or the Firearm: Unlike the age-old question, "Which came first, the chicken or the egg?" the response to this question should unequivocally be the bullet! All too often, both novice and experienced big-game hunters feel the rifle is the most crucial piece of equipment for deer hunting. The correct choice, however, is the bullet. It is not the rifle that knocks the deer down. As army types like to describe it, the rifle is simply the delivery system. What kills the deer is the amount of impact shock, penetration, and the destruction of internal organs caused by the projectile, or bullet, delivered by the rifle. A rifle is basically a tool that helps pinpoint the projectile to a specific area in order for the bullet to cause the maximum amount of damage. Therefore, when thinking about your next rifle purchase, don't think about the caliber of the rifle first. Begin with the cartridge, then decide what rifle you feel will deliver the projectile most effectively.

Color of Clothing Deer See Best: At the US Department of Agriculture's Veterinary Laboratory in Texas, several doctors examined the eyes of anesthetized deer using electron microscopes. Their study determined that deer do indeed see colors. In a similar study done in Michigan, biologists used conditioning techniques that provided food when deer responded correctly to certain colors. What stunned the biologists was that the deer they tested responded correctly to all the different colors they were shown 95 percent of the time! Many other studies over the last decade have been done by scientists, biologists, doctors, and even zoologists. The general consensus of these studies seems to be that deer see a variety of colors. Deer don't see well into the red end of the color spectrum, and they see colors best within the blue end. Some say deer see into the blue spectrum better than humans do. So what's the conclusion for deer hunters? Research seems to suggest to avoid wearing blue jeans or a blue denim jacket when deer hunting.

Cottontail Deer: Deer are similar to cottontail rabbits in some ways. They often will seek the most impenetrable cover available to escape detection and will remain totally still as hunters walk within feet of where they are hidden. When flushed from cover, they often

Deer often seek thick cover, just like rabbits. They frequently stay motionless as hunters walk within feet of where they are hidden. Photo Credit: Canstock Photo Inc./RonRowan.

travel a circuitous route that eventually takes them back to the location they were rousted from. A good tactic to use after spooking a deer from cover is to stay close to the area where the deer was jumped. Find a spot to conceal yourself, and wait for the buck or doe to return.

Copper Premium Bullets: For the green deer hunter or anyone else who wants to reduce the amount of possible contaminates caused by lead, avoid shooting your deer with lead bullets. Instead, give serious consideration to using all-copper premium bullets. All-copper bullets will eliminate even the slightest possibility of lead toxins corrupting the meat of the deer you kill. In a study done several years ago at the Minnesota Department of Natural Resources, the bodies of dead sheep were shot with lead bullets. The researchers then examined each animal with X-rays and CT scans to determine the volume of lead fragments and their distance traveled from the point of entry wound channel. Interestingly, lead fragments traveled up to eighteen inches from the point of entry of the lead bullet.

Corticoids: The rutting odor of a mature buck will cause an immature buck's adrenal cortex to produce corticoids. Corticoids impede further testicular development and function. This causes a sudden drop in the production of testosterone that reduces aggressive behavior by young male deer, which helps to decrease the social tension and competition by immature bucks.

Crepuscular: This is another term for nocturnal. It refers to any animal that is exceptionally active after daylight. Deer are crepuscular, as they are most active at night. Now you can bamboozle your hunting buddies by saying you didn't see a buck because he went crepuscular instead of saying he went nocturnal!

Deer Canine Teeth: Did you know the first deer had fangs? The modern day whitetail deer got its beginnings millions of years ago, probably right alongside of man's ancestor, *Australopithecus*. The Tertiary and Quaternary cervids, which scientists depict as extruded canine teeth made their slow but deliberate ascent up the evolutionary ladder. Therefore, Mother Nature—or evolution—had to develop a pecking order for whitetails that would not include a high risk of males killing one another. Her answer was to evolve whitetails without long canine teeth and instead have them grow antlers from their skulls that could be used for wrestling with each other. Antlers are perfectly designed for battles that will not generally cause fatalities. Because evolution is an ongoing process, a million years from now, future hunters may be stalking whitetails with Dracula fangs! There are still a few modern-day deer, including the Chinese water deer and the muntjac deer of Asia, that are not as social as other deer. These two species still have fangs! The Chinese water deer, however, has no antlers, and the muntjac has rudimentary antlers. The whitetail deer has evolved to be much more of a social herd-like animal, and hence it no longer needs long canine-like fangs.

Deer Foods: It is easier to list the foods whitetails won't eat than what they typically do. An adult deer eats about ten pounds of food per day, and researchers claim there are 614 different foods that whitetails eat. With many of the newer food plot seeds hunters are planting—including Swede, Pasja, and Appin—there are probably more than 614 foods deer presently consume.

Deer Memory: Despite what some hunters believe, deer are not capable of long-term memory. In fact, they have very short-term memory factors.

Deer Tracks: Anyone who emphatically claims they have a foolproof ability to differentiate between buck and doe tracks is either fooling themselves or trying to fool you. Large tracks don't mean anything. Because each deer is an individual, like people, some have big feet and some have small feet. The presence of a deeply set dewclaw or drag marks in snow or on bare ground only suggests that the deer that left the imprint was a heavy bodied animal and, as it walks, it

My son Peter Cody checking a field of mixed winter-hardy clovers including Kura, Marathon Red, and Giant Ladino. All of these are favorite clovers of whitetail deer. Photo Credit: Fiduccia Enterprises.

slightly sinks into the snow or soft ground. There are indicators to help make a better educated guess about a deer's sex by its tracks. The line of travel is a good guide. Bucks tend to walk in a straight line, while does tend to wander somewhat irregularly as they walk. Female deer generally walk pigeon-toed, and their tracks demonstrate an erratic line of travel. A buck's feet, however, turn outward slightly, and this can be easily seen in the tracks.

Deer Yards: While most adult deer can withstand punishing cold temperatures, they can't tolerate consistent wind associated with extreme cold. Such weather conditions can cause them to lose body heat at an alarming rate. This is why most deer in northern regions have a behavior to group up in low-lying areas, dense stands of pines, or swamps that have good stands of conifer cover—all of which will substantially reduce the speed of the wind. Some biologists claim deer use the same deer yards for many years if necessary. It is also claimed that deer will migrate long distances—up to twenty or more miles—to reach their traditional deer yards.

Defecation: In the winter, deer poop a lot less than they do during the other three seasons. In spring, summer, and fall, when there is plenty to eat, deer will defecate about thirty-six times in a day. In winter, when food is much more limited, deer reduce their defecation to about ten to twelve times per day.

Dispersal: Young buck dispersal occurs when female deer drive yearling bucks from their home range to prevent inbreeding. Sometimes a young buck will travel up to several miles before establishing a new home range of his own. The yearling bucks driven from your land become resident bucks of your neighbor's lands. Interestingly, the same phenomenon acts in reverse. Yearling bucks driven from neighboring lands are likely to establish residence on your property.

Edge: All hunters have read or heard about hunting deer in edge-type habitats. Edges are among the most significant habitat features within the whitetails' world. An edge is where the woods meet a field or a field adjoins with another change in the habitat or environment. The reason deer are seen so frequently in edge-type habitats is that they provide an abundance of good cover and, more importantly, a wide diversity of nutritious vegetation, particularly in spring and early summer.

Exocrine Glands: All the external glands of a deer are referred to as being exocrine, which means outside in Greek. The most recognized exocrine gland is the tarsal gland. Other glands that are considered exocrine include the metatarsal, pre-orbital, forehead, interdigital, and salivary glands.

Fasting Metabolism: Hunters often wonder how deer can survive a harsh winter. It is due to a survival tactic known as fasting metabolism. All members of the deer family experience a slowing down of the basal metabolic rate each winter. It usually begins in December and lasts until late March. Like the onset of the rut, the actual timing of the slowed basal metabolic rate is set off by latitude. By decelerating their metabolism, deer require less food and use their stored body fat more slowly. Once fasting metabolism is underway, deer are unable to eat more even if the food is available. This is why game departments often say feeding deer in winter serves no real purpose. Biologists say that a deer's food intake during this period is substantially reduced by 50 percent or more.

Flehmen: An old world German phrase used to express the lip-curling, deep breathing behavior of male deer and other male animals. Male deer use this to ascertain if a female deer is in prime estrus and ready to accept the sexual overtures of a buck. The buck breathes in the scent deeply while raising his nose high in the air. Then he curls his upper lip, which plugs his nostrils shut. This blocks the scent inside, where it saturates the sensory nerve endings in the epithelial lining. With his muzzle held high, the buck exhales through his open mouth, forcing some of the scent molecules past his vomeronasal organ. This organ tells the buck exactly what state of estrus a doe is in.

Flexible Cartilage: The reason whitetails are able to make razor-sharp turns and other maneuvers at a moment's notice is because their front legs aren't connected to their shoulders with a ball-and-socket joint. Instead they are

This magnificent buck is checking the air in order to detect the estrus pheromone odor of a doe. Photo Credit: Ted Rose.

This buck has seen, heard, or sensed something that made him uneasy. Deer foot stomp for a variety of different reasons. Photo Credit: Depositphotos.

attached via an extremely flexible cartilage. This construction enables an average buck to make standing leaps of about eight feet long and running jumps thirty feet in length.

Foot Stomping: When a whitetail deer stomps its foot repeatedly, it is displaying mild to intense anxiety. Female deer stomp more often than male deer, particularly mature bucks. Foot stomping is meant to provide visual, audible, and olfactory signals to other deer, which express that imminent danger is looming. Deer stomp with one foot but sometimes alternate the stomping from one foot to the other. On some occasions, deer will stop stomping and use a stiff-gait walk toward the direction of the potential danger and circle around it in an attempt to identify through sight and scent what frightens them. Deer also use a foot stomp to display that they are in a self-protective posture and, therefore, the message to a potential predator clearly communicates that it has lost the element of surprise. Other deer are forewarned by feeling the vibrations, seeing the foot stomping taking place, hearing the stomps, and smelling the olfactory signals. When a deer repeatedly stomps its feet, the interdigital gland deposits excess interdigital scent on the ground. It warns not only nearby deer but also deer passing the area at a later time.

Funnels: I am often asked to describe exactly what a funnel is as related to deer hunting. A funnel is nothing more than any natural corridors—including gaps, ravines, or gorges—between mountains, along creek bottoms, as thin strips of land lying between ponds or lakes, or any other natural passageway or natural cut in the terrain. Funnels made by man include gateways, narrowing woodlots, bushy fencerows, and concealed passageways along roads and houses. All offer quality hunting opportunities within or along them.

Gonadotrophic Hormones: Photoperiodism governs the behaviors of all members of the deer family, such as deer, elk, moose, caribou, etc. As daylight begins to shorten

Bucks often mount other bucks to demonstrate they hold a higher position within the pecking order. Photo Credit: Ted Rose.

in late summer, the pineal gland receives less light with each passing day. This influences the pituitary gland, located at the base of the deer's brain, to produce a gonadotrophic hormone that initiates the testicles of a buck to enlarge, which causes an increased production of testosterone in the buck's system.

Hierarchy: This term is more accurate to describe whitetail social structure than dominance. True dominance takes place more often with canine and feline creatures that urinate on four borders of a prescribed and well-defined boundary line. Other canines and felines who trespass are chased back across the borderline and, if caught, are severely injured and often killed. Complete dominant behavior does not exist within the world of the whitetail deer. Therefore, dominance in deer is much more precisely defined as a pecking order within a hierarchy.

Instinct: A reaction by a creature without predetermined thought is said to be instinctive.

Lead Deer: It may surprise many hunters to hear that deer live in a matriarchal society where one doe assumes the top rung of the hierarchy ladder. She leads a small herd of fawns, yearlings, older does, and immature bucks, all of whom are her blood relatives. All deer herd groups are headed by one mature doe that is experienced and cunning.

Licking Stick: Researchers first discovered how male deer use licking sticks during the early 1980s. Licking sticks are generally thin, resilient saplings about one to two inches in diameter but sometimes smaller. A buck will usually snip the sapling in half at about thirty-six inches from the ground. He will deposit his forehead scent on the sapling and then quickly follow up by repeatedly licking the stick, hence the term licking stick. They particularly like to leave the scent from behind the antlers and ears on licking sticks, too. Licking sticks act as scent-post magnets to all deer. Bucks of all ages are attracted to licking sticks and will go out of their way to deposit their own scent on any licking stick within their home range. Female deer are attracted to licking sticks, as well, and are quick to deposit their scent on them.

Life Span: A wild deer's expected life span is said to be ten to twelve years. Larger ungulates, such as elk and caribou, have slightly longer expected life spans of twelve to fifteen years.

Market Hunting: This practice was legal from about seventy-five to one hundred fifty years ago in many states across the country. Depending on where it was practiced, it had a devastating effect on deer herds nationwide. A hunter in New York claimed to have killed more than twenty-five hundred whitetails before he died in 1850. Records from Delaware maintain a hunter took eighteen deer skins a week to a trading post for forty-seven consecutive weeks. Gladly, market hunting for deer was banned about sixty years ago.

Motorized Vehicles: Whitetails don't demonstrate that they have much concern or fear for most motorized vehicles. Deer are often seen standing along highways feeding as cars and trucks zip by them sometimes only scant feet away. I have often been on my tractor working our fields and have had deer walk into the field as I was disking or cutting a plot. Sometimes deer will allow me to ride within a few feet of them while I am on the tractor, riding my Arctic Cat ATV along our trails, or even when I drive a pickup truck into the fields. I have discovered the key to keep deer in the woods or fields from reacting negatively to any ATV, truck, or motorized vehicle is to keep the speed below 7 mph.

Nontypical Antlers: I am often asked what causes a deer to have nontypical antlers. There

This doe seems to be standing by the speed limit sign in order to remind motorists to slow down! Photo Credit: Ted Rose.

are a few factors that cause this. I suppose the most common factor that initiates the growth of a set of abnormal antlers is accidents. The injury happens while the antlers are soft and still growing. Antlers that are injured oddly retain some sort of warped factor to grow back odd-looking antlers from year to year. However, each new set may not necessarily be as abnormal as the first set of nontypicals were. When the antlers are damaged because the injury site occurred to the pedicels, however, the deer will usually grow a nontypical set of antlers for the rest of his life. Another factor that can cause deformed antlers is an injury to the foot or leg. Although the injury may cause antler irregularity, the oddity usually doesn't last more than a season or two. The last possible reason for disfigurement to a set of antlers is caused by a genetic marker. Biologists are not sure why or how this occurs.

Olfactory Advertisement: First and foremost, the word olfactory relates directly to a creature's sense of smell, including the whitetail deer. An adult whitetail buck deposits a surprising amount of scent when making or refreshing a scrape or rub. Odors are left from a combination of glands, organs, saliva, urine, and feces. There are odors left by ten of the buck's glands, including the interdigital, tarsal or hock, metatarsal, pituitary, pre-orbital, preputial, nasal, salivary, and forehead glands. There are also glands behind the buck's antlers and in front of the ears, and they will leave scent from those two areas, as well. Bucks also deposit scent from the vomeronasal organ, mentioned previously, which means they leave a minimal amount of scent from fifteen different body locations.

Olfactory Bulb: Located in the roof of the deer's nasal passage are tiny hair-like cilia, or nerve endings, that ensnare inbound molecular odors and direct them to the olfactory bulb, which sends them directly to the brain, where they are received as chemical impulses. The brain then decodes them into individual odors.

Other Deer Movement Time Frames: According to some scientists' research, the most movement of deer during the rut occurs at about 7:45 a.m. The data suggests that the time frame can vary up to a half-hour on either side, dependent on where a hunter is located in a certain time zone. I have found there is a predictable and pronounced deer movement pattern in and out at 7:30 a.m. during the rut. In fact, it carries through most of the deer season, as well.

Ovulation: Like all mammals, a female deer in her peak estrus cycle releases an egg. It is discharged from her ovary into the fallopian tube and then on to the doe's uterus, where the buck's sperm fertilizes it. An interesting fact about ovulation that perhaps goes unnoticed by some hunters is that the rutting odor of a buck and his rut behaviors actually help to stimulate the doe to ovulate. So there are some beneficial reasons for a buck's tarsal and other glands to make him stink like a bad boy.

Palatable: When I was giving a food-plot seminar, an attendee asked me to explain what foods deer find most palatable. My answer was all the foods that are edible to them! There is some confusion about the definition and use of the word palatable. Foods that deer find palatable are foods that deer can consume. The food items—there is a long list of them—may or may not be the most nutritious or desirable to the deer, but the deer can eat them. More nutritious types of plants, such as those used in food plots (clovers, grains, brassicas, etc.), provide more value, therefore the deer find their delectableness or palatability more pleasing.

Papillomas: Most hunters have killed a deer or have seen deer killed by other hunters that have large wart-like growths on them. These growths are scientifically referred to as Cutaneous Fibroma Papillomas. They are also known by a more common name: papilloma cysts. Biologists say they are caused by a virus that is spread from one deer to another by flies and midges that bite the deer. I have witnessed some large fibromas—some as large as a softball or larger. Thankfully, a majority of fibromas are harmless to deer. The ones that do cause problems are those that grow near a deer's eyes. Cold weather kills the repugnant flies and midges. When the weather is frigid for extended periods of time, it can cause the fibromas to freeze and fall off. Biologists assure us that the meat of deer that have fibromas is not affected in any negative way and is safe to eat. I

The papilloma growth on this buck may look unsettling to most hunters. While they are not pleasing to look at, they do not cause any harm to the meat. Photo Credit: Ted Rose.

respectfully reserve judgment on that, but I'm somewhat of a Sheldon (from *The Big Bang Theory* TV show) about such things.

Pedicel: The extensions that protrude from the front of the deer's skull plate form the base that antlers grow from. The pedicel develops on the skull where a special coating of flesh, known as the periosteum, has formed a base.

Pedicel Transplants: Here's a creepy science-fiction-type fact about deer. Research was performed on deer by Drs. Goss and Hartwig, who surgically removed the periosteum pedicel skin from a deer's skull and replanted it on different parts of the deer's body. Rudimentary antlers grew wherever the doctors implanted the periosteum! Yuck! You have to wonder what that looked like. Now that's a definite case of Frankenstein nontypical antlers, huh?

Perlation: A question I get often by hunters and nonhunters alike goes something like this: What causes all the boney bumps so often seen at the bottom of some deer's antlers? The pimple-like boney bumps on a deer's antlers are scientifically referred to as perlation. These protrusions are most often seen jutting out of the main beams, usually around the bases of the pedicels and above them for a few inches. Immature bucks generally do not have any perlation on their first set of antlers. As a buck gets older, however, each new set of antlers becomes more and more adorned with perlation. Perlation is said to aid bucks by shedding the bark of trees they rub. I happen to like antlers that are heavily embellished with perlation.

Perlation is a term used to describe the tiny bumps often seen on buck antlers. It is plainly visible at the pedicels and at the bottom of this buck's antlers. Photo Credit: Ted Rose.

Photoperiodism: This phenomenon is the single most important influence that triggers the whitetail deer's breeding cycle, or rut. Photoperiodism is the amount of daylight that occurs within a twenty-four-hour period. No other force governs

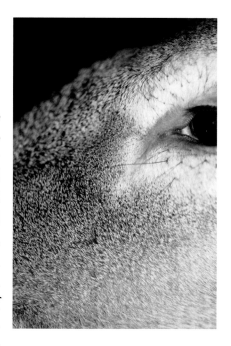

The length of daylight that is perceived through a deer's eyes is transmitted by electrical signals to the pineal gland in the deer's brain. Photo Credit: Ted Rose.

when animals get the inherent urge to mate, migrate, hibernate, end hibernation, and even have their young, with the type of meticulous precision photoperiodism provides. In deer, the amount of daylight perceived through the eyes by the optic nerve is then transmitted by electrical impulses to the deer's pineal gland, a small pinecone-shaped gland located at the base of the brain. It then sends chemical signals to the endocrine system to release hormones through the animal's bloodstream. When the whitetail deer's system detects a lessening of light, the body automatically begins to release the signals to the deer that the mating season is upon him or her. It is photoperiodism within specific latitudes and longitudes that kicks off the rut—not the moon phase, cold weather, or any of the other unscientific and, more importantly, unproven theories that people claim cause the onset of the rut.

Polyestrus: If a doe is not bred by a buck during her first estrus cycle or if she is mated by a buck but does not become pregnant, she will come into her estrus period every twenty-eight to thirty-two days until she is successfully bred.

Polygamous: Both male and female deer are polygamous because each will mate with other males and females.

Popliteal Gland: This is one of the lesser-known deer glands that is not often considered by biologists to be important during the rut. It is a tiny gland hidden in the fat in front of the deer's haunch. Some hunters strongly believe that if it is not removed when dressing the deer, it will cause the meat to have an unpleasant taste.

Researcher: I often use this term in my writings about deer anatomy, biology, behavior, and hunting strategies. It refers to an individual or group within the scientific community that participates in a specific study to discover new information or confirm

The buck that made this rub line wanted to be sure his olfactory message was seen and smelled by all other deer in the area. Photo Credit: Fiduccia Enterprises.

existing theories—in this case about whitetail deer. I have studied whitetails by observation in the wild and by video documentation for fifty-one years. With each passing year, I learn new information patiently gathered by researchers within the scientific community.

Rub Lines: This refers to a group of trees that are rubbed by a buck within a series of closely located saplings more or less in a straight line, which are most often made by a buck going to or from his bedding area. In my hunting experience, I have been unable to establish if rub lines are made by a buck to demonstrate a specific visual or olfactory purpose. I have tagged these types of rubs with a term: rubs of convenience. A buck simply makes them because they are there, and as he moves to and from his bedding haunts, he casually pauses to rub a group of saplings along his trail.

Rubology: Okay, I'm busted. There is no such word as rubology. I made it up. For me, rubology is the study of all the dynamics regarding buck rubs. For example, mature bucks with large antlers frequently rub small trees. However, immature bucks with small antlers seldom rub large trees.

Selenium: Each year when I hire a farm-based trucking firm to spread truckloads of inorganic minerals on our farm, I also have them include the trace mineral selenium. Selenium salts are toxic in large amounts, but trace amounts of this mineral are necessary for cellular function in many animals and other organisms. Deer that live on soil depleted of selenium have a higher than normal rate of stillborn fawns. Plants also require selenium, mostly in trace amounts.

Sexual Maturity: All of the deer species' (Cervidae) males and females are able to breed once they reach one and a half years old. But within the male society of deer, being capable of breeding doesn't mean one-and-a-half-year-old bucks actually get

Both female and male deer are able to breed once they reach one-and-a-half years old. Photo Credit: Depositphotos.

the opportunity to breed. Bucks occupying the higher positions within the hierarchy limit most, if not all, of these young bucks from mating with does. This is primarily accomplished through olfactory signpost markings. The wide variety of biochemical odors adult bucks deposit at scrapes, rubs, overhanging branches, and licking sticks cause these younger bucks' brains to produce and release into their systems corticoids, which suppress a younger buck's sexual drive, or libido, which curtails the aggression of the rut. By the corticoids limiting most of the younger bucks from breeding until the following year, the one-and-a-half-year-olds get the opportunity to develop into stronger, larger males who will pass on better genetics.

Spongiosa: During the growing process of an antler, a buck receives nourishment from the outside and inside the antler. The soft core of the antler, which is made up of bone matrix, is called spongiosa. Sometime in early August, the supply of blood is cut off to the spongiosa, and it dries out at the base of the pedicels. From that point in August to sometime between December and March, the antlers continue to dry out, and eventually they fall off. During the rutting season when bucks are sparring or engaging in all-out fights, the spongiosa is still moist, and it provides pliability that prevents the antlers from snapping at the base, which lessens tine breakage, as well.

Tails Up: Tail size and coloration identify the three types of North American deer—whitetail, mule deer, and blacktail.

Singleton: Singleton is the proper term to describe the birth of one fawn. Two fawns are twins, three are triplets, four are quadruplets, and five are quintuplets.

Warm weather during hunting season will often keep bucks bedded for longer periods during daylight hours. Photo Credit: Canstock Photos.

Warm Temperatures Slow Deer Movement: Many research studies have determined that warmer temperatures overwhelmingly affect deer movement. This is particularly the case during the month of November. When November air temperatures climb above 45 degrees, studies have concluded that deer activity noticeably begins to drop off, and in some instances, deer movement simply comes to a standstill altogether.

Chapter Five

For the Love of the Hunt

"I make no apologies, concealments, or socially correct rationalizations for why I hunt and why I 'kill' deer. I hunt them, not harvest them. I draw life's breath from pursuing game, not suffocate from it. I celebrate a bone-chilling, frigid morning, not despise it. I find comfort in the solitude of the hunt, not fear it. I bear witness to the end of an animal's existence during the hunt, not avoid the reality that mortality is inevitably part of the hunt. In the end, I am a predator. I hunt, I kill, and I eat. As a hunter I embrace the kill, I don't make excuses for it."
Peter Fiduccia, 1984

Some anthropologists theorize that several million years ago, a four-legged chimpan-zee-like hominid, also known as a great ape, dropped from a tree. Once its feet were firmly planted on the ground, it carefully scanned the savanna on all fours looking for the presence of predators. Not able to see over the high brush and prairie lands, he began to cautiously push through the tall grass in search of food. Without the slightest warning, a large feline predator pounced from the cover, and with a single bite to its prey's neck, the cat instantly snapped the small hominid's spine.

According to evolutionary biologists, about four million years ago in Africa, another similar primate jumped down from the canopy above. Before leaving to forage for fruits and nuts, it, too, first vigilantly scrutinized the savanna grasslands in search of potential predators. This time, however, the creature known as *Australopithecus afarensis* had evolved. Instead of looking through the grass on all four legs, this early hominid stood up on its hind legs and cast a wary eye both through and over the top of the grasslands. Only after she found no predators close by did *Australopithecus afarensis* have

Photo Credit: Fiduccia Enterprises.

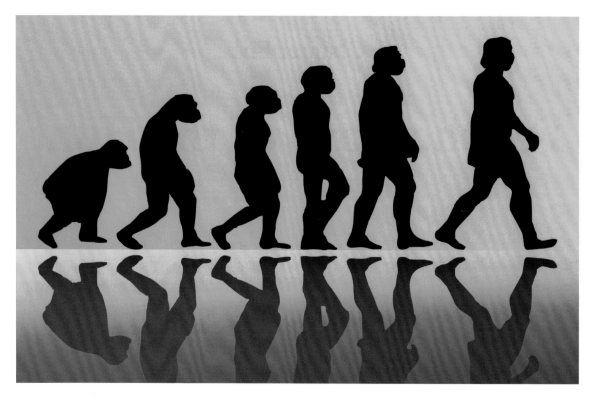

The earliest bipedal hominin is considered to be either Sahelanthropus and/or Orrorin. Either of the two are said to be the last species between chimps and humans. Ardipithecus was a full bipedal, that arose somewhat later, and the early bipedals eventually evolved into the Australoithecines and later into the genus Homo. Photo Credit: CanStock Photos.

the chance to safely forage for her fruits and nuts. After gathering her bounty, she walked upright back to the safety of the trees, climbed up into the canopy, and ate what she had collected. Through the eons of time, there are countless similar examples of evolutionary arms races between predators and their prey with a steady ebb and flow between hunters developing new successful tactics for attacks and the prey evolving defensive adaptations to counter them. These adaptations are often portrayed between hunter and prey as reciprocal—with prey and predator acting as two sides in a ceaseless evolutionary battle that science refers to as coevolution.

About 1.9 million years ago, a new larger longer-armed and longer-legged bipedal hominid with the body blueprint of modern humans came onto the evolutionary scene. This hominid was different in several ways than his predecessors. The crucial

During humanity's evolutionary periods, the rule of coevolution states that man and his prey were kept in a constant state of development. Photo Credit: CanStock Photo.

divergence was that *Homo erectus* had developed a big brain—an engine that required more energy than just fruits and nuts could supply. So, *H. erectus* became the first hominid hunter and consumer of meat.

However, Mother Nature wasn't finished sculpting her hominid models yet. About 250,000 to 300,000 years ago—a mere blink in evolutionary time—Mother Nature evolved *H. erectus* into the larger brained, fleet-footed *Homo sapiens*. They were hunters and gatherers during that era, and according to Harvard human evolutionary biologist Daniel Lieberman, "Our species [*Homo sapiens*] was as fit as today's pro athletes." One of their most extraordinary behaviors was that they left Africa around fifty thousand years ago and steadily marched into every inhabitable crevice on planet earth. About ten thousand years ago, during a time known as the Neolithic period, another

About ten millennia ago all other hominids became extinct leaving only Homo sapiens as the sole surviving hominid on earth. Photo Credit: CanStock Photo.

evolutionary step forward took place. As the sole hominid left on earth, *Homo sapiens* moved across the planet, settled down where they could, and began to raise crops and domestic animals for food consumption to survive.

This period is the time frame during which I feel a genetic departure took place in our DNA makeup—a separation that defines why some of today's post-industrial *Homo sapiens* hunt and some of them don't. A genetic marker is a gene or DNA sequence with a known location on a chromosome that can be used to identify individuals or species. It can also be described as a variation that may arise due to a mutation or alteration in the genomic loci that can be observed. My conjecture is that some of today's *H. sapiens*, the ultra-modern "us," still harbor a hidden genetic marker that keeps some of our brains strongly bonded to principally being meat-eating hunters and others bonded to simply being gatherers, or nonhunters. While there

Throughout human kind's development, the hunting of game, gathering of available food stuffs, and eventually raising farm domestic animals played a dominant role in our survival. However, our earliest relatives' instinct to hunt for meat was primarily responsible for the eventual growth and extreme development of the human brain. Therefore, there is no doubt that many modern humans still harbor the hunting gene and the deep yearning instinct to hunt. Photo Credit: CanStock Photo.

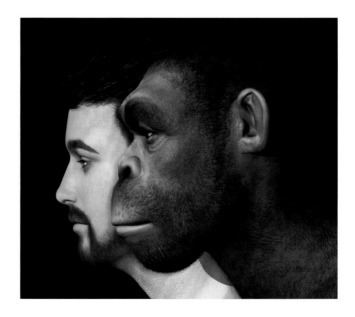

are no specific scientific facts about my supposition, I strongly believe in it. Those of us who actively seek out the hunt simply for the love of it must, in my mind's eye, have a hunting marker within our chromosomes that encodes the genetic instructions responsible for the urge. It may well be a marker that is efficiently concealed deeply in our DNA and not yet identified by those in the scientific community; realistically, scientists are justifiably too busy identifying genome markers to help cure diseases rather than spending their valuable time trying to document a marker that compels some people to hunt.

There is absolutely no doubt in my mind that those of us who hunt don't do so predominantly for food or survival anymore. As a species, we no longer have to work hard to acquire food, nor do we work as diligently to survive. Instead, those who hunt do so to satisfy a genetic bonding with the pursuit of game.

In the end, this is why I feel some people are inexplicably drawn to and have a deep connection with the craving of the hunt, yet other people have equally confounded feelings and abhorrent aversions to hunting. To some degree, my theory about having an inherited hunting gene also explains why some hunters excel and others have to work harder at it because of the coding variants in relation to hunting. All hunters who have inherited the hunting chromosome possess an instinctive aptitude to pursue game. If you nurture the awareness, you will inevitably develop higher levels of hunting skills that are naturally coupled with more hunting success. Lastly, by embracing the hunt for what it realistically is—the killing of game—you will become a hunter to whom the hunt matters most.

Chapter Six

Trailing and Recovering Gut-Shot Deer

It was mid-October, and first light brought with it a brisk chill in the air. Most of the colorful fall foliage was still on the trees. I directed Jeff Venti, a guest of mine, toward a tree stand on our land called 5-Point. I watched him for a few moments as he hoisted his bow up the stand and got comfortable, and then I headed to my stand. About thirty minutes later, Jeff called me on the two-way radio. "I saw a big doe walk down the ridge, and when she stopped thirty yards from me, I arrowed her. Can you come over?" I arrived at the stand about fifteen minutes later, and I asked Jeff if he knew where his arrow hit. He replied, "I think it hit her in the lungs."

After a short search around the hit zone, we located the arrow. The moment I picked it up, I knew it was a bad hit. The arrow smelled foul and had bits of green-looking mucus on it. There was some coarse, short, light-colored hair that had reddish tips on it, as well. I turned to Jeff and said, "I'm

It is crucial to try to locate deer hair at the hit site a bow. Gut-shot hair will be coarse, short, and lighter in color with reddish brown tips. Photo Credit: Fiduccia Enterprises.

Photo Credit: Fiduccia Enterprises.

sorry to tell you this, but this is a gut-shot deer." I knew we were in for a long and careful trailing job if we were to recover the doe.

When a deer is shot in the paunch with a bow or firearm, it reacts in specific ways. The first point to remember about a gut-shot deer is that they will definitely die, but it sometimes takes them hours to succumb to their wound. Once it was confirmed that Jeff gut-shot the doe, I decided it was best to let her lie down for a few hours before trailing her.

Believe me, it is never a good idea to quickly take up the blood trail of a deer hit through the stomach. When they are pushed too quickly or hard, they often go for long distances before lying down again. Sometimes they can cover a mile or more, which makes for an unnecessarily tedious tracking job that might never end successfully. On average, however, most paunch-shot deer travel about five hundred yards before lying down for good.

Around 1 p.m., about five hours after the deer was hit, my wife Kate—who, like my son, Peter Cody, is an excellent blood trailer—Jeff, and I went back to the hit zone. We marked the exact spot of the hit with an orange survey ribbon. Ten yards from that, we discovered the first evidence of blood and hung another orange ribbon there. Over the next one hundred fifty yards, there was not a lot of blood to be found. It is common for gut-shot deer to leave a scarce amount of blood to trail. We only located a few drops here and there as we advanced slowly. While Kate and I did most of the searching, Jeff was looking ahead for the deer in case she was bedded down ahead of us. If that should occur, he would be ready to make a shot if needed.

About an hour later, we located our first good sign: a bloody deer bed where the doe

When blood trailing a gut-shot deer, it is wise to proceed slowly. Most often there will only be a few drops of blood here and there. By moving too quickly, it is easy to overlook a drop or two of blood. Photo Credit: Fiduccia Enterprises.

had stopped to rest. That is worrisome when tracking gut-shot deer; as soon as a deer beds down, the wound begins to clot. I decided to slow our trailing pace down even more. Within seventy-five yards, we found yet another bloody deer bed. Then, as often happens when on the trail of a deer hit in the abdomen, the blood trail ended. After searching around the bed for twenty minutes trying to locate more blood, I had a reality check. What if we can't find this deer?

We decided the best option was for the three of us to split up. Kate suggested that the deer might head for water, and I agreed. It isn't unusual for a paunch-shot deer to seek out water. Kate slipped down the ridge a bit and started toward our ponds. I headed on somewhat of a straight line, where I thought the deer might continue going. Jeff took a higher route that paralleled the ridge. Kate hadn't gone more than one hundred fifty yards when I heard her call out to me, "Peter, I've got her!"

This incident happened several years ago during the start of the New York archery season. Like all ethical hunters, Jeff did his best to place his arrow in the so-called bread basket. But, as any experienced hunter realizes, a projectile doesn't always end up where it is supposed to. In fact, the possibility of having a thought-out, well-placed shot miss its intended mark and end up wounding a deer instead of killing it quickly is part and parcel of every hunt. It is an unfortunate scenario, but it is also a reality of hunting. Inevitably, most—if not all—hunters will wound a deer. It has happened to me, and most likely it has or will happen to anyone reading this. When it occurs, however, the question becomes, how well prepared is the hunter to track a blood trail of a gut-shot deer effectively enough to recover it? Blood trailing a wounded deer is like most things about hunting—it requires patience, practice, and experience to become a well-honed skill that is performed well.

Although gut-shot deer don't generally leave a lot of blood to follow and because they can go for miles after being hit, most hunters

Many blood trails leave behind a lot of blood, but that doesn't always mean the deer has been mortally wounded. Learning how to interpret the color, texture, and amount of blood found can be very helpful in recovering a deer. Photo Credit: Fiduccia Enterprises.

think that they are difficult or impossible to find. Nothing can be further from the truth when it comes to deer shot in the paunch. When armed with just some basic information about gut-shot deer, most hunters will recover the deer more often than not. But first they have to become acquainted with how a gut-shot deer reacts from the instant it is hit.

Body Language: When a deer, buck, or doe is hit in the paunch, it may demonstrate little to no reaction from the hit, particularly if it is hit with a broadhead arrow. Deer hit when bow hunting may lunge forward slightly and stand for several seconds without moving. Then they may walk away slowly. Sometimes after they walk away, they will stop and stand for long periods of time. The entire body usually appears hunched up, and their heads are hung low to the ground. In some instances, gut-shot deer may hunch up at the time of the hit and then trot off slowly with their legs spread apart slightly. This is especially the case when they are hit by a bullet. If they feel nothing is on their back trail, deer will lie down as quickly as they can. As I mentioned earlier, it is important to remember when trailing a gut-shot deer that all deer hit in the abdomen will die. If that is kept in mind, the hunter is more likely to find the deer sooner rather than later.

Arrow Evidence: Once a hunter establishes how the deer reacted after being hit, the next clue will come when discovering the arrow. When the arrow is found, check it closely for particles of food or green-brown particles, which indicate the arrow may have hit an intestine. Use your nose to detect a foul odor. If the arrow passed through the paunch, it will smell foul and blood on the arrow will appear dark. Any hair discovered—and hair will always be at a hit site from a firearm or bow—will be coarse, short, and lighter in color with reddish brown tips.

Firearm Evidence: When deer are gutshot with a firearm, the trailing is sometimes much easier, as there is more damage done and the entry and exit holes will bleed more profusely. But don't get cocky and think that it will be an easy tracking job. It might, but it also might not be. When a hunter uses a firearm and gut-shoots a deer, the deer will exhibit the same body language as when hit with an arrow. However, there is usually more hair left at the hit site and, as stated, more blood. The hunter should still give the deer a few hours to lie down and expire from its wound. Pushing a deer shot with a firearm could also mean the deer will travel long distances after being hit and possibly end up never being found.

Gut-shot blood will be darker and may contain brown or green matter. Dissimilarly, bright red blood is evidence of a heart, lung or muscle shot deer. The frothy pinkish blood here is a sure-fire sign the deer was hit in the lungs. Photo Credit: Fiduccia Enterprises.

Color of Blood: The blood that is found at the hit site and along the trail will provide a wealth of information about whether the deer was indeed gutshot. Wounds to the stomach are more than likely to leave dark-colored blood behind. It is also probable the blood will contain brown or green matter from the paunch or intestines. In contrast, bright blood is left when deer are hit in the heart, lungs, or muscles. Sometimes it is possible for a broad-head arrow or bullet to hit vitals and muscles, as well as the paunch. This will result in both dark and bright blood being left behind.

It is important to know a little about the deer's anatomy in relation to gutshots. There is a notable difference between abdominal and intestinal wounds. A deer's paunch, or to be more precise its rumen, is the first section of its stomach, where the partially digested food is held. It is later regurgitated for additional chewing and sent to another compartment of the deer's four-sectioned stomach. The intestines, however, are cylinder-like tubes that go from the stomach to the anus.

You can easily see why many seasoned trackers would much rather trail a gut-shot deer than a deer shot through the intestines. Another negative about trailing deer shot through the intestines is that they leave even less of a blood trail than gut-shot deer do because intestinal wounds rarely bleed externally. One last off-putting note about deer shot in the intestines is that they usually travel much farther than gut-shot deer do. Some seasoned trackers have told me deer can easily go a mile or more before expiring from their wound.

Similarities: Most paunch-shot deer share similar characteristics. The blood trail will not be easy to follow. They bed down soon after being hit as soon as they realize they are not

Gut-shot deer seek water to quench their thirst. Some say deer will also submerge themselves in water to sooth the discomfort of the wound. Photo Credit: Ted Rose.

being pursued. They rarely die while walking or running off and rather die while bedded down. They often bed in several places before they are too weak to move to yet another bedding area. While not every gut-shot deer will eventually look for water, enough do for it to be noted.

On the Trail: When actually tracking a paunch-shot deer, don't expect to find blood at the hit site or soon thereafter. Most times gut-shot deer don't begin to bleed until they have gone fifty or more yards from where they were hit. Be aware that the blood trail is bound to diminish. It is often necessary to get down on hands and knees to pick up droplets of blood from gut-shot deer. The farther the deer travels, the better the chances are that the wounds will plug up with matter from the stomach or intestines.

While it is always better to wait at least four to six hours before trailing a gut-shot deer, it is better, when practical, to wait overnight. If rain is predicted, wait a few hours if possible and then begin your search. It is true that the rain will further diminish the

GUT SHOT

When hit, this deer may show little or no reaction, but may just slowly walk away. In some cases, "gut shot" deer may hunch up at time of hit and then run slowly with legs spread apart slightly. He will lay down quickly but remember that all gut shot deer die. Keep at it and you'll find him sooner or later. Check arrow closely for particles of food in the case of a stomach hit, or green slime in the event that an intestine was hit. Use your nose. If you hit the gut you can smell it on the arrow. Hair will be coarse, short, lighter in in color with reddish brown tips. If pushed to soon, this deer can go for miles and may never be found. If possible wait at least four hours before trailing. Eight hours would be better. You can look forward to a very smelly "gutting" job.

This card summarizes the location of a projectile hitting the gut area, as well as vital tips to aid hunters in recovering a gut-shot deer. Photo Credit: Fiduccia Enterprises.

blood trail, but by waiting, you increase the chance that the deer may have already died in its bed.

As with all types of blood trailing, the overriding factor of success in finding wounded deer is never to give up—or at least never give up too soon. Dogged determination is the key factor for success in finding wounded deer, which means check out likely nooks and rabbit hideaways. The bottom line is, as I'm fond of saying about deer hunting, if you're not in the game you lose, and that is especially true in this scenario.

Chapter Seven

Mock Scrapes: Create the Illusion and Score

In this chapter, I will discuss how to build a mock scrape to ambush a buck who comes in to investigate your counterfeit illusion. Before doing so, however, it is important to understand how bucks make rubs and scrapes and what the two olfactory and pheromone signposts are meant to communicate to other deer. However, I won't be talking about how to make a mock rub—I have done so in other books, including my last book *White-tail Tactics—Cutting Edge Strategies That Work!*, available at www.deerdoctor.com. But I do want to include what a buck does at a rub in this chapter, which will demonstrate all the behaviors a buck undertakes when making a rub and how much odor he painstakingly deposits when creating both rubs and scrapes.

Without question, the most observed buck sign found throughout deer season are buck rubs and scrapes. Each year, countless hunters plan their hunting strategies that include intercepting a buck, particularly a mature buck, at either a scrape or a rub. I

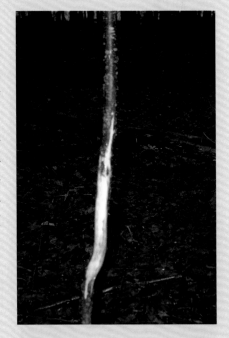

Many articles and TV shows claim that buck rubs are a primary place to ambush a mature buck. Countless research studies, however, dispute that assertion. Photo Credit: Fiduccia Enterprises.

Photo Credit Ted Rose.

would bet dollars to donuts, however, that a majority of bucks actually taken each deer season are killed near some type of natural vegetation or at food plots. Other bucks meet their demise along deer trails, particularly during the rut. The fact is, not nearly as many adult bucks as might be expected are actually taken at traditional signposts, such as rubs and scrapes. I'm not suggesting that rubs and scrapes don't offer good hunting opportunities; they do. A mature whitetail buck can be taken near a natural scrape or rub, but this will mostly be by hunters who can recognize which rubs and scrapes to hunt and which ones to avoid.

To dramatically increase the chances of killing a buck at a scrape, hunters should seriously consider building a mock scrape. The reasons a mock scrape dramatically improves the odds of taking a buck over a natural scrape will be discussed later in this chapter. However, I assure you a mock scrape will help a hunter considerably in taking a buck—even a mature buck.

Buck Rubs

Over the last two decades, much has been learned and reported by naturalists and scientists about the meanings of buck rubs. Research has concluded bucks make rubs as visual and olfactory signposts to communicate a variety of messages to other deer. A rub is where bucks leave eight to seventeen different glandular biochemical odors on

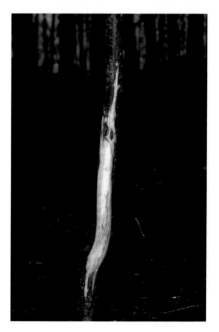

and around the tree they rub. The variety of glandular scents include interdigital, preputial, sudoriferous, tarsal, metatarsal, pineal, pre-orbital, anal, nasal, popliteal, salivary, and preputial glands, as well as scent from their urine, feces, seminal fluid, and antler bone. They also deposit scents from an organ located in the roof of their mouth called the vomeronasal organ. Each of these odors is unique to a particular buck.

In my years of experience, I have found some success when hunting natural rubs and scrapes. With that said, it isn't always easy for hunters to identify which

Bucks of all ages make rubs on tree trunks of varying diameters. Rubs are not only scent post markers; deer are attracted to them visually too. Even the sound of a rub being made can attract bucks and does. Photo Credit: Fiduccia Enterprises.

scrapes and rubs will provide top-notch action and which ones won't. The first task is to understand all the components associated with these two types of olfactory and visual signposts and the times they are made throughout the deer season. Rubs usually start to appear before the hunting season with rubbing behavior peaking during the rut and continuing—albeit with less activity—well into the winter after most hunting seasons have ended. Scrapes, on the other hand, usually start during the pre-rut of October and peak during the primary rut of November, although they can generate some buck activity during the post rut of December.

Rub Behaviors

An individual buck uses several different markers to advertise his new rub. They include the acoustic sounds antlers make, as well as the noises of his hooves jostling the forest debris. Many bucks will also occasionally vocalize while making a rub. The high visibility of the newly made rub and the combination of scents from a variety of glandular and other body odors that are deposited at the rub site serve as markers, as well. Each odor expresses a buck's presence, his identity, his age class, and his level of rutting status to other deer. The combination of all the odors releases specific pheromones that say to other deer, "Hey, it's me, Bucky-Boy!" Other deer smelling the rub or scrape will be able to decipher by the odors everything they need to know about the buck that made the rub or scrape, especially where he currently ranks in the male pecking order.

When a buck makes a rub, he purposefully acts out several behavioral mannerisms. As he approaches the intended tree, he is already depositing tiny amounts of interdigital scent with each step. The buck then stops short of the site by several yards to perform a behavior known as rub-urination. He vigorously rubs his back legs together and urinates over his metatarsal and tarsal glands, which drips the mixture of scents to the ground. When he finishes the rub-urinating, he squats slightly and squeezes his rump muscles, which causes pressure on the preputial gland—an exocrine gland

This gargantuan buck is performing the behavior known as rub-urination. Photo Credit: Ted Rose.

located within the penile sheath—which makes the gland emit a fluid unique to the buck that also falls to the ground.

Next he approaches the tree and, before doing any rubbing, sniffs the tree repeatedly. Biologists don't know exactly why the buck sniffs the tree before he begins to rub it or do anything else. Over my fifty-one years of observing deer, my speculation is that while the buck is sniffing the tree, he is also exhaling from his nostrils, thereby ejecting scent from his nasal glands—located inside his nasal passageway—onto the tree. I also surmise the buck sniffs the tree repeatedly to determine if he is satisfied with the amount of nasal scent he deposited.

The buck then licks the tree trunk over and over and, in the process, deposits scent from his salivary glands—located inside the mouth—and from the vomeronasal organ on the roof of his mouth. The enzymes in the saliva also contribute to the scent left on the tree trunk the buck is about to rub. The vomeronasal organ serves some of the same purposes as the nose. It is used primarily to take in estrus odors and evaluate the status of a doe's estrus cycle via her urine. He does this by curling his upper lip in what is called a Flehmen gesture. While lip curling, the buck will suck air into its mouth so whatever odor it is sniffing makes contact with the vomeronasal organ. It is said that the analysis of urine through the vomeronasal organ may also help synchronize the breeding readiness between bucks and does to ensure both sexes are in peak breeding condition at the same time.

After sniffing and licking the tree, the buck will begin to enthusiastically rub his antlers

against it, which places odors on the trunk from his sudoriferous glands, more commonly called forehead glands, found beneath the skin on the buck's forehead. As the buck rubs, he presses his forehead hard against the tree several times, which releases more forehead glandular scent each time. These glands are found beneath the skin on the buck's forehead. During the onset of the breeding season, they get considerably larger and emit more odor and secretions. The more mature a buck is and the higher he ranks within the social status of his bachelor group, the more sudoriferous secretions and odor he will produce.

Bucks with racks of this size often will rub huge tree trunks. This buck was photographed as he licked the tree bark repeatedly prior to rubbing it. Photo Credit: Ted Rose.

But the buck is not finished rubbing yet. As he rubs the bark bare, he deposits additional odors—some on the tree and some around the ground—from his penile, pre-orbital, anal, and preputial glands. At times he will even leave seminal fluid at the site. Before leaving, the buck will urinate again and defecate, too. Although no one has ever proven it, I think the buck also leaves a specific odor on the tree from his antlers. I have no way to verify my hypothesis, but it seems to be a reasonable deduction, particularly in that I can detect a slight odor from freshly shed antlers.

Once the rub is complete, it is a marker meant to communicate a variety of messages to other deer visually and through scent. Some rubs made by bucks are destined to used yearly and are therefore known as "signpost" rubs. What actually takes place at a rub is so much more than what hunters thought a buck did at a rub as recently as twenty years ago. Then, many academics and hunters believed the primary purpose of a rub was to help the buck shed his velvet and strengthen his neck muscles in preparation for the rut. Thanks to research, that notion is no longer valid.

Hunters who make mock rubs will learn just how visually attractive they are to passing bucks and does. The mere sight of a new rub generates instant attention and response from a curious deer. For more information about how to make a mock rub, visit my website and read the chapter in my book *Whitetail Tactics—Cutting Edge Strategies That Work!*

Before moving on to discussing scrapes, let me address an ongoing controversy about large- and small-antlered bucks and the size of the trees they rub. I doubt anyone reading this book hasn't heard in a deer camp or a hunting chat online the old adage that a large-antlered buck only rubs large trees and a small-antlered buck only rubs small saplings. I'm here to tell you that simply is not so. I could write an entire chapter about this one subject. But to keep things flowing here, trust this: Large-antlered bucks often rub trees as small as saplings. Small-antlered bucks and spikes, though, are not adverse to rubbing everything from a small saplings to larger diameter tree trunks rub large trees.

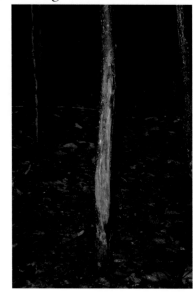

This is a classic example of a young "signpost rub." They are rubbed by numerous bucks from year to year which scars the tree permanently. Bucks will return to rub signpost rubs repeatedly for many years. Photo Credit: Fiduccia Enterprises.

Natural and Mock Scrapes

The first and foremost component for hunters to realize about natural scrapes is that they are not all created equally. Gathering as much information as you can about scrapes will be your key to using this mother of all deer signs successfully. Unfortunately, as I have often complained, the amount of misinformation about deer behavior and hunting strategies being disseminated today is problematic, as much of it is fabricated. This is particularly true when it comes to hunting with scrapes.

Too many hunters are led to believe that finding any scrape, even a primary one, is like grabbing the brass ring of success. They have been told all they have to do after locating a scrape is stand and wait patiently until a buck comes by—a strategy that could keep a hunter waiting until the cows come home.

A little-known fact about buck scrapes is that a notable percentage of all three natural scrapes aren't revisited and refreshed nearly as often as many hunters are led to believe. In fact, hard-core statics by researchers have proven that the chance of killing a buck or doe while hunting over a natural scrape is slim. That is not the case with a man-made scrape, as I'll explain later in this chapter. Now let me be clear, I'm not suggesting a buck can't be killed over a scrape; Lady Luck can see to that. But I wouldn't suggest the realistic odds are in your favor. I often recommend that

This buck is putting the finishing touches on his scrape by placing scent on the over-hanging branch just above it. Biologists have done numerous studies that suggest bucks are infrequently killed over scrapes. Photo Credit: Ted Rose.

when hunting natural scrapes, choose one accompanied by an overhanging branch and, much more importantly, includes a licking stick near it. The buck will take both the overhanging branch and licking stick (individually) into his mouth and chew the edges. This behavior often ends up fraying the ends of both the branch and the stick. When you find a scrape that has an overhanging branch and a licking stick, there is a strong indication that the scrape is being actively attended to by at least one buck. If you follow that advice, you will increase your odds of ambushing a buck at a natural scrape.

I should mention that the size of a secondary or primary scrape has nothing to do with the age class, antler size, or social importance of the buck that made it. A secondary scrape can be about three to four feet in diameter, and a primary scrape can be several feet or more in diameter. Not many natural scrapes are the size of car hoods, but there are a few that can be found of that size.

While false and secondary scrapes are generally nothing more than random markings, a primary scrape has considerable importance. Primary scrapes are the natural scrapes used by several different bucks and does over the course of the whitetail breeding season. Primary scrapes will be revisited and refreshed throughout the rut. Similar to secondary scrapes, they are most often made in the same locations by bucks year after year.

Types of Scrapes

Naturalists, biologists, and other academics refer to the names of scrapes with scientific terms. Most accomplished hunting pros and outdoor writers who refer to scrapes use slightly less technical designations. There are three types of scrapes that bucks make. They are called false scrapes, secondary scrapes, and primary scrapes, also known as a hub, territorial, or home-range scrape.

Each type of scrape appears at a specific time during the fall breeding season. While adolescent bucks—one-and-a-half- to two-and-a-half-year-olds—make all three of these scrapes, adult bucks of three and a half years or older most often only make secondary and primary scrapes, although some will make false scrapes on occasion. Adult bucks will usually make secondary scrapes in areas that does use regularly. When they make primary scrapes, they paw out earth in more secretive cover generally along the borders of their home range.

A buck applying scent to an overhanging branch above a secondary scrape. Note the number of rubs behind him. Photo Credit: Ted Rose.

Secondary and primary scrapes principally act as longer term visual and olfactory signposts to other deer during the rut than the brief false scrapes do. Secondary and primary scrapes act to alert other deer as to which bucks are claiming particular patches of dirt or areas within their home range. Not all scrapes are equal. Some are made indiscriminately, and others are made with more purpose and intent. The most important primary scrapes serve entirely different purposes than the other two.

All bucks refresh and scent-mark their own scrapes and rubs, as well as scrapes and rubs made by other bucks. Even female deer will mark scrapes and rubs with their urine, feces, saliva, and sudoriferous glands. Doe do so during the breeding season to help them determine which bucks are using what areas within their home range. Sometimes, a doe in peak estrus may not only freshen up a buck scrape, she may actually make a smaller scrape alongside the buck scrape. On rare occasions, some adult does have been documented making their own scrapes within their home range.

False Scrapes

The first scrape to appear in the deer woods is the randomly placed false scrape. These small circular scrapes are usually not much larger than the diameter of a large pot meant to cook pasta sauce—about twelve to eighteen inches across. Some are larger, but not many are. Bow hunters are generally the first to see these because false scrapes

are usually created by bucks in early October, when bow hunters are afoot in the woods. Bucks make false scrapes as a reaction to the first estrus odor of the year.

Mother Nature is perfect is her overall scheme. The pre-rut scrape-making scenario goes like this. She makes sure the rut begins by having all the mature does in any given herd—throughout the same latitude—who are in prime breeding condition come into a brief twenty-four- to forty-eight-hour estrus cycle. In any given area, then, a few of the healthiest older does come into heat. Like any female mammal, when a doe is in her prime breeding years, her estrus period

False scrapes are usually the first to appear in the woods every fall. Photo Credit: Fiduccia Enterprises.

is timely and reliable, unlike younger or old female deer, whose estrus periods are irregular or late.

So now the woods are permeated with estrus scent, and the drama of the pre-rut begins to unfold. A buck causally begins to make his way toward a food source, and he picks up the pheromone odor of estrus! The reaction is immediate. The buck's senses begin to go slightly awry, which is totally understandable; he has waited a year for sex. Somewhat demented by the estrus scent, the buck is instinctively driven to create scrapes to advertise his prowess to the few female deer in heat. While bucks up to three and a half years old mostly partake in this ritual, false scrapes are generally made by juveniles one and a half to two and a half years old that are not yet in their prime breeding years. Each buck is so excited that he builds not one or two sizeable scrapes but a dozen or more tiny ones. The adult bucks realize they don't have to waste a lot of unnecessary energy making false scrapes. They instinctively understand they have first choice at mating with does because adult females in their prime breeding years will intuitively seek out the most virile males.

You have seen these scrapes in October. One day there is no visible sign of the rut other than a few possible rubs. The following day, these little scrapes appear throughout the woods. When first made, false scrapes are bare to the ground and free of leaves and other forest debris. I have never seen any false scrape that was accompanied by an overhanging branch or licking stick. The lifespan of a false scrape is brief—perhaps two to three days. After that, the scrapes are abandoned. They are no longer bare to the ground and are quickly covered over by leaves. False scrapes are completely worthless to hunt over.

I'm going to make a short diversion at this point to share a tactic. While false scrapes are valueless, they provide significant rut-date information. When you find a fresh false scrape, meaning it is bare to the ground, it will be the mechanism that you can use to accurately determine when the primary and post ruts will occur. Once you have located a fresh false scrape, jot down the date—don't leave it to memory. You can bet that if you count twenty-eight to thirty-two days forward, the primary rut will be in full swing! By extrapolating from the date of the first false scrape and counting fifty-six to sixty-four days forward, you will have the primary dates of the post rut! The post rut can be the most dramatic of all three phases of the breeding season. The late rut is a time when some of the adult female deer and some yearlings that were not successfully bred in November come back into heat. It is also the time when some of the seven- and eight-month-old fawns come into their first estrus periods, which all account for a breeding stage that can see a significant spike in buck activity.

Secondary Scrapes

The next classification of the three types of scrapes is called a secondary scrape. This is the most prevalent and observed scrape of the three. Secondary scrapes are seen along fencerows, wooded trails, pinch points, funnels, near food sources, near bedding areas, and, most often, along well-used doe travel corridors. Bucks usually make scrapes on dry ground because it helps retain urine and glandular odors longer.

Secondary scrapes are made mostly made by adolescent two-and-a-half-year-old and some three-and-a-half-year-old late teen, hormonally driven bucks. Similar to all male adolescents, they think they are made of steel and are indestructible. A comparison would be the fights many of us had in the schoolyard. They get emotionally charged by ripping up the earth and thrashing vegetation to show off their prowess. Bucks that are four and a half years old and older have no need to be braggadocios. Adult bucks make secondary scrapes in areas that are more heavily traveled and favored by does. Their scrapes will appear narrow and longer in length rather than circular due to the way they make the scrape. The buck will make several long pawing strokes with his front hooves, then he will deposit a variety of scents. He will rub his pre-orbital, sudoriferous, and salivary glands on an overhanging branch above a secondary scrape to signal his intentions to does and competitive bucks. The secondary scrapes rarely include as much of the glandular and other scents that a buck deposits in a primary scrape, and they hardly ever include a licking stick.

Secondary scrapes are a larger than false scrapes, at about two to four feet in diameter. Photo Credit: Fiduccia Enterprises.

Secondary scrapes are notably larger than false scrapes. Generally, the diameter of a secondary scrape can be about two to four feet, although sometimes they are slightly larger. These scrapes are usually made from late October to early November. As noted, they are not regularly active. A hunter may get lucky and kill a buck at a secondary scrape, but this will mostly be because he or she happened to be at the right place at the right time. But when it comes to deer hunting, there's nothing wrong with being lucky rather than good. With that said, I would strongly suggest not to waste your valuable hunting time sitting over secondary scrapes in hopes of taking a buck, especially an adult buck. Secondary scrapes have more value than false scrapes, but they are close to worthless.

Primary Scrapes

As a reminder, primary scrapes can also be referred to as hub, home-range, and territorial scrapes. I mention this in case you ever read an article or discussion about scrapes that uses one of these alternative names. It will stop any confusion regarding if there are other types of scrapes. When it comes to a buck making a primary scrape, the same principle is applied as when buying a business or real estate—location, location, location.

When you locate a primary scrape, you will know it. Its size will be the foremost indicator. A primary scrape will be at least several feet in diameter and sometimes larger. At times, they can be the size of a pickup truck hood, albeit that's uncommon. It will always be found in deep cover, it will always be bare of forest debris, it may sometimes have an obvious deer track in it, the bare earth will sometimes be stained with a wet spot of urine, it will always be slightly depressed in the middle, it will always have an overhanging branch that is frayed at its tip, it will almost always have a licking stick nearby, and it will always have a detectable odor of musk and urine. Before leaving, check to see what type of tree or brush the buck made his scrape under; it will be made clear why soon. These are all key components that help you correctly identify a primary scrape. This is the scrape that bucks routinely return to, scent check, visually investigate, refresh, and safeguard.

I recommend you don't hunt a primary scrape after discovering it. Here's why: There is a high probability that a buck is bedded down within one hundred yards or so wind-checking the scrape, and a single mistake by you can blow him out of the area. Another important reason is based on a research study done on the time of day adult bucks visit their primary scrapes the most. As might be expected by veteran hunters, about 65 percent of all primary scrapes are visited and refreshed by adult bucks under the safety of darkness. So the odds are against anyone trying to hunt a primary scrape during daylight. Yes, you can get lucky, but the flip side of that coin is you may waste a lot of valuable hunting time and end up never seeing the buck during legal shooting hours.

Build It and He Will Come!

If it's not the best option to hunt a natural primary scrape, what should a hunter do? Now is the time to employ the killing tactic of building your own primary mock scrape! To create the most effective illusion, make your scrape slightly smaller than the natural primary scrape you discovered. It will require some planning and tools. Before you leave for the woods, make sure you have showered and washed your hair thoroughly with an unscented soap. Also wash your clothes and the soles of your boots the evening before with an unscented soap. Prior to leaving for the woods, spray your clothing and equipment with a scent eliminator. The tools needed will include a leaf rake, latex gloves, unscented boot coverings like delivery men use when they enter a home, a snip, and a pair of flat-tooth pliers. You will also need deer scent. Here's what I use when I make a mock primary scrape: Buck Stop's Gland-U-Lure, Deer in a Bottle, straight buck urine, straight tarsal scent, interdigital scent, forehead scent, and Love Potion No 9: A Fatal Potion of Pheromones Check my website to see the types of brands I use under Mock Scrape Scents at www.deerdoctor.com.

Once you have found a site in good cover to build your primary mock scrape, remember that there should be a small sapling, the licking stick, within five yards of the site where you will be making the scrape. An adult buck looks for a licking stick to be accompanying a primary scrape, so remember to create the entire illusion. If a sapling isn't available in the spot you choose, use a stout branch two to four fingers around and stick it firmly into the soil to

Create the entire illusion, and then make sure there is a licking stick within five yards of the mock primary scrape. Photo Credit: Fiduccia Enterprises.

imitate a licking stick. Don't forget to fray the end of the licking stick. Try to match the tree or brush you will be making your scrape under to the type of trees and brush deer prefer to make scrapes at in your area. Now you know why you made note of the type of tree the buck used.

You will also want to create a licking branch out of an overhead hanging branch. There is a difference between a licking stick, which is a sapling growing near the scrape site, and the overhanging branch from the tree that the scrape is under. To make this, select a stout branch and cut it with a knife about a quarter of the way through. It is crucial not to cut too deeply, or it will break off. Cut it just enough to let it flop a little from the rest of the branch. The branch should be

This buck is depositing scent onto a stick-licking (a.k.a. overhanging branch). Photo Credit: Fiduccia Enterprises.

about forty-two to sixty-eight inches high. I generally settle at about fifty to fifty-five inches. When you are finished making the overhanging branch, apply forehead gland scent with a clean scent pad to the end and along the branch. You can do the same thing to the licking stick just before leaving the area.

Now it's time to play in the dirt. Before beginning, I liberally spray the teeth of the leaf rake with buck urine. Then I start my work directly beneath the overhanging branch. I begin removing all the forest debris from the ground in an area about forty-eight to fifty-six inches around. This is truly one time in life that size matters! While you are building your scrape, remember scent is also paramount. You're imitating a trapper, which means you are taking every precaution in eliminating human scent.

Deer Scent

When you're making a mock primary scrape, the calendar will dictate using deer scents that bucks are used to smelling that time of year—October 28 to November 10, give or take a few days.

The scents I use to create a mock-scrape include: Buck Stop's Gland-U-Lure, pure tarsal gland scent, Bob Kirschner's Trailmaker (Interdigital scent), Mimic-Scrape scents, and Love Potion No. 9—A Fatal Attraction of Pheromones (a proprietary blend of rutting buck urine and estrus doe urine). Since Love Potion No. 9 is a scent I own, I don't want to over promote it here. If you don't use it, apply any other quality doe estrus and rutting buck urine you are comfortable with.

Finally, as you leave and reach about twenty yards from your newly made scrape, squeeze or spray several drops of tarsal gland scent onto the forest floor along with a *few* drops of interdigital scent. Also place several drops of Love Potion No. 9 and/or your other mix down as well. Repeat this once more when you get about fifty to seventy-five yards from the mock scrape. When returning to hunt the scrape, put a liberal amount of Love Potion No. 9 (or your other mix) on a boot pad and walk in. When you reach the scrape, walk a circle around it and then walk toward your stand. When you are about twenty yards from the stand, hang the pad on a branch then go directly to the stand. By following this procedure it will help create a realistic illusion that even an adult buck will find hard to ignore.

Hunt your mock scrape three times a day every other day at different times, such as from dawn to 10 a.m., 11 a.m. to 1 p.m., and 2 p.m. to sunset. Use all precautions entering and leaving the area to prevent being detected. If at all practical, go in and leave the stand using different entry and exit points. Use a variety of tactics, including calling with estrus doe blats and buck grunts and other similar rut tactics. Each day you should see more and more buck activity at the scrape. If you haven't seen a buck during that time, freshen up the scrape with the scents, rest it a day, and hunt it again for longer periods each day. Hunting the stand for longer periods means taking extra care with human scent elimination. You're hunting an adult buck!

Don't deviate from creating the entire illusion or look for shortcuts. Pay meticulous attention to wind direction each time you hunt the stand. If on any day you are going to hunt the scrape and the wind is blowing toward potential bedding areas, hunt somewhere else that day.

By understanding the information within this chapter, you will take your scrape hunting to higher levels. When this tactic is executed correctly, your mock primary scrape will be as real to the buck as a natural primary scrape.

Chapter Eight

Natural Tarsal Glands: The Ultimate Buck Decoy

In 1963, I read *Shots at Whitetails* by Lawrence R. Koller. Even at that time, the book had already become a hunting classic. The following year, I began deer hunting. I planned my deer hunt with a mind filled with stories written by the well-known outdoor writers of the 1960s who publicized New York State's north country trophy buck hunting opportunities. Each fall, the pages of the big three magazines of that era—*Sports Afield*, *Outdoor Life*, and *Field & Stream*—had a least one story touting where to go to hunt for whitetails in New York State's Adirondack Mountains.

In October of 1964, I painstakingly packed my hunting gear into my father's 1963 Ford Galaxy XL. On a cold late Friday evening, I left Bay Ridge, Brooklyn, New York, and headed due north. Several hours later, I arrived in the Adirondack Mountains to stalk whitetail deer for the first time. I parked along an old logging road outside the small hamlet of Childwold, located between the villages of Tupper Lake and Cranberry Lake. With only a few hours of sleep in a cold car, I got up before dawn, dressed

This is the village of Tupper Lake. Other than the vehicles in this photo, the town looks very similar to when I hunted the surrounding woodlands in 1964. Photo Credit: Tupper Lake Postcard.

Photo Credit Ted Rose.

in my hunting gear, and made my way into the woods. I was hunting on International Paper Company land. I had read an article that IPC opened this tract of thousands of acres of lumber land for public hunting for the first time in one hundred years. I was determined to kill a buck. Unfortunately, I did not.

The northern zone portion of New York State's deer season usually opened on October 25, about a month before the southern zone of New York's deer season did, which remains the same today. Over the years, it became a tradition for me and my hunting buddy Howie Crofts to make the northern zone opening weekend. Over the next dozen or more years, I cut my deer-hunting teeth, so to speak, throughout the Adirondack Forest Preserve's 2.6 million acres—housed within the six million acres of the Adirondack Park. I rattled, called, tracked, and sat on many a stump for countless hours, hunting and studying deer throughout those mountains, including the Keene Valley, Lake Placid, Newcomb, Old Forge, Big Moose, Indian Lake, North Creek, and a village called, of all things, Deerland.

About now you can justly wonder—what does all of this have to do with this chapter? Well, the quick answer is, the Adirondacks are where I first learned about the effectiveness of using a natural tarsal gland of a deer to attract a buck. During my third deer season, 1967, I drove my '67 396 Super Sport to a tiny community called Newcomb. After hunting for a few hours in the morning, I left the woods about 10 a.m. and went to Minerva to buy a sandwich. When I got out of my car to walk to the general store, I was mesmerized by a twelve-point buck that was strapped to the roof of a station wagon. The hunter of the big buck had it proudly roped securely to the roof's metal railings. As I write this, I can still clearly recall how I stared at that buck for several minutes in what some might call a stupor. Sometime during my trance, a gratified old-timer and another hunter, clad in the red and black wool "camo" of the '60s, approached me.

"Nice buck, ain't he, boy?" the older looking one said. (I later found out his name was Sal.)

I don't recall replying, but I must have said something because a long conversation ensued about how he killed the buck.

He continued, "My friend Curly here kilt a buck nearly identical to this 'un yesterday. After I helped Curly hang him on the deer pole, I skunned out the tarsal and hung it from a tree branch this morning by my stand. Then this ol' boy come a walkin' down the trail as perty as ya please. I kilt him as he stuck his nose into that stanky gland!" A note of ironic interest at this point: Curly was as bald as a cue ball.

My jaw was probably hanging wide open by time he finished his account of the hunt. Looking directly in my eyes, the old-timer then said, "How bout I skun my buck's tarsal gland out for you boy? You can use it this afternoon to try to get you a buck. It'll work for ya. All you need to do is hang it on a branch and wait for a buck to come check it out. With any luck at all, you'll be skunning out your buck by evenin'."

The fact is, after he made the offer I nearly peed my pants from unbridled anticipation! I watched intensely as the old-timer took his knife out of its sheath and began to skillfully separate both tarsal glands from the insides of the buck's rear legs. With a wide smile on his face he said, "Take a deep whiff of this, boy." I did. I must have grimaced because both hunters broke out into thunderous laughs. "Well, looks like we gotcha, eh boy?"

Little did they know, to me the gland didn't stink badly. Quite to the contrary, in my mind it was rife with the aroma of sweet success. I offered to buy the boys coffee, and we went back into the general store and spent the next hour talking about what a tarsal gland is and what it does. By the time I left the store, I was well versed in the biology of the gland and its value as a natural lure to attract bucks and hot does.

By 1 p.m. that afternoon, with snowflakes the size of quarters slowly drifting to the ground, I hung the tarsal gland on a low branch of a sapling oak. I was tempted to hang both of them, but both Sal and Curly had warned me only to hang one. I walked back to my ground stand, which was about fifty yards from where I hung the gland. I sat on my red plastic Hot-Seat—you will only know what a Hot-Seat was, how it smelled, and what it looked like, if you are over forty—and leaned my back against a wide old oak. As the snow began to cover the ground, I heard a noise. I was pretty sure it was a grunt made by a buck, but since I had never actually heard a buck grunt in the wild, I wasn't sure.

Luckily, I knew enough to sit motionless and wait patiently. In less than a few

Deer of both sexes communicate a variety of different messages through odors emitted from several of their glands, organs, natural oils, fluids and steroids. Photo Credit: Ted Rose.

minutes, I heard what I thought was another buck grunt. Before I could question myself, the buck walked straight to the tarsal gland as he repeatedly grunted lowly. I carefully raised my lever-action Marlin Model 336 Gold Trigger 30-30, pulled the hammer back, placed the crosshairs of vintage Redfield Wideview Accu Range 3x9 scope on the buck's front shoulder, and fired. The buck instantly fell quietly to the snow-covered forest floor. I rushed to him and poked him in the eye several times with the barrel of my rifle—as instructed to do by many an outdoor magazine writer in their articles—to safely make sure the deer was dead. I grasped his antlers with both hands, held them tightly, and proudly examined his two eight-inch spike antlers.

Today, using a natural tarsal gland isn't as new a tactic as it was in the 1950s and '60s, and natural tarsal glands are not used as much by a majority of deer hunters these days. More hunters are apt to use tarsal gland scent in a bottle sold by a reliable deer-scent company. For the most part, this chapter is about a few different ways a hunter can use a natural tarsal gland—either one removed from a deer taken by another hunter or from a roadkill deer where it is legal to do so. I want to be clear that I have also used tarsal gland scent from a bottle for dozens of years in many of the same applications I will discuss here, and I have had good results. But according to my records, when I used natural tarsal glands, I have had slightly better success. Before discussing the different types of tarsal gland tactic applications to attract a buck or doe, I would like to define the tarsal gland in more detail.

Tarsal Gland

The tarsal gland is an external gland located on the inside of a deer's hind legs. It secretes fatty substances called lipids. The standard definition of a lipid is, "Any of a class of organic compounds that are fatty acids or their derivatives and are insoluble in water but soluble in organic solvents. They include many natural oils, waxes and steroids." Some biologists and hunters claim it is the most essential whitetail deer scent gland. I can neither confirm nor deny that contention.

Deer of all ages and both sexes use the tarsal glands to communicate with each other all year long. Some recent research and articles have suggested that the mix of bacteria species that live within the gland is unique to each deer. Its individuality has been compared to the fingerprint of a human. The odor makes it possible for each deer to specifically identify another. Equally interesting is that the tarsal gland odor is said to be able to transmit, via the deer's olfactory senses, another deer's age, sex, state of pecking order, breeding condition, and sexual receptiveness. In male deer, it is also said to communicate a buck's state of belligerence.

During most of the year, the gland is light tan in color. During the breeding season, or the rut, the gland turns dark brown. As the rut nears its end, it is almost jet black. From the onset of the pre-rut and through all three rut phases—pre-, primary, and post—bucks urinate over the tarsal gland constantly. The urine clings to the long thick hairs of the tarsal glands to turn them darker and darker as the breeding season progresses. When the staining runs down past the tarsal gland itself to discolor the lower leg, as well, it is a significant indication that the buck is mature.

Deer use their tarsal glands and the pheromones expelled from them—which are mostly made up of lactones, or any of a group of internal esters derived from hydroxyl acids—as both a visual and olfactory signal. In mature deer, the tarsal glands emit a more pungent aroma than they do in immature deer. When excited, the hairs on the tarsal gland stand erect. The upright hair can be seen from quite a distance by other deer. There is little doubt that this gland is one of the more important glands to whitetails—and hunters.

Any experienced hunter who has harvested a buck or doe during the peak of the breeding season knows how pungent a tarsal gland smells. The odor has come to be associated with deer hunting. However, some may not know that the tarsal gland is used in a behavior performed by male deer called rub-urination.

Rub-urination is what a buck does from the first time he begins to disperse his tarsal gland scent during the breeding season. He places his two rear legs together and presses the tarsals tightly against each other. Then he squats slightly and begins to urinate so it flows over both glands. Then he squats a bit lower and excretes fluid from his preputial

This buck's jet black tarsal glands appear wet—a sign he has been urinating and depositing preputial gland fluid over them. Photo Credit: Ted Rose.

gland over the tarsal glands. Next, the buck rubs the tarsal glands together several times vigorously. Because of all these aromas, fluids, and pheromones, it is reasonable to understand why natural tarsal glands are such powerful decoys as deer attractants.

The tarsal glands—as well as the other male glands including the pre-orbital, inter-digital, nasal, salivary, forehead, and, to some lesser extent, the metatarsal and the vom-eronasal organ—play a vital role during the rut. One other gland, though, may vastly increase the success of using a natural tarsal gland. It is the preputial gland, and it is located within a buck's penile sheath. Some biologists reason that the preputial gland serves two purposes: It is used for lubrication and may also contain sperm. The scientific community is still not entirely sure about what exactly this gland does. I will discuss this gland and how it might be used in combination with the natural tarsal gland near the end of this chapter. They are all used in various degrees of depositing—or sniffing and tasting—pheromones when a buck makes a scrape, rub, licking stick, or overhanging branch. When a hunter creates a fake rub or scrape, the tarsal glands serve as the primary attracting scent.

Natural Tarsal Gland Tactics

The first part of this tactic requires knowing how to remove the tarsal gland from its former owner. The older the buck is, the better the tarsal gland will work. Be assured, though, the tarsal glands from an adult doe will also work quite well. From the instant you decide to use the gland as a decoy, it is highly advisable not to touch it with bare hands. Nothing will dampen the success of this tactic faster than contaminating the gland with human scent. Wear latex gloves to remove it and when you use it in the field. When it is skinned off the deer, make sure you take more rather than less. Cut a liberal amount of hide from around the hock to ensure you have an ample amount to hang. Whether you are using it immediately or not, place the tarsal into a plastic bag so it doesn't get polluted with unwanted scents. Do the same immediately after removing it from the branch of the tree.

There are a few different ways to use a natural tarsal gland to attract competitive bucks, curious subordinate bucks, or estrus does from the simplicity of hanging a tarsal gland on a branch to creating a more sophisticated decoy that includes a mock rub or scrape. I have had success with each of these tactics. I have found my optimum response period takes place mostly in the early pre-rut or post rut. While I have had good success using a natural tarsal gland during the primary rut, it hasn't been as effective as

When tarsal gland hairs stand up like they are on this buck, it is a sure bet he is about to urinate over them. Photo Credit: Ted Rose.

the other two rut phases. Some other pros support my results but can't or haven't offered a hypothesis as to why.

My common sense theory is that during the primary rut there is an overabundance of tarsal aroma distributed throughout the woods by live bucks. They are dispersing other glandular scents, fluids, and odors from their various glands and organs. There is no doubt in my mind that they react to the salubrious odors left by live bucks breeding does more than they do from a tarsal gland with a scent that isn't as fresh or powerful. During the pre- and post rut phases, however, tarsal odor is less prevalent. Thus, bucks will be more apt to investigate tarsal scent during the pre- and post rut. This is just my working theory, but it beats the snot out of saying I don't know why I get more response in early and late rut than I do during the primary rut.

Hang It

If a hunter doesn't intend to use a tarsal gland in conjunction with building a mock scrape or rub, the quickest and easiest strategy is to simply hang a natural tarsal gland on the branch of a tree and wait for a buck to respond to its scent. Be sure the gland is as fresh as possible when you use it. If it has been used for a few days, remember to take it down wearing latex gloves at the end of the day's hunt, and keep it refrigerated until it will be used again. Although this tactic will work, over the years I have found it will work better when you create the entire illusion.

Mock Scrape

To fool a buck as much as possible, a tarsal gland should be used in combination with the a mock scrape or rub. Making a scrape doesn't require a degree in rocket science.

This is a natural primary scape found on our land. I made my mock scrape about the same size, and included an overhanging branch and licking stick. I used commercially made tarsal scent instead of a natural tarsal gland Note the size of this scrape compared with the cross bow lying in it. Photo Credit: Peter Cody Fiduccia.

Make it big enough to mimic a primary scrape of an adult buck. They are considerably larger than the false scrapes of October and the secondary scrapes of early November. Primary scrapes are almost always found in thick cover between food and bedding areas.

Two days before the opening of the 2014 firearm deer season, I made a mock scrape along the edge of my primary sanctuary in an area called Kate's Woods East. I didn't use a natural tarsal gland, as I hadn't yet killed a buck nor had anyone else, so I used a tarsal gland scent instead. I made the scrape large enough to be seen from a blind on a hillside about two hundred yards away. I started hunting the blind around 1 p.m. No sooner did I settle in than I saw a good-sized antlered buck cruising through the sanctuary woodlot. He ran back and forth several times and then left the area. About half an hour later, a good-sized doe started sniffing my mock scrape. It was obvious that she was interested in what she smelled because she stayed within ten yards of the scrape for twenty minutes before a young four-point buck showed up. He made the doe really nervous, and although she wanted to bolt off, the scent from the scrape kept her glued to the spot. Over the next two hours, the buck chased the poor doe in circles almost continuously. Every time he got close to her, she would lay flat on the ground. Finally, she gave up, and when the buck least expected it, she snuck off by crawling into some high weeds and then running into other cover.

I realized she was in estrus and would most likely come back to the mock scrape soon after the young buck disappeared. I hoped she would have a buck in tow if or when she returned. She did return, and when I saw her come out of the pines above my blind, she was making an absolute beeline to the mock scrape. As she ran to it, I caught movement out of the corner of my eye. Not thirty yards from my blind was a dandy eight-point buck hot on the trail of the doe. I never allowed him to reach her. Most interestingly, after I shot the buck, the doe didn't bolt off. Instead she stayed by the scrape even as I approached the dead buck. It wasn't until I started dragging him out that she finally ran off.

Although I didn't use a natural tarsal gland, I mentioned this hunt for a couple of reasons. One was to drive home the point that using tarsal scent from a bottle can work. I also wanted to make the point of how creating a mock scrape helps to dramatically increase the success of using tarsal glands along with a scrape.

For detailed instructions on creating a mock scrape, see the previous chapter, "Mock Scrapes: Create the Illusion and Score."

Mock Rub

You can also use a natural tarsal gland with a mock rub. When a buck, whether it is an immature buck or an older animal, sees a freshly made natural rub, he instantly recognizes the highly visual object—deer can see rubs from long distances—as an olfactory signpost. They're naturally and characteristically curious about rubs, and they have an inherent need to investigate them. That point alone will help draw a buck to the mock rub that a tarsal gland is hanging from. The buck's senses tell him he must inspect and mark the rub with his scent to communicate his presence and status to other bucks and does within the area. As long as nothing happens to set off an alarm to the deer, he has no choice but to inspect the rub because his instincts demand and urge him to do so.

Not a lot of deer hunting tactics work on such basic sensory and instinctive levels as mock rubs do. There is no question that a mock scrape with a natural tarsal gland will attract a buck. When a buck responds to a scrape, however, he does so with a little more caution than when he responds to a rub. A buck, particularly an adult buck that is high in the pecking order, instinctively knows a primary scrape is often watched closely by other bucks lurking in nearby cover. In my experience, mock rubs generate

This hunter is starting to create a fake rub as a visual and olfactory lure to decoy both bucks and does into the area. Photo Credit: Fiduccia Enterprises.

slightly more response than mock scrapes do, but both are extremely effective tactics when used correctly.

Remember when creating a mock rub that it should not appear to have been made by Godzilla, right? You want it to suggest by its length, shape, and trunk size to any interested buck that the rub was made by another buck who can be easily intimidated, which is the key to all types of visual, audible, and scent-decoying tactics.

Now take the natural deer gland and hang it four to five feet above the ground. If the tree doesn't have a branch that low, screw a small tree step into the tree and hang the gland from it. Before hanging it, rub the gland along the entire portion of the rub. Around the base of the tree, squirt several drops of pure buck urine.

Walk back from your mock rub about ten yards and put down about ten to fifteen drops or a few good squirts of the straight buck urine on the forest floor. Aim the spray as a buck would in several directions but not all over the place. A doe would urinate in a single spot; a buck's penis will dangle back and forth while urinating. By doing all of this, a hunter creates the entire illusion.

Preputial Gland

As I mentioned earlier, male deer also deposit scent and fluid from the preputial gland, which is located within a buck's penile sheath. Although the scientific community is still not entirely sure what this gland does, I intend to test the preputial gland's value as an additional natural deer attractant over the next few deer seasons. My plan is to remove the penis and testicles of a buck after it has been killed and hang the penile sheath and scrotum next to the tarsal gland. My reasoning is based, as all my proactive Spider Syndrome deer-hunting strategies are, on common sense deductions.

Since my experience has proven to me that rutting bucks and estrus does respond well to natural tarsal glands, it is my deduction that they

This buck's body posture demonstrates he is about to expel fluid from his preputial gland down onto to his tarsal glands. Photo Credit: Ted Rose.

should respond equally well to the preputial gland and scrotum, too. I can only believe the combination of the natural odors, fluids, and pheromones—endogenous, internally produced chemical signals secreted by deer, as well as other animals—of both the tarsal gland and the preputial gland and scrotum will help to create the entire illusion—a phase I coined in the early seventies to go along with my Spider Syndrome tactics. While you may want to try using the preputial gland along with the natural tarsal glands now, I forewarn you that I have no hard evidence or experience at the time of this writing that using it will help. For the purpose of this chapter, I will stick to discussing how to use a natural tarsal gland. You can decide for yourself if you want to include the penile sheath and scrotum to emit the preputial pheromones.

I would also like to include a brief overview of some of the other glands of a white-tail deer. When a hunter knows more about deer glands, it can only help. Each gland or organ emits pheromones, secretions, and an unbelievable combination of compound chemicals. These olfactory chemical messages act to alert, calm, attract, frighten, identify, and even assist in establishing a deer's rank within the herd.

By understanding each gland or organ and what the deer uses it for most, hunters can create olfactory illusions that will help to attract, hold, purposely spook, and even intentionally direct deer in specific directions! Combining the scents of deer glands with different tactics will increase your deer sightings and success. Plan to use the tips shared here—you may end up taking a buck of a life-time this season!

Interdigital Gland

The interdigital gland, located between the toes of the hooves, is commonly used by whitetails. It is a small sac that opens from a duct. When squeezed, the sac emits a yellowish substance with a potent odor that reeks of rancid cheese. The odor emitted from each deer's interdigital gland is unique to that particular animal and helps identify it to other deer.

Each time a deer puts its hoof on the ground, the gland emits a tiny amount of interdigital scent. The scent enables other deer to identify and follow a particular deer if they choose to. The odor from the interdigital gland also aids deer in identifying when a transient deer is in their range. When interdigital molecules begin to evaporate, the odor of the track changes, and that may be how deer and predators can judge the freshness of the track and which way the deer is moving.

Interdigital scent is also used to warn other deer of potential danger. When a deer stomps its hoof, it deposits an excess amount of interdigital scent. In doing so, it alerts other deer to danger through scent, sound, and sight. A deer coming upon excess interdigital scent immediately knows there is, or was, potential danger in the area. It is alert and will mill about nervously for several moments in an attempt to decipher the odor. It will then either walk back in the direction it came from or take a wide berth around the scent left. Deer rarely, if ever, walk directly over it.

Interdigital Tactics

This scent can be used in a few ways to attract, intentionally spook, or change a deer's travel route. To attract deer with this scent, it is important not to use more than a couple drops of interdigital on a drag bag or the sole of a boot before walking toward your stand. Once you are within thirty yards of the stand, walk a circle completely around it and move directly to the stand. Deer will often follow the scent with their nose held tightly to the ground. Interdigital scent can be used to intentionally roust deer

from thick cover, such as blowdowns, standing corn, laurels, etc. When a likely patch of cover is spotted, place several drops of interdigital scent on the ground. Stomp your foot several times and blow an alarm-distress snort. To create the entire illusion of a deer signaling danger, position yourself so your scent is blowing toward the cover. This tactic can be used without including the alarm-distress vocalization.

Interdigital scent can also be used to purposely change a deer's direction of travel toward a particular stand instead of having it take another trail. It works especially well

I use a commercially made Interdigital scent called Trailmaker (www.deerdoctor.com) "to stop, attract, intentionally roust, and even change a deer's direction from one trail to another." Photo Credit: Ted Rose.

This buck is depositing forehead gland scent along with other scents from its pre-orbital glands, saliva, and Jacobson's organ (VNO) on the overhanging branch above a scrape. Photo Credit: Ted Rose.

where two well-used trails intersect. Simply place several drops of interdigital scent several yards down the trail you don't want the deer to travel, as the excess scent indicates a deer encountered potential trouble at the spot. Once a deer smells the excess interdigital scent, they will briefly pause, become skittish, and quickly head back from where they came or turn down the other trail leading to your location.

Forehead Glands

The forehead glands are between the top of the deer's eyes and the antlers. They become active in September and get progressively more pronounced throughout the rut. The potency of these glands is directly associated with the deer's age and social status. The forehead glands produce an oily substance that makes the hair around the eyes darker. As a buck rubs a tree or overhanging branch, his forehead scent is deposited to act as an olfactory communication message to other deer. It advertises the social ranking, current breeding status, and age of the buck leaving the scent. The older a buck is, the more trees and branches he will mark. Some biologists believe that the odor from the forehead gland pheromones left on trees and other vegetation helps bring does into estrus.

The Forehead Gland Tip

Unfortunately, at this writing forehead gland scent is not available commercially. I have only taken it from a dead buck. The best way to do this is to take a clean rag while wearing plastic gloves and rub it vigorously against each gland. Or press the rag to the glands and squeeze the oil from them with your gloved fingers. Place the rag in a zip-top plastic bag, and seal it immediately. When making mock rubs or scrapes, remove the rag and wipe it on the rub or overhanging branch over a scrape. This has proven to be an excellent strategy. I have seen both male and female deer investigate mock rubs and scrapes I created using forehead gland scent.

A buck vigorously rubs his pre-orbital glands on the overhanging branches to deposit sebaceous and sudoriferous odors. Photo Credit: Ted Rose.

Pre-Orbital Glands

The pre-orbital, or lachrymal, glands are the tear ducts located on the inside corner of the deer's eyes. There are a few sebaceous and sudoriferous glands located at the tips of each pre-orbital gland. Some researchers feel these glands do not produce a lot of odor, but others disagree with that analysis. Deer often rub the corners of their eyes on vegetation, overhanging branches, and twigs. Many other researchers, including my good friend and former business partner Dr. Leonard Lee Rue III, feel that deer use these glands for self-marking purposes. Therefore, it appears deer do deposit scent from their pre-orbital glands purposefully. The pre-orbital gland's primary function is as a tear duct. It is also believed to be under muscular control and may be opened to emit odors. It is also said pre-orbital glands are more visible in mature bucks and signal aggressive behavior to other bucks.

A Pre-Orbital Scent Tactic

This is another glandular scent that is not made commercially but can be collected the same way as forehead gland scent. It will help create the entire illusion when making mock rubs and scrapes. I get slightly better response from deer when I include the pre-orbital scent on fake rubs and scrapes. But it involves a considerable amount of effort to collect it from a dead animal.

Metatarsal Glands

Metatarsal glands are inside a light tan-colored circle of hair about one and two-thirds inches in length located on the outside of the hind legs between the toe and the hock, or heel, on whitetails. Some naturalists and biologists feel the gland is atrophying, or getting smaller through evolution, because deer no longer need or use it. Therefore, it

The metatarsal glands are on the outside of the hind legs. They no longer have ducts. Biologists claim the metatarsal glands may be atrophying. Photo Credit: Ted Rose.

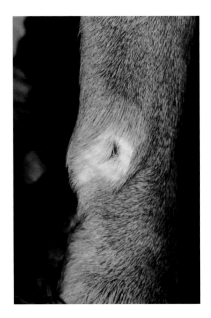

has no viable purpose anymore. This is thought to be the case because the metatarsal glands no longer have ducts. Still, others believe the glands emit a pheromone that deer use for communication and as an aggressive odor to warn off other deer during the rut.

Metatarsal Gland Scent Tactic

Because the glands are not totally understood, be prepared for anything to happen when using metatarsal glandular scent. Over the years, I have tried it several times. Sometimes it has helped to attract deer, but not often enough to make it a worthwhile tactic.

I have provided information about four more glands below. None of them are made commercially that I know of, and it's not practical to try to obtain scent from these glands or organs to use as a hunting tactic. But, it is important to know about them and the purposes they serve.

Nasal Glands

These two almond-shaped glands inside the nostrils help a deer detect odors. Some researchers feel they are used to lubricate a deer's nose. It is also believed that deer use their nasal glands to leave scent on overhanging branches and at rubs.

Vomeronasal Organ

This organ is often referred to as a buck's second nose! It is obviously not a nose at all, but it does serve some of the same functions and purposes as the nose. The next time you take a buck, look at the roof of its mouth. You will see a diamond-shaped formation with a small passage leading into the palate. This is the vomeronasal organ also known as the Jacobson organ.

This buck seems to be enjoying the odor he is passing over his Jacobson's organ (VNO). The Vomeronasal organ alerts a buck to the exact stage of a doe's estrus condition. Photo Credit: Depositphotos.

The vomeronasal organ is crucial to bucks during the rut. During this time, its primary function is to analyze doe urine. The buck curls his upper lip and sucks air into his mouth, which is also known as a Flehmen gesture. Any urine scent gathered passes over the organ. The buck is immediately able to evaluate if it contains estrous pheromones. If it does, the buck will know if it has been left by a doe that is close by or if the doe passed through the area recently. This helps the buck avoid chasing after does that may not be ready to breed for twenty-four or more hours. When the vomeronasal organ detects a high volume of pungent estrous pheromones, the buck immediately pursues that particular scent until he locates the hot doe that deposited it!

According to researchers, the vomeronasal organ is capable of detecting the exact state of estrus the doe is currently in to within hours. Analysis of urine through the vomeronasal organ is thought to synchronize the breeding readiness between bucks and does, and it ensures that both sexes are in peak breeding condition at the same time.

Salivary Glands

These glands are inside the mouth and produce saliva, which contains enzymes to help digestion. When a buck rubs a tree, he always licks the rubbed trunk and deposits

Bucks mouth the ends of overhanging branches and licking sticks repeatedly in order to deposit the enzymes found in their saliva onto the branch. Photo Credit: Ted Rose.

the salivary enzymes on the tree. He also does this when he rubs twigs and branches at scrapes. When a buck makes a licking stick, he takes a small twig or tiny sapling into his mouth and places it between his teeth. Then he gently pulls his head back to fray the end of the twig or sapling. It is thought that the buck does this to deposit scent from his salivary glands on the licking stick, as well as on overhanging branches at scrapes and on rubbed trees.

Well, there you have it—an explanation of how to use tarsal glands, and perhaps the preputial gland and scrotum, and the odors they emit to help attract a buck or doe. The information provided about the other glands and the pheromones they disperse will help any hunter to attract a buck or doe. By using each glandular scent correctly—and by using them sparingly and not using too much each time—you will increase your sightings and, hopefully, the number of deer you bag.

As an ending side note about removing natural tarsal glands: Many old-timers believe that if a knife blade touches the tarsal gland when the hunter is dressing out the deer, the scent or any fluid from the gland that gets on the knife will taint the deer meat. According to many biologists and butchers I have talked with, the tainting talk is nothing more than an old wives' tale. With that said, I would recommend playing it safe rather than sorry. I'm always careful not to let my knife blade come in contact with any part of the tarsal gland while I'm field dressing and removing the hide from a deer I have shot.

Chapter Nine

How to Locate a Buck's Fall Range

One of the more perplexing questions about deer hunting revolves around buck movement patterns. In late summer, a hunter can be scouting a field for a week straight and see half a dozen bucks, including a few large-antlered keepers each time. The following week the same bucks go MIA. This seemingly unexplainable disappearing act presents a monumental and frustrating puzzle to both the veteran and novice deer stalker. Where have all the big boys of summer gone? Unearthing the answer to that question can be a task some hunters aren't able to solve easily. Discovering how to find bucks, especially mature bucks that leave a particular property in late summer, can be one of the more important skills a deer hunter can master. After all, just the task of scouting to find adult bucks on any hunting property requires a lot of work. It doesn't happen just as a matter of luck. It takes time, patience, persistence, and a solid game plan. Sure, a hunter can get lucky and happen to locate a buck he wants to focus on during the hunting season without putting

In a recent deer movement study done at Penn State University it concluded 50 to 80 percent of one-and-a-half-year-old bucks disperse to establish new home ranges, irrespective of deer population, deer density, or suitable cover. Photo Credit: CanStock Photos.

Photo Credit: CanStock Photos.

much effort into it, but luck isn't the usual way this works out. To develop a consistent method for finding the larger antlered bucks, you need a dedicated plan of action and top-notch scouting tactics.

But there is a hitch to merely locating a good buck in summer. What you really have to discover is whether or not he is a resident buck who intends to remain on the land. The issue revolves around an instinctive biological occurrence known as FBD, or Fall Buck Dispersal. FBD is an abominable and frustrating natural phenomenon in the world of the whitetail deer.

In my last book, *Whitetail Tactics—Cutting-Edge Strategies That Work*, I included a chapter entitled "Adult Buck Dispersal and Other Buck Movement Patterns." It went into the subject of Fall Buck Dispersal in painstaking detail. For that reason, I won't repeat it here. Basically, some bucks that leave lands in late September or early October to relocate on their fall ranges don't return until the following summer. This conduct is part and parcel of their instinctive buck behaviors. On the other hand, some bucks who venture off to fall ranges do return in November. This is predominantly true when the land they just left contains a healthy population of adult does.

When bucks disperse to their fall range, they can travel both near and far. Some bucks may only move several hundred yards from their summer feeding range, but others can literally move a mile or more. In fact, research has documented that some adult bucks disperse as far as a few miles from their summer range!

A summary done by Long and Associates, a private research firm, revealed the mean distances traveled by young non-migratory bucks ranged from 1.9 to 23.6 miles! Photo Credit: CanStock Photos.

While the disappearing act of relocating bucks is understandably baffling and exasperating to hunters, it should be somewhat consoling to us all that we are not alone. Countless veteran and novice hunters have been faced with the same problem. I, too, have been afflicted by the conundrum of Fall Buck Dispersal.

So what does a hunter do to locate bucks that have suddenly left their lands and moved off to their fall ranges? They should become what I term surreptitious scouters.

A mature buck approaches two younger bucks displaying body posture (ears pinned back) that lets the immature bucks know he ranks higher on the pecking order. The young bucks may be new arrivals that have dispersed from other areas. Photo Credit: CanStock Photos.

Summer scouting is quite different from fall scouting. In summer, a hunter locating a buck to focus on requires nothing more than good scouting practices. The methods a hunter uses to scout in fall, though, will be the absolute key to success. When a hunter uses flawed approaches in fall scouting, it can quickly make a buck nervous and uncomfortable. It can also unnecessarily alert him that he is being watched or stalked. Both these elements can be reasons for a buck to leave a piece of ground he is comfortable with including in his fall range.

Generally, I see three to four mature bucks over the summer as I plant, mow, or do other work around the farm, which usually turns out to be my early summer way of scouting my property. In July, however, I pinpoint an adult buck and an alternate buck to hunt in the upcoming deer season. That's when I begin my summer scouting in earnest. For instance, last summer, in 2014, I gathered ample video of nine adult bucks feeding in my food plots. This was more mature bucks than I usually see or would have anticipated seeing in our food plots.

During the last two weeks of July of that summer, I spent four evenings a week in a blind called Big View. The blind offers almost total seclusion for me to scout from. It looks out over more than twenty acres of fields planted with a wide variety of food plots—swede, chicory, clovers, an assortment of small grains, and the soft and hard mast from our apple, pear, peach, and chestnut trees. I videotaped deer entering my fields and noted carefully where they entered and exited. Some came from locations on our land, and others came in from neighboring properties. Interestingly, almost all of them left by heading in different directions than where they came from. Mostly, I wanted to qualify statistics about the adult bucks. I jotted down their times of entry, where they entered from, the wind directions, and every other component I saw.

By my birthday—August 31—I was still seeing Mr. Broken Rack, the Twins, and Crooked Rack feeding in the food plots regularly. The largest antlered bucks of the nine I nicknamed the Big Five. They had already shed their velvet and had begun changing

Five mature bucks gather in a food plot in late August. Discovering their fall ranges after they shed their velvet required the use of trail cameras. Photo Credit: Ted Rose.

their patterns. They entered the fields later and left much sooner than they did in July and August—a sure sign they were preparing to leave for their fall range. I knew things were about to start changing. If I hoped to kill one of the Big Five summer bucks, I had to make a solid plan to locate where they were living in late September.

I was beginning to fear perhaps one or two of the Big Five might be bucks whose home ranges were someplace else. I know that some bucks' fall and summer ranges aren't the same. I understand that clearly. So what was I to do? It turned out that all I needed to do was what most deer-hunting tactics require—developing a practical and pragmatic fall scouting game plan. The strategy had to include a variety of the best stealth scouting methods I could assemble.

Our 192 acres are connected to 121 acres of land owned by two of my cousins and another 130 acres of unhunted land we have access to. The 443 total acres encompasses a lot of different terrain and, more importantly, a lot of diverse vegetation. I hoped some of the Big Five Houdini-type bucks were living and feeding on the fall foods harbored on these lands. My fear was that some of them might be setting up fall ranges on properties outside of our 443 acres.

Unfortunately, in early September, I had to leave for three straight weeks to produce three television shows in Newfoundland, Canada, about moose, woodland caribou, and black bear hunting. But before I did, I set out eighteen trail cameras over the 443 acres in a wide variety of prime locations. This is one of the key factors for finding truant bucks.

I returned home from Newfoundland in the first few days of October. The following evening, I couldn't wait to get to Big View to see what was going on. Did the big boys return or would they still be fugitives? Before my wife Kate, son Cody, or I could count on taking one or more of the Big Five bucks, I had to find out where they were residing since I left. For one thing, bucks are wired to lay low this time of year, which makes them much less visible.

Buy the best trail cameras you can afford. Like scopes, binoculars, ammo, and other crucial gear, trail cameras are hunting "tools." The old adage "use the right tool for the right job," is top-notch advice and definitely applies to trail cameras. Photo Credit: SPYPOINT.

So what can you do to locate the bucks that left for fall ranges? Well for starters, don't scout by walking the property. I gave up traditional scouting techniques years ago. The only thing this type of scouting accomplishes is that it alerts adult bucks to oncoming human pressure. While there are exceptions to this rule, an overwhelming number of adult bucks will absolutely not tolerate more than a few human disturbances within their core fall areas. After they are jumped one or two times, they pack up shop and relocate. It may not be far, perhaps only a few hundred or so yards, but that can be enough to put them on a neighbor's land. There is no logical reason to educate a buck to your presence.

The answer is technology—use trail cameras to locate bucks in fall ranges. While this may seem obvious to the more experienced hunters reading this, it may not be to a lot of other hunters. One of the easiest ways to catch a good buck on camera is to set it over a bait pile. Before doing so, however, check your game laws. Bait piles are illegal in some states. If bait piles are legal to use, though, it will provide you with a quicker and more effective way of gathering quality photos of possible bucks to hunt. I keep my cameras set out for at least seven days; sometimes I double that if I suspect there is a quality buck in the area.

If the state where you hunt doesn't allow using bait piles even outside of deer season, all is not lost. Strategically locate a few cameras out around a food plot. Set a camera up in the middle of the plot, then set a few in more in areas with good vantage points, such as along inside corners. If you have my book, *The Shooter's Bible Guide to Whitetail Strategies*, there is an entire chapter dedicated to hunting inside corners or in a high traffic area in the corner of a field. I also like to set cameras up on light trails that parallel heavier deer trails, as they are deer runs often used by adult bucks.

To capture bucks like this on camera in open food plots, hunters have to know what plots are most palatable during key times of the season. Photo Credit: Whitetail Institute.

However, just including cameras around random food plots isn't the best tactic. If you know what plots the deer are feeding in most, that is where you want to set up your cameras. Some plants provide better nutrition and palpability than other plants do at different times of the year. Knowing which the deer are eating most when your cameras are out will increase the number of quality photos the cameras capture of adult bucks.

I like to set up cameras in more generic areas, as well. The tried-and-true travel routines do pay off with good photos, too. In this case, I set them up in funnels, along creek beds, around my ponds, in thickets, and along fence posts. One excellent way I have found of attaining quality images of mature bucks, particularly in the fall, is to place a camera on or near an area where I know bucks have created what is called a signpost rub. These rubs are almost always made by mature bucks. I consider a signpost rub as any tree that a buck has rubbed for at least three consecutive years. Some signpost rubs have been hit by bucks consistently for dozens of years! Bucks usually make signpost rubs on Black Ash trees—also known as brown, swamp, and basket ash—so it is important to be able to identify the different ash species. The black ash usually grows in damp soil and tends to establish itself in swamplands, along stream and riverbanks, and even in spring seeps on hardwood ridges. Black ash is native to the North Central region of the United States, including the Great Lakes, and it extends to the northern parts of the East Coast and into Canada. When a signpost rub is located, it is a prime spot to place a camera.

Today's cameras are more high-tech than ever before. Many come with field scan time lapse, video options, and a mode that allows the user to take images at set intervals for specific periods of time. They can even be set to take photos by the minute. I know what you are wondering—what are the best model choices for cameras? Most made by reliable companies such as Cuddeback, Wildgame Innovations, and Bushnell will perform well and are reliable and sturdy. My first choice are cameras made by Spy-Point.

When buying a trail camera, purchase only units with the type of accessories you feel best fit your needs. It will save you time and frustration, and help you get the best images possible. Photo Credit: Cuddleback.

Scouting with cameras will teach you a lot about the buck you are after. Once you have captured a buck on camera, record how often the camera took his photo. This will definitely demonstrate where he is and how often he is visiting that area. If the camera only captures him a couple of times within the seven to fourteen days it was set out, he is probably on the edges of his home fall range area. Move the camera until it gets at least a dozen images of him. Then you know you are closer to an area where you can hunt him. It should go without saying that it is crucial to establish the direction he approaches from and what direction he leaves. Evening images will be much more telling. Just like a rub line, they will show a more reliable pattern to his travel than do the morning images, which are generally much more random by comparison. Lastly, pay particular attention to the times he is captured on camera. It will help you establish a time to ambush him. You may be surprised to discover that a lot of adult bucks have movement patterns from 10 a.m. to 2 p.m.

I don't waste any of my valuable hunting time with a buck that is showing up on my cameras only at night. Sure, I could get lucky and kill him during daylight, especially during the rut. But bucks captured on camera only at night are generally bucks coming from long distances to feed on food plots or hook up with an estrus doe. I prefer the concept

Trail cameras help to take the guesswork out of where hunters should set up their stands. Photo Credit: Summit Treestands.

of surprise when I'm hunting an adult buck. If I have him on camera or, better yet, I have seen him from a secure and distant blind during daylight hours in fall, he goes right to the top of my list as a key-target buck.

The information received by trail cameras will also be definitive about where to place a stand. The hunting strategies to take adult bucks remain constant. Set up cameras in the fall with scent control in mind. Using latex gloves to set out cameras is an excellent idea. All other rules of scent control should be adhered to, as well. Also establish different routes in and out of the areas where you want to capture photos of bucks. If you miss connecting with a photo of him the first time, rest the area a few days and then return to set up a camera again. The element of surprise is an overlooked tactic, whether it is used when placing trail cameras before season or when actually hunting.

For instance, we have owned a 192-acre farm since 2001. Over the past fourteen years, we have taken some average bucks and some real wall-hangers. Most times the larger antlered bucks were taken while using a combination of different hunting strategies, including antler rattling, deer calls, making mock scrapes and rubs, and a variety of other proactive tactics. Sometimes they were taken the old-fashioned way by stump sitting, or hunting from a blind or stand and waiting for a good buck to amble by. All of these have proven over the years to be fun and rewarding hunting methods.

However, I have taken the largest antlered bucks on our farm during off hours when most hunters are not in the woods. I have killed several good bucks from 10 a.m. to 2 p.m. Cody took his largest buck—the second largest deer taken at our place—at 10 a.m. Kate has taken bucks during that time frame, as well. Hunting during those time periods often surprises an adult buck that typically doesn't encounter heavy hunting pressure at that time of day.

Over these fourteen years and through all the different types of tactics used on our farm, I developed a record of where to get the most photos of deer—particularly adult bucks. I keep this information close to my vest and share only with Kate and

My two cousins Leo and Ralph Somma drag a two-and-a-half-year-old buck taken by Ralph (right) on his land that borders my property. It was shot as Ralph still-hunted back to his cabin. The buck regularly fed in our food plots on our property. Photo Credit: Fiduccia Enterprises.

Cody, and I forewarn you, keep the information you gather on adult bucks with your cameras to yourself. Share it and you'll have to accept the consequences. Do I need to explain that philosophy or repeat it? Within a short period of time, you will develop an acute understanding of where to set your camera up, as well.

As I mentioned earlier, some bucks' home ranges are close, and some are much more distant. Bucks that have fall ranges near their summer ranges are usually home-bodies. They tend to have much smaller fall ranges than bucks who wander large distances from their summer range. This behavior also has a snag to it. If you set up a camera in an area of a homebody buck, you might experience the phenomenon I call overexposure. Basically, the camera will capture dozens—if not more—images of the same buck. For instance, I once had two cameras set up within one hundred yards of each other, and they both captured dozens of images of the same buck. Obviously, he didn't like to roam far from his core area. Should this happen to you, extend the range of the two cameras to two hundred to three hundred yards apart in more promising areas.

If the bucks you have been watching all summer disappear in late September, don't panic. Instead, use more secretive scouting and other high-tech locating methods to find them on their fall range and plan how and where to hunt them from that point on. Despite the many excuses I have heard for why summer bucks disappear—"They've gone totally nocturnal," "They were killed by poachers," "Hit by vehicles," "Coyotes ate them all up," "There's a cougar in my area," and countless other explanations—fall buck escapees can definitely be found. It just takes a little more homework to find them!

Using stealth scouting techniques will significantly limit tipping your hand and educating any buck you've pinpointed to hunt prior to the start of deer season. Be confident in your relocating skills. As exercise trainer Tony Little was fond of screaming on his TV commercial to sell his exercise machines: "YOU CAN DO IT!"

Finding bucks that have dispersed in fall requires investigative work that is best achieved using trail cameras. Photo Credit: CanStock Photos.

For recommendations please see the accompanying sidebar (Best Wildlife Scouting Camera Reviews 2015) below. It includes a list of wildlife spy cameras equipped with the latest technology, those that perform reliably, and those that can stand up to rugged use and foul weather. Most of today's models are also capable of producing high-quality images and even video. What they can't do is make a reservation for you at your favorite restaurant.

Best Wildlife Scouting Camera Reviews 2015

The following list of trail cameras have come a long way from the first models produced. Today's wildlife spy-cameras are hi-tech equipment that can be viewed as tools by hunters rather than gear. Many produce hi-resolution HD color images, shoot video, and some include many other neat options. They will help take your deer scouting to the next level. Scouting cameras come in a wide range of costs from very affordable to pricey. The more expensive units, however, include many more options that are sure to be impressive. I have included the Manufacturers Suggested Retail Price alongside each unit. All prices were listed at the time of this writing.

SPYPOINT Cellular Trail Camera: This unit is now available within the United States. The Mini-LIVE-4GV cellular camera wirelessly sends photos via the 4G (EV-DO) cellular network on the mySPYPOINT server. Photos can be viewed quickly wherever there is internet access (computer, cell phone, or tablet) making it easy to see all the images taken. Not having to go afield to retrieve and see the photos keep hunting sites undisturbed, saving hunters time and money. The mySPYPOINT online management service also allows you to organize your photos, change the settings of the camera, and get the camera's latest status including signal strength, battery level, used memory space of the SD card, used data quota, etc. A real benefit of this unit is that if it is stolen, it is possible to know the location of the camera with GPS coordinates. This camera does not require a SIM card. This unit works with Verizon 4G (EV_DO cellular network within the United States. It is advisable to verify Verizon's coverage is available in your area. MSRP is $599.00 but don't let the price of The Mini-LIVE-4GV cellular camera scare you. SpyPoint makes a wide range of cameras that will fit within anyone's budget. For more information including the price go to www.spypoint.com.

Primos Proof Cam: The new Primos Proof Cam shoots images and video. The Proof Cam 01, 02, and 03 cameras are all designed to simply take images, HD video or HD. The time lapse images are based on what hunters want but without other stuff they don't use. The 02 and 03 models have a .4-second trigger speed and three-second recovery rate, 12 megapixel images and Low Glow (the 02) to 100 feet or Blackout LEDs (the 03) to 80 feet that provide great nighttime images. Visit their website for more info and pricing at: www.Primos.com.

Bushnell Trophy Cam Aggressor HD: This Bushnell unit offers a lightning fast 0.2-second trigger speed along with a one-second recovery time, extended nighttime photo range and one-year battery life. Other features include 14 megapixel HD image and 1080p HD video that includes audio. The unit comes in either Low-Glow or No-Glow models. The SMRP is $179.99. More info at: www. Bushnell.com.

Moultrie A-7i: The Moultrie A-7i is built on the same engineering principles of its best-selling A-5 wildlife camera. Incredibly, this unit is among the lowest priced invisible flash cameras on the marketplace. It includes a functional black LED array design for taking better photos. Moultrie also improved the A-7i regarding better resistance to the weather and reliability. The unit also provides three-image multi-shot capability, reduced detection delay time, and more. This is a very affordable unit with a SMRP of $89.99.

Comanche Outfitters Kodiak Series: Comanche Outfitter's new line of Kodiak Series wildlife cameras all come with the type of features hunters want in their trail cameras. The Kodiak Series line includes a 12 megapixel image sensor, 720p HD video recording with audio, 40 invisible infared LEDS and an advanced motion detector. The Kodiak Series cameras can record for months on a single set of batteries because they include a "standby" motion detection setup. Wireless access is available from up to two hundred feet away from a smartphone and free app without other external remotes or accessories. Visit their website for more info and pricing at: www.kodiakCamera.com.

Tactacam: A simple touch of a button record hunts with the Tactacam. This small unit is packed with super features to capture your big buck moment. A 12mp sensor provides terrific HD video in two settings: 1080x30fps and 720-60fps. With one simple touch of the recorder it begins video-taping all the action. The lens is optimized for bow, crossbow, or firearm use. The Tactacam has terrific low-lux capabilities which allow it to record well in low-light situations. The camera is always in focus even through branches and also offers vibration indication. Additional features include a camera that is water-proof tested to thirty meters and shock resistant for up to .50 caliber rifles. It comes with the stabilizer, scope, gun, universal and other mounting systems. The SMRP is about $280. For more info: www. tactacam.com.

Check out other camera models at the websites below.

Browning - www.browningtrailcameras.com

Covert HD—www.covertscoutingcameras.com

Cuddeback—www.cuddeback.com

Eyecon—www.eyecontrailcameras.com

HCO Scoutguard—www.hcooutdoors.com

Chapter Ten

When the Weather Turns Sour, Buck Hunting Turns Sweet!

Let me begin this chapter by requesting it be paid particular attention to. I assure you the following information is important and, if adhered to, will help the success of your deer hunting. It will also dramatically increase your odds of consistently taking an adult buck year after year. If you doubt anything you just read, please skip this chapter and go to the next one. (That's light-hearted sarcasm. Please read the entire chapter carefully.)

My first book, *Whitetail Strategies—A No-Nonsense Approach to Successful Deer Hunting*, was written in 1995. At the time, I had been deer hunting for thirty-one years. Over those three decades, I discovered the extraordinary importance all the components of weather play in relation to deer and deer hunting. Now, twenty years later, I still claim that a hunter

During my five plus decades of hunting whitetails I have discovered that both does and bucks will move more than most hunters believe they will in all types of foul weather—including heavy rain, snow, wind, dense fog and particularly during extremely cold temperatures. Photo Credit: Ted Rose.

Photo Credit: Pond5.com/Wildlifephotoguy.

who thoroughly understands the whole enchilada of weather and deer hunting will be a more informed and much more successful deer huntsman or -woman.

I have acquired a lot of personal knowledge on the subject of weather over my fifty-one years of pursuing deer and other big game throughout North America and Africa. But interestingly, I continue to learn about how weather influences all aspects of daily life, particularly movement, within the world of the whitetail deer. I share much of what I have learned about weather and hunting with you in this chapter.

To emphasize that a hunter can never know enough about how weather plays a role in deer hunting, I'd like to share a story. In 2008, I read a most enlightening source of information about weather. It came from a book titled *Trophy Bucks in Any Weather*, written by Dan Carlson. Carlson, a former meteorologist, is a lifelong big game hunter. His information is down-to-earth and easy to absorb and apply, and I highly recommend his book to all of you. Purchase it at your earliest convenience. It will go into much more detail than I can provide in a single chapter. Carlson shares his knowledge of the subject based on his years of education and his former professional occupation.

I can state unequivocally that I have seen and taken some of the largest antlered bucks in inhospitable weather conditions. I consider inclement weather to cover rain, snow, wind, ice, fog, and extreme cold. These are the types of harsh conditions that, unfortunately, encourage some hunters to pull the bed covers back up over their heads rather than go hunting. I should also state clearly that over the last several years, a lot of my hunting in excessively foul weather, at least on our land, has been done from enclosed blinds—with heaters! I'll be sixty-nine this summer. It's getting a little more difficult each year for me to hunt in tough weather conditions, especially in northern upstate New York's frosty temperatures and blustery November winds.

To validate, however, that I continue to hunt outside of a blind in foul weather

when necessary, please go to YouTube and look at a late December moose hunt I produced in Newfoundland, Canada, at Red Indian Lake Outfitters & Tours. The TV show also documents

Deer will definitely move in foul weather, including frigid temperatures. I have discovered extreme cold temperatures will actually cause more daylight movement than normal. Photo Credit: Ted Rose.

I killed this bull after outfitter Fred Thorne of Red Indian Lake Outfitters called it in during sideway blowing snow squalls and temperatures below 15 degrees Fahrenheit. Photo Credit: Fiduccia Enterprises.

and emphasizes a much more pertinent point about hunting in terrible weather—it can provide hunting success.

During that hunt, I spent three days climbing mountain ridges and walking along wind-blown ridge tops and bone-chilling bogs glassing for moose in twelve or more inches of snow. Those three days saw a combination of abominable weather. One day we hunted in heavy rain, and the final two days were in freezing glacial-type cold with high winds and blowing snow and sleet.

On the afternoon of the next to last day of that hunt, with my fingertips nearly frozen solid and my face cheeks burning from the pellets of sleet and blowing snow, we stalked up a mountainside. From the crest, we glassed a group of moose that contained several cows and four good bulls. With a stiff wind blowing snow in my face, I ended up killing a terrific bull as he stood in a bog watching the cows. When the .308 150-grain Winchester XP3 smacked into his shoulder, he instantly fell nose first into the snow. He was dead before he hit the ground. In the type of weather that isn't really fit for man or beast, I took my second largest bull moose to date. It proves once again that, whether you're hunting for moose, deer, or any other big game, it is important to realize that the game can and does move more than anticipated even in the foulest of weather conditions.

As I have written in more than a dozen other books, when hunting gets tough, don't be hypercritical of your deer hunting skills. More importantly, don't base your foul-weather hunting on what TV personalities—including me—can do. We all get to hunt in prime locations with private leases or with outfitters whose lands don't get the type of heavy hunting pressure most hunters encounter. Under these circumstances, TV personalities don't have to be overly concerned about seeing mature bucks. (Again, I don't want to sound like I'm pointing fingers, so I include myself here.) Why?

Because many of these types of hunting situations—leases, private ranches, or hunting with outfitters—harbor adult bucks or other game. Over my fifty-one years of hunting overall and thirty-two years of professionally hunting on television, I have hunted all types of property from heavily pressured state lands to private leases to game lands opened only to a particular outfitter who is licensed to hunt them. In areas such as this, mature deer move at dawn, midday, and dusk no matter what the weather might be—aside from the most extreme conditions.

In heavily hunted areas, state lands, small properties surrounded by other lands, and even on privately owned properties that have heavy hunting pressure, only a small percentage of bucks make it to adulthood. Therefore their daytime movement habits are different from those of the mature bucks in lightly hunted areas. I conclude this from personal experience. For instance, although we don't exert a lot of hunting pressure on our 192 acres, our deer are still affected by the heavy hunting pressure our neighbors place on deer.

That brings me to my next point. What do the heavily hunted bucks most of you see like about moving more in foul weather? Deer really can't avoid nasty weather. Sure, they can seek the heaviest cover, such as a stand of thick pines, to lessen the wind, reduce the amount of snow on the ground, or degrade the water from a heavy rainfall. But none of these options really help deer avoid harsh weather—they just lessen the conditions a little.

Consequently, it doesn't really matter to them if they are bedded down or moving about in bad weather. In a moderate to more substantial rain or snowfall, deer may move more because they realize they can move more quietly in this type of weather. Another foul-weather hypothesis I have—and many of you have, as well—is that deer may be aware that during foul

I took this buck at 10 a.m. on state land. He was chasing a doe in a snowstorm. The photo was taken after the snow had stopped. Photo Credit: Fiduccia Enterprises.

Over five decades of hunting experience has taught me to expect to see deer, particularly adult bucks, even in heavy downpours of rain, sleet, or snow. Photo Credit: Ted Rose.

weather they encounter less human scent and have fewer actual run-ins with humans. It may also be that they have a high survival rate when they move about in terrible weather conditions.

The repeated result of deer encountering a lack of predation when moving in bad weather encourages them to repeat the action. As they become mature, they have made moving about in inclement weather a habit. This is substantiated by fifty-one years of keeping written and video logs that show deer moving during snowstorms, frigid temperatures, high winds, snow, or rainstorms. I have also established that adult bucks will move more during daylight hours, particularly between 10 a.m. and 2 p.m., during stormy weather.

One of my favorite inclement weather conditions for hunting is rain. Despite this, I rarely go bow hunting in the rain, as I don't like to risk losing a deer because the blood trail was washed, and I don't hunt once the wind and precipitation exceeds a steady 45 to 50 mph. Other nonhunting winds and precipitation include strong gales, whole gales, or hurricanes. However, I never miss a firearm hunt when it is raining as long as the weather doesn't reach those extreme conditions. Over the past five decades, my records have also provided hard-core evidence that virtually one-third of all my adult buck sightings throughout North America have taken place in moderate to heavy rain.

In the early eighties, I was a licensed New York State guide. In a heavy downpour of rain, I placed a client hunter on a stand I called the Buck Tree in a commercial apple orchard called Och's Orchards. While the rain soaked us both to the bone, I called and rattled in a dandy eight-point buck. The buck was shot at 3:30 p.m. When we approached to field dress him, we noticed he looked like a drowned rat. He had obviously been out and about in the rainstorm for a considerable amount of time.

My records also conclude hunting in the snow, even when the temperatures are frigid, is similar to hunting in the rain. Deer, especially adult bucks, will be on their

This buck seems oblivious to the snow piled up on his face, antlers, and back. He is most likely on the move to estrus does and/or food. Photo Credit: Ted Rose.

hooves and moving. What makes hunting in the snow even more exciting is a buck will leave a record of his tracks in the snow that can tell where he moved and about how long ago he traveled in that direction.

As I mentioned previously, it doesn't pay to hunt in extremely windy conditions. Deer tend to lessen their foul-weather movement in high winds. The one element that can penetrate the remarkable hide of a deer is extremely cold wind, particularly for long periods. When this happens, it makes deer use up precious energy at a time when they can't afford to do so. Deer often bed down in low-lying areas or in a stand of heavy pines for protection from the elements in these conditions. But even under such hideous weather, mature bucks do move every now and then. And that's enough of an opportunity for any of us, eh?

Other important factors that can alert a hunter to prepare for better hunting opportunities include an approaching cold front and falling barometers. Generally, any approaching front can trigger the barometer to fall. It can drop like a rock or fall slowly, depending on the strength of the approaching front. Most meteorologists agree that a cold front can initiate a precipitous decline in the barometer, while warm fronts cause a more controlled drop. Once a cold front takes hold in an area, the barometer begins to rise.

In my hunting experiences and logs, I have noticed that falling barometers cause a sharp increase in buck movement. Bucks generally begin to move just before a cold front arrives. The movement may not last long, but it does occur.

The key element to success when hunting in falling barometers and cold fronts is timing them right. If you get out too early or too late, you run the very real risk of

When the barometer begins to drop, deer will move to any available food source to eat. This buck is chowing down on old leaves. Photo Credit: CanStock Photos.

missing the opportunity completely. Check the weather forecasts during the day often on your smartphone. If a daytime cold front is predicted, make the necessary adjustments to hunt it in a timely way.

The reason for a sharp increase in buck movement during a falling barometer may be that bucks instinctively know the changing pressure will increase doe movement, especially toward preferred food sources. Many times when I have hunted in weather conditions that include a drop in barometer, particularly if it is a sharp drop, I have noticed bucks increase their rubbing and scrape-making behaviors.

In all types of foul weather, I like setting up in areas of food sources. This is especially the case during cold fronts. Setting up in known travel corridors that lead to food sources is a high-success bet. Remember that once a falling barometer begins to rise again, particularly if the front remained hung up for a long period of time, deer will also move better.

When it comes to hunting in inclement weather, the one adage I steadfastly apply to my deer hunting is that you definitely can't kill a buck from bed. So the next time the rain is coming down sideways, the snow is falling, the winds are blowing, and the temperatures are icy cold, especially if there is a falling barometer to indicate a cold front, get up and get out. There's good hunting to be had.

Chapter Eleven

Don't Drive 'Em, Nudge 'Em Along Instead

This chapter is not about how to drive deer as much as it is about how to gradually move deer from cover toward a stander or standers. The drives I am referring to can include as few as two or as many as six to eight hunters. A small drive's primary goal is not to have deer, particularly adult bucks, run past a stander at a high rate of speed. Instead, the objective is to have a buck or doe sneak off slowly and pass a stander at either a relaxed or brisk walking pace or, in the worst case, a slow trot.

There are many ways to move deer, starting with a one-person drive up to a drive that can include an army of hunters clad in orange. In the case of large drives with a throng of hunters moving through the woods whooping, hollering, and banging sticks against trees, deer instantly fly off helter-skelter in all directions. Some deer inevitably cross the paths of hunters in stands. The large drive is definitely not my style of hunting. For a lot of reasons, I have an intense distaste for large deer drives. I

Large multi-hunter drives often end up with standers seeing bucks hightailing from the pushers at a warp speed of 9.9. Getting a clean shot at this buck would be difficult at best and, more importantly, could wind up with an errant shot wounding the buck. Photo Credit: Ted Rose.

Photo Credit Ted Rose.

want to state a clear disclaimer, however. I don't ridicule, begrudge, disparage, or want to prevent anyone who enjoys partaking in large organized drives from doing so. After all, the practice of large deer drives has its roots firmly planted in deer hunting tradition.

Over my fifty-one years of deer hunting, I can count on five fingers—or probably fewer—the times I have participated in this type of drive. Each time I came away from the experience totally unsatisfied even though on each occasion a good buck or two were killed by some lucky standers. One such drive took place in about 1988 in a New Jersey town noted for having most of the available hunting grounds on private property that is heavily posted. The area is also known for harboring a high population of adult bucks.

I was graciously placed in a stand along with several other hunters who took up positions along prime deer escape routes or other high-potential areas where deer were expected to run past. On that drive, I saw a good buck, and I readily admit I raised my shotgun and tried to get the buck in the scope. Thankfully, the buck was running so fast I had absolutely no ethical choice but to not shoot at him. Seconds after the running buck passed me, shots rang out. By the drive's end, two respectable adult bucks were taken.

In 1984, I was part of a huge deer drive in Pennsylvania. To my best recall, there were at least twenty hunters involved in the drive, although there may have been a lot more. By the time it was over, I saw at least forty deer. Several of them were bucks, but to this day, I'm not sure how many points a single one of those bucks had! They were all moving as if their tails were on fire; it would have been unethical to shoot at any of them. Again, the drive ended successfully with two eight-point bucks taken. Please note, that was twenty or more hunters and two bucks.

The last large organized deer drive I took part in happened in 1990. It took place on a large section of land in Sparta, New Jersey. The land was owned by a well-known wildlife authority, naturalist, and hunter of the era who has since passed on. Because he was not part of the drive, he shall remain nameless.

Once again, the drive included more than twenty hunters. Kate and I were posted together on a mountainside. She was hunting, and I was the cameraman. As a large herd of deer, some twenty strong, ran down the mountainside toward us, Kate lifted her shotgun and took aim at a buck. At the same instant, a shot rang out from above us. The buck escaped, but Kate and I could hear buckshot peppering the ground near us! Fortunately, the pellets were totally spent by the time they reached our area. We escaped without injury but made a decision to never participate in such a large drive ever again. The saddest and most shocking part to the end of the hunt was not that shotgun pellets hit near Kate and me, but rather the unbridled elation that two standers shot bucks!

With that said, however, I would like to repeat what I mentioned about large drives earlier. I genuinely don't begrudge hunters who want to participate in them. I understand that it is a tradition that has long-established roots in hunting. Large drives are probably the origin of hunting tactics for big game. Driving deer is part and parcel of a social affair to many hunters during the season. I understand it is a highly effective way of taking a buck, particularly after hunting pressure has many bucks hanging tight in thick cover. I also recognize that large deer drives can be one of the better ways to ensure putting venison on the table. To me, however, these types of drives seem more about a hunt to kill, rather than a kill of a hunt.

Miniature Drives

Drives seem to happen most during times when other hunting tactics aren't working to their full potential, including still hunting, decoying, using deer calls, rattling, and stump sitting. That's when most hunters who don't normally use deer drives as a strategy decide to try moving them from thick cover with a bunch of standers and drivers. Before thinking about rounding up a posse of hunters to drive deer through a section of land, however, think about using a miniature drive that includes far fewer participants instead.

Moving deer slowly from their hiding areas involves some honed combinations of strategies: still hunting, stand hunting, knowing escape routes, good shooting skills, and, more importantly, understanding the wind. When these tactics are merged, the subtle push or nudge of a miniature deer drive offers a safe and exciting sport. All the hunters must be well

Hunters putting on mini-drives with just a couple of drivers and standers have a much better chance at seeing deer move by their stands slowly. This is particularly true during the rut. If a doe moves slowly away, so, too, will the buck. Photo Credit: Ted Rose.

organized, follow a specific tactical game plan, and perform their respective roles without a fault.

A point I would like to make about small drives has to do with its nomenclature. Small drives are better classified as a tactic to slowly nudge, move, gently push, encourage, or bump deer along rather than actually driving them. From this point on, when I use the term drive, it is more appropriate for you to change it in your mind to one of these other words. I only use it because it is a customary, comfortable, and accepted term.

The first time I realized lesser drives could be a valuable deer hunting strategy was in the late eighties. I was hunting a six-hundred-acre parcel of land that I leased in Warwick, New York. All but 111 acres of the property was on a steep mountainside and along the ridgetop. One afternoon during a steady snowfall, I was gradually making my way up the northwest side of the mountain. That approach most often provided me with a wind that was either in my face or cutting across me at an angle. Over the years I'd hunted the land, I noticed that when it snowed the odds were I would jump a bedded buck as I reached the ridge's crest. My analysis was that the snow allowed me a more silent approach. When I reached the top of the slope, I had to climb up a few feet to get onto a ledge that overlooked the mountain's plateau. I suppose any slight noises I may have made must have alerted the nearby bedded bucks I had encountered.

So on this particular snowy day, I made a plan I thought would work to bag a buck in the event one was bedded at the ridgetop. I returned home, as there were no cell phones in those days, called my friends Felix and Randy, explained my idea, and invited them to hunt with me. The plan was that Felix and Randy would be the interceptors, or standers, and I would drive the buck from its bed if one were there. I sent Felix to a tree stand location that looked over a deep and narrow draw that deer would regularly use to move up and down the mountainside. It offered a vast amount of terrain to look over. It was the same tree stand that former Yankee Wade Boggs favored when he hunted with us several times in the past. Many times, I had watched does and bucks use this deep, narrow funnel to get to the bottom of the mountain to feed in the fields below. The bucks I had jumped during snowstorms always took this escape route down the mountain. Randy took a position in my favorite tree stand. It looked over a much wider draw that started at the top of the mountain to the bottom of the ridge.

When Felix and Randy were settled into the stands, they radioed me that they were in position. I started up the mountain with the snow falling down more heavily

I have a long-standing tradition of helping to drag bucks out of the woods for my successful hunting companions. This is the buck Felix shot on the "mini-bump" drive, as it walked past his stand. Photo Credit: Fiduccia Enterprises.

than it had earlier. As I got to within fifty yards of the ridgetop, my plan was to slow my pace even more than usual. It took me about twenty minutes to cover the remaining distance to where I had to climb onto the ledge. As I crested the ridgetop, I stopped momentarily in hopes that a buck was bedded someplace close. If it were, it would either see, hear, or scent me. That's when I saw him. A good-antlered buck was already standing fifty yards from me and was looking around. I would have taken him myself, but by now it was snowing so hard I had trouble seeing him clearly in my scope. I'll never really know what made the buck move, but a few seconds later I watched him slowly walk away from my direction and toward the mouth of the narrow draw Felix was watching. His body language confirmed to me he had no sense of alarm. Nothing had frightened him enough to send him running off frantically, but something didn't feel, smell, or look right, and he decided to leave.

Within several seconds from when I first saw him, the buck was out of my sight. I cautiously made my way to the head of the funnel. I watched intently, hoping to get a shot at him, but the opportunity never developed before he disappeared from my view. I stood there hoping he would stay on the known escape route that would take him down to the bottom of the ravine and inevitably to Felix. I was sitting on a stump eating a Snickers bar when the mountainside belched from the muffled report of Felix's .30-06. Felix told me later that day that he killed the buck as "it slowly walked past me while browsing on twigs." Hence the success of the miniature drive was born as one of my deer hunting strategies.

There is a common theme about hunters who employ small drives—they plan every detail carefully, perform the drive quietly and alertly, and the drive most often ends successfully. The key to small killer drives is to keep bucks from realizing they are being actually driven. Instead, small drives, or miniature pushes, as I like to refer

Small drives and mini- bump drives typically end up having bucks walk past standers instead of running past them. Photo Credit: Ted Rose.

to them, try to nudge deer from potential bedding and hiding areas in a more natural way. These pushes can admirably be labeled a strategy. Deer that are gently encouraged to leave their beds by one or two imperceptible pushers toward standers are much more likely to slowly move off in the direction planned by the hunters who are nudging the deer along rather than vigorously driving them.

There are some important basic points, however, that are pertinent to all drives but especially to miniature ones. It is vital to know that deer prefer to escape by moving into the wind. This helps them to identify any potential danger that lies ahead of them. Unfortunately, it is virtually impossible to place standers upwind of deer without the deer detecting them, but this problem can be avoided by using tree stands. This is why most drives, large or small, are conducted downwind or with a crosswind. Downwind pushes work best when they are kept short. When making small drives, it is wise to plan approaches for each potential site to be driven. Before starting, check the wind direction and then decide which push to execute.

Unlike large drives that can cover huge areas of land, miniature drives are most successful when they cover five hundred or fewer yards. All deer, particularly adult whitetails, would much rather sneak away using cover during a push rather than run. On miniature drives, the intent is not to frighten the wits out of deer but rather to suggest through normal walking noises that it is time to move.

Blockers or Standers

For a miniature drive to perform to its maximum success, one rule that is essential is to pay attention to the blockers, or standers. They must at all costs ease quietly into position so deer don't hear, see, or smell them. Therefore, standers must know precisely where they are to go. They must keep the wind in their favor the entire time and use all the stealth they can muster to slowly and quietly reach their prescribed stand locations. Here is where one of the biggest mistakes is made in small drives. The blockers must be provided enough time to reach their stands slowly and quietly. If they are rushed, the entire success of the drive is jeopardized and doomed to failure. Once on stand, blockers should be alert during the entire push—even more observant than they would be when posting on a stand waiting for a deer to amble by naturally.

The Nudge and Bump Miniature Drive

On miniature drives, it is the responsibility of the pushers to get the deer up and moving without causing them to panic. Preferably, the objective is to make the deer feel like they're making calm, calculated choices rather than sensing they are being pursued by a group of predators. When deer are nudged from cover, they will inevitably be more undisturbed and predictable. The whole principle of the nudge drive is to coax deer, particularly adult bucks, to make their way past one of the standers by an anticipated escape route.

When moving deer slowly on miniature pushes, the drivers benefit from a buck's tendency to sneak in and out of a preferred bedding or hiding area the same way each time, as long as the route has kept him safe and the bedding area has not been driven aggressively.

This drive is specially designed for two to three hunters, such as with two standers and a slow-moving and silent driver. A few factors come into play on this push. One of the key elements is the pusher must be somewhat familiar with where bucks usually bed, particularly during heavy hunting pressure. Another is to totally commit to steadily but slowly walking through the given area to be nudged as unhurriedly as possible while trying to be as quiet as possible but not totally silent. It is important to make a footfall a little harder than normal or to gently scrape a boot over some leaves. Any one or a combination of these tactics is enough to encourage a buck to get up and sneak off on one of his favored escape

This young hunter is perfectly positioned should a buck be nudged past his stand. He is using a YPOD shooting rest to ensure himself of a well-placed shot. Photo Credit: YPOD.

routes. This tactic depends on the buck's keen sense of hearing working against him, which puts the advantage in the court of the hunter on stand. It bears repeating that shooters must enter the area first without being detected by deer, and they must down-wind of the land that will be driven.

In all small drives, it is best, when practical, to put the shooter either in a tree stand or on a high point of land so he or she has a better view. A high point of ground may be only a few feet higher than the surrounding ground, but it helps. Many of you have seen on our television show that an overwhelming number of our deer, moose, caribou, and other game are taken with one-shot kills. The reason for this is not that we are Annie Oakley-type sharpshooters. What accounts for such accuracy is that we use shooting sticks, specifically Hip-Sticks, to steady our aim. A good rock-steady rest is the key to killing deer on any hunt, but it is more important on a deer push.

Moving steadily but slowly is another crucial element to the success of this drive. The key is to constantly keep moving so deer don't have time to slip behind you. Sometimes when a pusher pauses, deer detect exactly where he or she is and allow him or her to walk past them, then they make their getaway from the back door. To avoid this, set a path out and slowly walk in a consistent zigzag through the area. The slow progression not only keeps approaching noise at a minimum, but it also allows ample time for scent to drift ahead of you if that option exists because of a mild breeze. Any deer detecting scent but not relating it to immediate danger because they don't see or hear anything will tend to move off slowly in the opposite direction.

The nudge drive works most effectively when used by as few as two or as many as four to six participants. Every time an additional nudger is added, though, it increases odds that the pushers will make more noise than deer will tolerate comfortably. That sometimes leads to the deer running by the standers instead of walking by them. In fact, if the plan for this drive includes four hunters, it is much better to use three standers and one nudger. If six hunters participate, use four standers and two pushers.

A small patch of ground with cover like this is perfect for a small nudge drive. Bucks and does feel secure enough in the cover to move slowly from one or two pushers. Photo Credit: CanStock Photos.

Learn from past experiences where you have unintentionally jumped deer or spooked them from cover and they ran off. Record to memory what direction the buck took to escape. After he has run off, look for his tracks and study the direction he took; the tracks will reveal a lot of pertinent information. If this is done prior to snow being on the ground, look hard for signs. Leaves will be kicked up or disturbed; look for skid marks in the dirt where the buck may have turned sharply, and keep an eye out for broken branches at knee- or hip-high spots. All these clues can help solve the mystery as to what escape route the buck took.

Advanced Small Push Tactics

Small nudge and push drives work best when a compact piece of ground is selected for the drive. Ideally the land to be pushed should contain the heaviest cover within the property. Look for areas that I call cottontail hideaways. In other words, big bucks like to hide in the sort of thick cover rabbits usually prefer. I have seen bucks totally disappear in cover that is barely able to conceal a rabbit! In cover like this, bucks don't move unless they are nearly stepped on. Other good cover examples include swales in the middle of agricultural fields, narrow gullies, woodlots, briar patches, patches of standing corn, or other similar plants that aren't over three to five feet in size, river bottoms, brush-choked ravines, marshes, bogs, swamps, pine thickets, and small two- to five-acre islands of woods in the middle of fields. All are excellent choices for small drives. Basically, you want to keep the area to be nudged manageable, so it has to be a reasonably small amount of land. These are my favorite areas for both types of drives. Any area larger than this can be sectioned off and pushed separately.

If the area to be pushed becomes too small, however, the number of standers has to be reduced accordingly. Otherwise, it is almost impossible for the standers to reach their respective locations without being smelled, heard, or seen by deer. In situations like this, it is practical to place a couple of standers a quarter of a mile or more away! They can intercept deer that have snuck out the back door or the side exit.

Timing is Crucial

It is true that many of the large drives I mentioned at the opening of this chapter will move deer from first light on opening day to the last glimmer of light at the close of the season. In contrast, small pushes work best not only after the season has been underway for a week or so, but also for much shorter periods of the day. Wait to put on small drives until the surrounding hunting pressure sends deer, especially adult bucks, into hiding.

It's Not Over Until the Fat Lady Sings

No matter what type of drive, there is one mistake that is commonly made by hunters. They often leave their stands too soon after the push is over. Once the drive has ended, particularly a nudge drive in thick cover, don't assume there weren't any deer in the area if nothing comes out. With over fifty-one years of hunting, I can assure you I have seen deer break from cover countless times after the drive has ended and the hunters are moving back to their vehicles or standing around discussing what took place. Always make a plan that will include at least some of the hunters remaining at their posts for a minimum of thirty more minutes. Many times a buck will get up and casually walk off after he thinks everything has calmed down. Other times, bucks that have escaped without being noticed sneak back to their favorite refuges. Keeping standers posted after the drive has ended can pay off in big dividends.

Drop Push

This can be an effective drive. One hunter takes a stand on a predicted escape route. One pusher follows the primary driver from about one hundred yards behind. Whatever zigzag route the primary bumper uses, the backup pusher zigzags in a manner that crisscrosses the original route.

This small drive also requires that both drivers walk at a snail's pace. However, the key point is that both hunters stop every twenty-five yards or so and wait five to ten minutes before moving again. This takes preestablished coordination. When a wise buck sees, hears, and potentially smells the approaching bumper, he will either try to sneak off ahead of the bumper, sneak around him, or let him walk by. If he moves

Seeing a buck walking at this pace is common on small drop pushes. Photo Credit: Ted Rose.

ahead of him, the stander gets an optimum opportunity for a shot. The driver can also get a shot if the deer tries to remain hidden or as it moves off on either side of the bumper. For safety reasons, the primary pusher can't shoot at a buck behind him. The pusher at the rear gets an opportunity if the buck passes alongside his route or directly behind him.

On small drives, it is always best to set the stander downwind. Once the pushers move past the standers, the drive doesn't end. The pushers should retreat from the area to leave the stander on stand for at least thirty minutes. Again, many times this single tactic has proven to be worthwhile as a buck or doe will return to its bedding area.

Other than thinking small for these types of drives, there are important factors that have to be paid attention to for small drives to work to their best potential. The fact is, no matter what type of drive is used, small or large, it is basically impossible to predetermine if deer are bedded within the area to be driven, if they will leave their cover, and exactly what route they will take to escape. A successful drive is a direct result of the hunter's knowing where the deer want to go and setting up the drivers and standers accordingly!

The best success comes from understanding deer behavior, as well as having knowledge of cover, terrain, and escape routes in your hunting territory. Check where deer trails lead and when they are used. Find bedding sites and favored feeding spots. Know where deer seek protection from the weather—heat, cold, sun, rain, and wind. All this information will help you know where to position standers depending on the time of day and weather conditions. Plans to put on a small drive work best when it is most likely that deer have settled into their bedding or hiding areas. This generally means putting on pushes in the late morning or at midday. All successful pushes also take the weather into prime consideration.

Two-Man Loop and Nudge Drive

When done correctly, two hunters can move deer as effectively as larger pushes can. This push requires one blocker to circle around the area of cover to be pushed and enter it as quietly as possible about two hundred to three hundred yards downwind. Once there, the blocker takes a stand on the ground to see into low-lying cover. The nudger slowly walks into the cover to nudge deer toward the blocker. The nudger should move through the area as though he were trying to flush out a cottontail rabbit. Most times, the blocker gets a prime opportunity to see and bag a deer. If the drive doesn't work by the time the nudger reaches the blocker, the nudger then loops wide and becomes a blocker at a new location two hundred to three hundred yards ahead. Now his partner pushes deer through the available cover toward him. This technique can accommodate more than two hunters if it is necessary to effectively cover more area.

Alarm-Snort Instinctive Drive

This push works particularly well anywhere swamps or other thick impenetrable cover exists. It can be done with four to six hunters. All but one hunter take stands at the far sides of the cover. Once there, they are to remain quiet and establish potential shooting lanes where expected deer might move through. The remaining hunter waits at least thirty minutes for the other hunters to set up and let things settle down. When the time has passed, the pusher then walks only about fifty yards into the cover while intentionally snapping a twig here and there. Once at his or her location, he or she waits about ten minutes and begins blowing several cadences of the alarm-distress snort call. Deer within the area will immediately react to the warning vocalization by trying to escape by sneaking out of the sides. If another stander or two is safe to include, they should block the back escape routes. On this drive, particularly when standers

are blocking the back door, it is essential for all participants to take extreme caution—as they would on any drive. In thick cover, it is wise to hunt with shotguns loaded with buckshot only—not slugs.

Lastly, many times small pushes end up being foiled before they begin. Deer are tipped off prematurely by hunters talking too loudly, making too much noise as they approach the area, or when hunters don't pay attention to the direction their scent is being carried before the

The versatile snort call is a primary tool when driving deer. It comes in very handy on an alarm-snort instinctive drive. It is no longer available in stores but can be found at www.deerdoctor.com. Photo Credit: Fiduccia Enterprises.

push even begins. To prevent this, always elect a person who will be in total charge of any push. This person should have complete familiarity with the land. If more than one person has equal experience, they should take turns being in charge of different pushes.

The more controlled a small drive is and the less complicated the push plans are, the larger the degree of success there will be. Teamwork is the name of the game on small pushes, as it is on all deer drives. When deer are taken, it will be a more satisfying experience, as well, as small drives are a more personal strategy than large deer drives.

Safety

One last crucial point about any type of drive, large or small, is that safety must be the paramount objective. Deer drives are inherently dangerous and can cause injury or even death. Use all the necessary caution and common sense that is available on every drive. Safety can't be overemphasized. Blaze orange hats and vests should be required for all participants. Shooting at running deer invites danger. Limit shots to prescribed areas. Be absolutely certain of your target and, equally important, what lies beyond the intended target.

Chapter Twelve

Secrets for Bagging Late-Season Bucks

Some of the best buck hunting can be had when temperatures become nearly unbearably cold. Brutally frigid weather forces all deer, including adult bucks, to feed as heavily as they can even during daylight hours in order to survive.

Many of the bucks I have killed over the years were taken during the coldest of days when I was most uncomfortable on stand. Over my first forty years of experience, hunting deer from tree stands or ground blinds in frigid temperatures was much more bearable. But I still don't miss a chance to get out when Jack Frost sets his sights on turning the tip of my nose, ears, fingers, and toes as white as snow. That's when I beat him at his own game and get dressed to kill—or when I set the Mr. Heater on high!

Shortly after the rigors of the three phases of the rut end in late December in most places, adult

Adult bucks typically move more in frigid conditions. I shot this buck in Saskatchewan, Canada, with temperatures that never got above five degrees Fahrenheit that day. Photo Credit: Fiduccia Enterprises.

Photo Credit: CanStock Photos.

During the late season a buck is instinctively driven to seek out any and all food sources in order to put weight back on before the harshest days of winter arrive. This buck is eating forage rape. Photo Credit: Fiduccia Enterprises.

bucks have one crucial thought process: survival. Their end goal is to make it through the severities of the remaining months of winter to see the next season. Living through a cold winter requires only one critical element: food and plenty of it.

Luckily for hunters, the later and colder the deer season gets, the more active and visible a mature buck becomes. Bucks are compelled by Mother Nature to seek whatever nutritious foods are remaining to regain enough weight to survive the winter. Because the young bucks have exhausted most, if not all, of their energy chasing after every doe they saw during the rut, now they are basically out of steam, and they, too, need to refuel their energy sources. The heavy feeding makes both adult and adolescent buck sightings more prevalent during the late deer season than commonly believed by most hunters. To add to this buck phenomenon, adult does keep food in high precedence, as well. When temperatures plummet, they make food an even higher priority. They become principally responsible for leading savvy old bucks out of hiding and into open food plots or other natural food sources even during daylight hours.

On the first day of a late season winter deer hunt in Saskatchewan, Canada, nearly two decades ago, I was posted on a knoll overlooking some woods that bordered a field. The temperature was an unbelievable -30° F, but the day was utterly calm. Within the first few minutes, I watched a doe that was about two hundred yards from my position repeatedly running into the woodlot and then back out into the field to eat. She did this about a dozen times. I decided to make a doe blat and call to her just in case there was a buck watching her from the woods. After several doe blats, she came trotting to my location at the edge of the woods. When she got there, I nearly fell out of my stand. There was a large buck with tremendous antlers behind her. As it turned out, I didn't get an opportunity to shoot the buck that day.

It was so cold that I was shivering badly, and when I went to raise my rifle, it shook noticeably. The buck caught the movement and disappeared in the blink of an eye. The

My largest buck. It scored 198 4/8 B&C inches. The entire week of the hunt was brutally cold, but the deer, particularly the bucks, were on the constant move. Photo Credit: Fiduccia Enterprises.

remainder of the week saw temperatures that never got above -30° F. Hunting for more than an hour or so outside was virtually impossible. Even when I hunted from an enclosed blind, it was difficult to stay longer than two hours.

Each day I saw several good bucks feeding in the grain fields we were watching, including the huge buck that escaped twice feeding in broad daylight. On the next-to-the-last day of the hunt, with an eye swollen almost completely shut from a sty caused by the intolerable freezing temperatures, I watched as the huge antlered buck once again entered the field. It was 11 a.m. when we went back to hunt the winter wheat field for the third time that morning. Not ten minutes after getting there, the buck walked out of the woods and joined a group of does who were feeding on winter wheat. They were about 175 yards from me, and I didn't want to shoot that far, as I was already cold. I decided to make an adult blat call. I blew the call three times before one of the adult does raised her head up from feeding. I made another call, and she started for my position, bringing all the does with her. The second she got out of the buck's sight, he came running in the same direction.

Minutes later, I placed the crosshairs just behind his front shoulder and squeezed the trigger. When the .270 WSM 150-grain bullet crashed into the deer, I realized it had hit further back than I was aiming. I was shocked that I missed my mark—so much so that I almost forgot to chamber a second round. As I put the scope on the buck again, I saw him run into the woods below me. When I got to the spot where he entered the woods, I noticed dark red, almost maroon, blood. This was a good indication that I had either hit the buck's liver or kidneys. The blood trail was easy to follow, and I found the buck not far into the woods.

The buck had sixteen atypical points with a lot of heavy mass throughout the entire rack. He green scored 207 1/8 Boone & Crockett inches and had a net score of 195 3/8 Boone & Crockett inches! A late-season hunt with temperatures that were almost too cold to stand was predominantly responsible for allowing me the opportunity to kill the buck. If he hadn't been instinctively motivated to pack on some pounds and restore some energy during the late season, he probably would have not been drawn to the winter wheat fields in daylight so many times during the hunt.

To further illustrate this point, a few years ago I killed an adult thirteen-point buck on our land. It was December 20, the last day of the New York muzzleloader season. While driving past one of our fields along a road at 8 a.m., I saw a small herd of does feeding. They were all eagerly taking one quick bite after another in a plot planted with a winter brassica, or forage rape, eating so fast you would have thought it was going to be their last meal. I credited what I saw to the fact that the temperature was in the low teens, the weatherman predicted it was going to fall even lower, and we were going to get several inches of snow as the day progressed.

I did my errand at work and rushed home to change into my hunting clothes. Within an hour, I took a stand in a field planted with turnips, swede, and sugar beets. It was 10 a.m., and the weather was still clear, but it had turned extremely frigid with the temperature hovering in the low single digits. As I sat in a blind named Little

View, it began to snow. I anticipated that the small herd of does I saw earlier would come in to feed before the food plots were covered in snow. I didn't have to wait that long.

Within an hour, a lone yearling doe emerged from the woods between the field I was watching and the field I had seen the does feeding in when I drove by. The doe ran into the field and began to chow down heartily on the turnip bulbs. As I watched her, I chuckled because she was eating so quickly I could see the food balled up like a baseball sliding down her gullet.

I shot this unusual antlered buck on a cold, rainy day in upstate New York. Photo Credit: Fiduccia Enterprises.

Not long after she came into the field, a dozen other deer, including three adult females, yearlings, and a few fawns, entered and began frantically eating in a plot planted with swede and another with sugar beets.

My anticipation began to get out of control, and I was getting edgy. I had to stop myself from turning my head in all directions to see if a mature buck might be lurking in the nearby woods watching the young doe and other deer. Moments later, a terrific buck trotted from the woods into the food plot. I didn't hesitate a second. I placed the scope on his shoulder and fired. When the smoke from my muzzleloader cleared, the buck lay dead in the middle of the food plot. It was just past 11 a.m.! The primary factor to killing a mature buck in a food plot at 11 a.m. that day had to do with the number of female deer that lured the buck from the woods and into the open field.

Over the years, I have taken several good bucks in similar cold weather circumstances. The first real intense cold snaps usually coincide with late-season hunting in much of the United States and southern Canada. The plummeting temperatures also kick-start the deer's physiological slowdown, although the changeover usually takes a few weeks to happen. Importantly, however, the transition instinctively spurs deer to feed heavily to fuel their still-high metabolic rates. This combination of factors is responsible for forcing deer, including adult bucks, to forsake their natural security and head to food sources before dark.

However, not all adult bucks end up feeding in open fields or planted food plots. Some still retain a certain degree of caution and feed on lesser foods in the woods—still arriving in fields at dark. So what is the strategy you can use for busting a late-season adult buck? There are three viable options: stand hunting, decoying, and miniature drives. Some suggest still hunting, but that time of year usually means crunchy snow or frozen ground, both

Many of our food plots include winter-hardy clovers, brassicas, and grains. This plot of pumpkins, rape, and chicory drew bucks almost regularly throughout the late December season in New York. Photo Credit: Fiduccia Enterprises.

My cousin Ralph lives in NJ and regularly hunts during that state's late January season. A time when foul weather is common. He shot this buck on his land a cold morning in NY soon after a snowfall ended. Photo Credit: Fiduccia Enterprises.

of which make for a noisy and impractical still hunt. The savvy hunter selects the tactic that the deer behavior and movement patterns suggest will work best!

Locate a Buck

Late in the season, deer begin to bunch up, especially if the temperatures are lower than normal. The easiest way to locate a buck during that time frame is to find an area where deer are concentrating. They will almost always be near food sources that time of year, so that's the first place to start your scrutiny. A good tactic is to drive along back roads and farm areas and to use binoculars to scan the corners of crop fields and pinch points from woods to second-growth areas.

This is the time to talk to people who are constantly on the road, including UPS, Fed-Ex, and school bus drivers, as well as farmers and other landowners. Someone will have information on where they have spotted a buck or bucks. All the investigations are to discover the feeding areas deer are currently using the most.

Information Determines Tactics

The information attained on deer concentrations will allow you to focus on where to scout with binoculars. In turn, what you discover or, for that matter, don't learn will help determine what strategy to choose. For instance, if it is established that a buck is using a feeding area during daylight hours, the best tactic will be to hunt that spot from a tree stand or enclosed blind if practical. It will be a high-odds favorite for busting the buck. If, on the other hand, deer are not entering the field

Bucks are much more sensitive to hunting pressure during the late season, especially when snow covers the ground. Jump a buck more than once from his lair late in the season and he'll hightail it to a safer area. Photo Credit: Ted Rose.

before dark but a good buck has been seen in the field after shooting light, then another strategy must be used. In a case like this, a hunter can either find a fresh deer trail that leads from bedding areas to the food source and hunt along the trail or try small deer pushes. Keep in mind, when deer are yarding or bunching together this time of year, they don't tolerate more than a drive or two before leaving the area for an extended period of time. They may not go that far, but it can be enough that you have to start your search all over again.

Caution is the Name of the Game

An important element to keep in mind when hunting late-season deer is that deer, especially adult bucks and does, are exceedingly careful after a season of being hunted. Jump a buck more than once, and he will revert to finding a safer place to eat in the blink of an eye. If you use caution, however, the buck will continue his daylight routine until something or someone forces him to abandon it. A natural occurrence for a buck to change his daylight feeding patterns, of course, is a dramatic change in the weather or wind direction. So it pays to scout with stealth.

Late-season hunting is a game of chess. It requires exceptional patience and thoroughness. Each time you hunt an area, you must exit as inconspicuously as possible or you risk blowing the deer out for a few days.

Owning a farm with lots of winter food plots, including winter clovers, brassicas like swede, rape, turnips, and radishes, and small grains, such as winter wheat, barley, and triticale, have taught me some valuable lessons about late-season hunts, particularly when a late season includes accumulated snow on the ground. Deer prefer to bed close to food sources to preserve their energy. I have seen up to forty

This is Big View blind. It overlooks more than twenty acres of fields that are bordered by woods on all sides. Many spots include pinch points and inside corners. Photo Credit: Fiduccia Enterprises.

deer bedded down within spitting distance of my food plots in the late season. So always approach an area that you intend to hunt as stealthily as is practical to avoid the potential of spooking not just a few deer but an entire herd.

Many of our enclosed blinds and tree stands that overlook our food plots and fields are situated where we can see deer feeding from downwind. Others are far enough away from the winter plots that we don't risk being seen or winded. All of them, however, offer the opportunity of having a straggler walk past the stand within gun or bow range.

If deer refuse to feed during daylight hours in the fields and food plots, the only other option is to take the hunt to them. Move to wooded or overgrown areas that have fresh signs that they are being traveled regularly, and plan an ambush accordingly. The best locations to ambush them are in pinch points. A more risky option is to get closer to the bedding areas. Either way, this time of year wary deer are vigilant, so extra caution is required.

Conclusion

Is late-season hunting for everyone? It is definitely not. First of all, for optimum success, it should not include your buddies unless you plan to push a piece of ground. To endure the unforgiving cold, snow, sleet, and whatever other weather comes along, it helps to be a cowboy, lumberjack, tough guy from Brooklyn, or a little brain-dead. It is lonely, extremely cold, and boring at times. One of the upsides is that you will probably not see another hunter. More than that, the unbridled satisfaction of enduring a hunt in severe winter weather comes into play when all the pieces of the puzzle fall into place neatly and you bag a dandy animal. Then all the hardships are quickly forgotten, including the uncontrollable shivering, running nose, chattering teeth, numb limbs and extremities, and the exquisite stinging pain of field dressing your trophy.

Chapter Thirteen

How to Kill the Infamous "Nocturnal" Buck

One of the most talked about phenomena in deer hunting camps, on outdoor television programs, in magazine articles, and in online chats is how hunting pressure causes bucks to disappear and go totally nocturnal. Many hunters claim that shortly after the firearm season gets underway, their trail cameras only get pictures of bucks at night. Many of them also claim after a week of hunting, bucks suddenly go nocturnal and are no longer seen feeding in fields during legal shooting light.

I readily admit buck sightings during daylight hours in hunting season, particularly as the hunting pressure increases, can become less frequent. However, the reality is that it is extremely unlikely any buck will remain bedded from shortly before dawn to shortly after dusk. Therefore, it is my firm belief that no bucks realistically go entirely nocturnal during the hunting season. Ask yourself this: If all bucks become totally nocturnal, how are any bucks killed

There is no arguing that hunting pressure can cause bucks to move a lot less during daylight. However, the reality of a buck becoming totally nocturnal is slim to none! Photo Credit: Ted Rose.

Photo Credit Ted Rose.

by hunters? At night? Of course not; they were killed as they moved about during legal shooting hours. Therein should lie the eureka moment—and a sense of optimism and anticipation—for all hunters who steadfastly embrace this false contention. When thought out, it is easy to see the irrationality of this idea collapses from its own weight.

The most credible reason why bucks considerably restrict their daylight travel is the obvious one: human encroachment. Without a doubt, it doesn't take deer long to realize the woods have exploded with humans. Deer begin to detect hunters and react by becoming less diurnal and somewhat more nocturnal. It is a natural instinctive behavior, particularly for adult bucks. Many times, this natural reaction only takes a few days of heavy human intrusion into their domain.

While deer may move a lot less than they did during the rut or prior to heavy hunting pressure, you can be sure they will move during daylight. Bucks may indeed hang back in the safety of a secure bedding area before moving toward a feeding area or searching for does during daylight hours. But inevitably bucks must feed and move, particularly in frigid weather. Another motivation for a buck to move during daylight is that even after the rut diminishes, a buck's inherent desire to breed doesn't just end. His testosterone is still at a level that urges him to move about in daylight hours seeking estrus does.

Many hunters claim categorically that all mature bucks become nocturnal shortly after they undergo heavy hunting pressure. Even adult bucks won't revert to being totally nocturnal. However, it is accurate that adult bucks lay low sooner and for longer periods of time than younger bucks do because of their survival experiences. They inherently know to curtail their daytime travel to short distances from their beds.

That being said, I have taken a considerable number of adult bucks between 10 a.m. and 1 p.m.—sometimes even as late as 2 p.m.

A significant number of them were by ambush tactics that allowed me to get close to their bedding areas. Any buck limiting his daylight wanderings may only

It's true that hunting pressure forces bucks to lay low and remain bedded for most of the day. However, the savvy hunter knows a buck can and will move sometime during the day. Photo Credit: CanStock Photo.

remain up and about during midday for thirty minutes or so, but they are indeed stirring. Older bucks innately know the safest time to travel is between 10 a.m. to 1 p.m., when hunting pressure is usually at it lightest. They will also move thirty minutes after dawn and thirty minutes before dusk. Most of the time, this puts them moving in daylight during heavy hunting pressure for a total of about ninety minutes per day. That's about four times less than they would be up and about during daylight at other times of the year, which can be six or more hours per day. Therefore, bucks do become somewhat more inclined to be nocturnal during the heavy human pressure of hunting season, but not totally.

On the other hand, deer have never been entirely diurnal creatures either. They are more inclined to be nocturnal ungulates to limit pressure from predators. Another often-overlooked factor by hunters who feel a buck has pulled a disappearing act is that a buck may have been taken by another hunter, killed by a vehicle, or eaten by a predator. Often, when a buck suddenly vanishes, the hunter is left with a false impression that the buck he or she is hunting is still alive. Unfortunately, as the hunting season progresses, it is commonplace for hunters to see fewer bucks because some have naturally begun to restrict their daylight travel, some have been killed, and some have relocated to sanctuaries and other safe locations. All these factors account for less visibility of both young and adult bucks.

Interestingly, over the three-week firearm season in New York, bucks begin to move about during daylight hours again as the season progresses. By the end of week two, most hunters have either bagged their bucks or run out of hunting time and gone back to work. With a lot less human intrusion, bucks once again sense they are less threatened and begin to move about more during daylight hours.

So how can hunters take bucks that are severely restricting their daytime movements? A paramount tactic is to ambush them as close to their bedding areas as is practical without alerting them. The formula is basic. The closer you set up to where the buck is bedded during daylight hours, the higher the chances you will get a shooting opportunity. You could intercept him as he comes into his bed or as he gets up and leaves the bedding area. You could even get an opportunity to take him in mid-morning. Bucks will often rise from their beds between 10 a.m. and 1 p.m. stretch, mull about the bedding area for several minutes, and then slowly move a short distance to feed or freshen up a nearby scrape or rub.

This is particularly true when the buck's bed is close to a concealed forest food source, such as chestnuts, acorns, or water. Sometime during the day, he will leave the security and comfort of his bedding area to seek out the safest route to these resources.

That's the simple fact that can't be overlooked when planning to kill the so-called nocturnal buck. He is even more inclined to leave his bedding area for sexual reasons. He may scent a nearby estrus doe even if the primary rut is waning. Again, keep in mind the less ground he has to travel to pass you, the better the opportunity will be for you to bust him during daylight hours. However, to be successful at this tactic, you not only have to remember no buck will remain bedded an entire day, you also have to totally believe it!

To further support that bucks do not go totally nocturnal, consider this: When there's low hunting pressure, how many times have you seen a buck enter a food plot or walk past a woodland stand within thirty to forty-five minutes of last legal shooting light? I suspect the answer is often. It is probable the buck could have been traveling hundreds of yards before passing a deer stand or entering a field or food plot. Conversely, a buck that has severely curtailed his daylight movements due to hunting pressure may only leave his bedding area thirty to thirty-five minutes before dusk. If he spends time stretching and mulling before heading to food sources or to search for estrus does, the buck may only leave his bedding area with fifteen minutes of legal shooting light left. When that happens, the odds of seeing him in a field or along a deer trail are slim to none!

Using a strategy that puts you much closer to a buck's bedding area is a two-sided coin, however. It can dramatically increase the chances of taking a buck that is lying low, but it can also alert the buck to your presence. To be consistently successful at this ambush tactic, it helps tremendously to know how to avoid getting busted by the buck. The first element to success is to know what bedding areas have high potential for a buck to use them. To discover active bedding area prospects, you require stealth-like scouting skills. But even with them, finding a buck bedding area is not always an easy task.

During the time of year that bucks begin to hold up, the foliage

Many times low laying bucks leave their beds with fifteen to thirty minutes left of legal shooting light and move slowly through the woods toward fields to find does and food sources. Photo Credit: CanStock Photo.

is all but gone. Buck beds that were seen earlier in the year may not have enough cover now. The best place to begin the search for a currently used buck bed, then, is in the heaviest cover within the property. Other high-potential areas, heavy cover or not, are sanctuaries or refuges. Any place that deer can retreat to and not have to worry about human intrusion—even during high hunting pressure—is an excellent place to shelter a savvy adult buck or two. It is a top choice for them to escape hunting pressure, and they know it. As long as the refuge rules are not violated by entering the sanctuary (see Chapter Nineteen), a hunter can be confident that a buck will be harbored within its borders.

In fact, when using an ambush tactic to take a buck with curtailed daylight movements, it is wise not to enter the security zone of any bedding areas, refuge or not. When I try to ambush a low-lying buck that I believe is in our sanctuary, I plan to use a stand that is set up along one of four perimeters that offers the best wind direction and is closest to where I think a buck or two may be hiding. The approach to hunt any bedding area must be cautious. You can get away with jumping an adult buck once or twice, but if he is disturbed in his bedding area more than that, the odds are excellent that he'll relocate to a safer spot.

Even though the prime directive (a *Star Trek* reference—I have to use at least one per book or risk being de-nerded) is to avoid disturbing the bedding area, it still has to be scouted. Again, this is best accomplished by doing so carefully from the perimeters. Don't expect the deer trails that lead in and out of potential buck beds to look as heavily used as trails used by does, yearlings, and fawns. The trail you're seeking should barely show deer are traveling it.

If it is a narrow trail that doesn't reveal a lot of tracks and either enters into or out of the area through thick cover, the more likely it is a buck trail. The thinner and deeper set into the ground the trail is, the better the odds are that it is a buck

A splayed track that is deeply set in a deer trail is a good sign that it was most likely left by an adult buck. Experienced hunters know that a mature doe can be heavy enough to leave a deeply set track as well Photo Credit: Ted Rose.

trail. If the trail or close by surrounding areas contain a two-and-a-half- to three-inch track that is slightly splayed, you are most likely on to an adult buck. Adult does can leave similar looking tracks, but they are usually accompanied by several other smaller tracks. Also look for signs of either fresh or refreshed rubs and scrapes when looking for bucks. Just because a buck is lying low and isn't moving much during daylight hours, he still instinctively leaves rutting signs as the rut winds down.

While refuges and areas of heavy cover are excellent options for buck beds, there are other areas you can consider. Bucks will congregate to hide anywhere hunting pressure is light. Another prime choice is remote hunting areas, such as those found in the Adirondack Mountains of New York or similar areas in other states and provinces.

On our farm, we intentionally leave the hay high from early summer on. We have discovered that bucks will often hide in the tall hay within thirty yards of a woodlot and, particularly, within our refuge. Don't ignore overgrown places. Treat bucks that have limited their daylight movements as if they were cottontail rabbits. They like to seek safety in the oddest places, which are often areas that hunters don't usually move through or expect. Another top location for adult bucks to seek cover on our land is in our swamp. They are there because we rarely go into the swampy area. All the areas and terrain I mentioned are places that can be found on public ground, too.

When it comes to hunting later in the season, if you've set your sights on an adult buck that is playing the daylight off-hour movement game, arrive to your stand as early as you can. The earlier you get there the better because the buck may still be on his way to the bedding area. In the evening, stay until the last moments of legal shooting light to catch the buck moving.

Unfortunately, if you live in New York State, this is not good advice. New York hunting hours are from sunrise to sunset throughout the entire bow and firearms season. By opening day, it is illegal to shoot at a deer before 6:47 a.m. It is also illegal during opening day to shoot at deer past 4:32 p.m. By the time bucks are moving less during daylight hours, usually the second week of the season, legal shooting light begins at 7 a.m. and ends at 4:25 p.m. By the last week of muzzleloading season in December, legal shooting light begins at 7:19 a.m. and ends at 4:23 p.m.! New York makes it tough to hunt a late-season adult buck that is traveling on a restricted time scale. If you live in New York, plan to hunt your semi-nocturnal buck from 10 a.m. to 1 p.m.

The sunrise-to-sunset law is unreasonable. It has irrefutably created a situation where a majority of hunters are needlessly tempted to violate the law. It would be judicious for the New York State Department of Environmental Conservation, a group of intelligent and hardworking individuals, many of whom are hunters, to reevaluate the sunrise-to-sunset law. It would be a catalyst to provide better hunting opportunities for resident and nonresident hunters alike.

A majority of whitetail hunters have told me they prefer to hunt in the morning rather than the evening. But when it comes to ambushing bucks that have cut back their daytime moving behavior, I have found the opposite is true. I have taken more adult bucks in the evening than I have in the morning. I strongly believe that other than the first few days of the opening of firearm season, most deer that get pressured, particularly adult males, are setting a course back to their bedding areas before the first hint of dawn colors the sky.

Conclusion

Yes, I agree that adult bucks have a tendency to become somewhat nocturnal. I absolutely don't concur that they go totally nocturnal, however. It is important to realize this semi-nocturnal behavior is short-lived, and it changes rather quickly as hunting pressure declines. It generally only takes a few days for bucks to be moving about more frequently during daylight hours. By applying common sense and stealth, you can bust a dandy adult buck during the time when mature bucks are laying low.

Chapter Fourteen

The Big Bucks of the Suburbs

I don't usually tell people that they have to get off the beaten trails or chase bucks into remote backcountry areas to successfully hunt them. The primary reason I don't recommend this type of tactic is that I try to relate my strategies and advice to practical hunting techniques. The fact is, the average hunter simply doesn't have the time to stalk deer in remote locations or even hike back into more local wild areas. Most hunters don't have such remote areas easily accessible within their usual hunting locations. Another reason for not suggesting hunting in remote backcountry areas is that this strategy isn't the only way to score on a trophy-class adult buck. I can emphatically state that a lot of mature trophy bucks, some with antlers large enough to make the Boone & Crockett record books, are killed within sight of suburbia throughout America every year. Even in states such as Montana, Maine, and Missouri, big whitetail bucks have learned to adapt by living, eating, and

Giant-antlered suburban bucks like this have all the elements needed (genetics, food, minimal hunting, and time) to mature into trophy-class animals. They often live and die in more suburban areas of the country than most hunters realize. Photo Credit: Ted Rose.

Photo Credit: Ted Rose.

mating within a stone's throw of civilization. No matter where you live, you have backyard bucks to hunt someplace close by.

I recognize most hunters, if not all, aspire to take an adult buck each season. Over the last fifty-two years, I have listened, read, and watched on television the many pros who give their viewpoints on what it takes to consistently kill mature bucks. One of the most commonly recommended tactics by other whitetail authorities is that, and I'm paraphrasing here, "Hunters must get off the beaten trails and hunt in the most inaccessible and remote areas available if they want to shoot a trophy." In my five-plus decades of hunting experience, I have found such advice is rather narrow-sighted. I agree to some extent that pursuing bucks in the idyllic backcountry areas can lead to a hunter bagging a mature buck. However, hunting in big wilderness areas, such as those found in Maine or New York's Adirondack Mountains, can also severely reduce a hunter's chances of seeing and bagging a deer, as deer population levels are usually less dense in these areas. Additionally, the deer living in remote areas, particularly adult bucks, simply have too much ground they can use to hide in or escape to avoid hunting pressure. Therefore, hunting off the beaten trail or getting far into the backcountry can often end up reducing the odds of killing an adult buck. I'm not saying it can't be

done, however. But realistically, only a specific number of hunters employ wilderness tracking and other backcountry hunting tactics successfully. While there are positive aspects to hunting adult trophy bucks in the backcountry, it doesn't mean it's the only way a hunter can score on taking a large-antlered adult buck. Therefore, if hunting closer to home suits your fancy, there are many suburban and even urban zones throughout the country, close to heavily populated areas, that offer terrific adult buck hunting opportunities.

To demonstrate my point I offer this. Over the years, I have had some experiences hunting

Backcountry bucks can roam far and wide, and may never see a human in their lifetimes. They have access to vast areas to escape into in order to avoid hunting pressure. Photo Credit: Ted Rose.

backyard bucks. I have taken a few respectable adult bucks with high-scoring antlers of 150 inches or more in areas that can definitely be called the suburbs. In fact, some could be more realistically described as urban areas within close but legal and safe proximity to houses, highways, and city limits. In Northeast states, such as New York, New Jersey, Pennsylvania, and Connecticut, deer, especially large-antlered mature bucks, have learned to adjust their way of life to avoid hunting pressure while living in such areas. They have discovered how to use small woodlots and other secretive places within populated areas to almost totally eliminate pressure and survive the hunting season. In many instances they live, eat, and mate just outside of city limits in backyards, cemeteries, golf courses, thickets along traveled roadways, and even within tiny woodlots that are often so small they are overlooked by most hunters. Many times, these areas provide no danger from hunting and enable bucks to get old enough to sport some impressive headgear.

A perfect example of this would be a buck I shot when I lived in Warwick, New York. Warwick is about fifty-five miles northwest of the George Washington Bridge. When I first moved there in 1975, it was mostly filled with dairy farms and commercial apple orchards. Over the years, it became a bedroom community for people who worked in New York City. Many of the dairy and apple farms were sold and converted to high-end housing developments. Large parcels of hunting land became much less common to find. Eventually, the area turned into a place where many of the adult bucks were killed on small five- to ten-acre settings. I had become a hunter of backyard bucks.

During one particular hunting season, I became alerted to a buck who would bed down in some heavy cover located less than one hundred yards from a nonhunting friend's house. Each morning, the buck would leave an apple orchard that was across the street from my friend's place, cross the road, and bed down within one hundred yards of his back deck. From my tree stand in the apple orchard, which was a couple hundred yards from his house, I could hear his dog barking excitedly each morning around 7:45 a.m. The barking would last for a while, and then it would end abruptly. While talking to my friend one day, I mentioned this to him. He replied matter-of-factly, "I know, his barking drives us nuts. He's barking at a buck that passes through our yard each morning. He stops barking when the buck gets out of his sight. He starts to bark again when the buck gets up and crosses the lawn as he leaves to go into the apple orchard in the afternoon." The conversation was an *aha* moment! I asked him if I could bow hunt his land, and he agreed.

The next morning with my newfound permission, I posted up on his thirteen-acre woodlot. I climbed into my tree stand, which was about seventy-five yards behind his home in the woods, hoisted my bow up, and made myself comfortable. I could see the cars driving along the road in front of his house from the stand. I actually watched his children get on the school bus and his wife leave for work while I sat patiently waiting for the buck to show up. Then, as I had heard happen so many times while in the apple orchard, his dog began to bark vigorously. It was 7:40 a.m., and as casual as you please, a buck was nonchalantly walking across the yard and totally ignoring the chained up black Labrador as he made his way into the small woodlot. When the buck reached the end of the lawn, he walked off into the woods about fifty yards, paused, circled several times, and bedded down. As I sat in my stand, I was amazed at how relaxed this big buck was. He paid absolutely no attention to the dog, the cars on the road, or a passing jogger.

For well over an hour the buck lay motionless in his bed. Finally, in an attempt to get the buck to move, I decided to blow an alarm snort vocalization. I figured it would be a good plan to get the buck to stand up and allow me a clean lane for my arrow to fly through. I took the snort call out and blew, hesitated for a second or two, and blew another snort. The alarm vocalization worked! The buck instinctively stood up to scan the area to find why another deer blew an alarm snort. I quickly drew my bow, placed the pin on the lungs, and sent the arrow toward its mark. By 9:30 that morning, I was dressing out a nice eight-point buck that field dressed at more than 180 pounds and whose antlers gross scored 137 inches—large enough to make the Pope & Young record books.

While I have lost interest in hunting backyard bucks, it is a strategy many hunters employ throughout countless areas in North America. If a hunter enjoys this type of hunting,

I nicknamed this buck, "The School Bus Buck." He would wait in the apple orchard until the school bus pulled away before crossing the road onto my friend's thirteen acres, where he would regularly bed down in a thicket of cattails surrounded by briars. Photo Credit: Fiduccia Enterprises.

then he or she certainly doesn't have to hike into out-of-the-way locations or remote wilderness areas to take a mature buck. There are countless suburban and urban areas across this country and in Canada that are adjacent to heavily populated places with terrific hunting opportunities. A classic example of this is the southern area of New York State. While a lot of the state's deer hunting is in rural farm areas or more remote locations in the Adirondack Mountains, a percentage is found right outside cities and towns. Westchester is about ten to fifteen miles from midtown Manhattan. While posting up in tree stands in Westchester, you can see the George Washington Bridge and the entire New York City skyline. Yet each year, bow hunters kill some the state's largest antlered bucks that have adapted to living in small woodlots throughout suburban Westchester. While maturing in these areas, deer, especially bucks, survive and thrive in heavily populated areas that are often not hunted. By surviving from year to year and season to season, they gain the most important element of all to becoming large-antlered adult bucks: age. Hidden and left alone during hunting season, many suburban bucks mature into four-and-a-half- to six-and-a-half-year-old trophy-class whitetails by simply adapting to this urban lifestyle.

Bucks are quick to figure out where hunters can't or won't hunt. Once such an area is located, an adult buck will secretly go about his business of survival somewhat indifferently to the houses, strip malls, factories, half-acre swamps, small estates, and mini gentlemen farms that they call home, particularly during hunting season.

This isn't the only strange place you'll find big bucks. Even in areas where there is a lot of open hunting ground, deer will often bed down in places that are overlooked by most hunters. Adult bucks are sensitive to hunting pressure. It doesn't take more than a few close encounters with hunters to forewarn a

Two young bucks learning to be backyard buck "survivors." Within a couple of years they'll get the time to grow sets of impressive antlers. Photo Credit: Ted Rose.

mature big buck of what is about to take place: predation. They adapt quickly to it and avoid it by bedding down only yards off a major roadway if necessary to escape pressure. They have learned from past experiences that by quietly bedding close to the road or in places often overlooked by most hunters as unlikely deer areas, they can allow people to walk right past them as they head for their stands a few hundred yards deeper into the woods. Once while I was hunting during the late January season in Hampton Bays in Long Island, New York, I saw a large-antlered buck bedded on an open grass lawn not more than twenty yards off the road! He was as safe as a bug in a rug because he was bedded between two houses that were only scant yards apart from each other!

It becomes clear, then, that it is not always necessary to get off the beaten trail to bag a mature buck with impressive antlers. If a hunter is inclined to take a large-antlered buck and doesn't mind sacrificing the romanticism or ambiance of a more traditional type of deer hunt, then hunting backyard bucks is certainly a worthwhile endeavor or tactic. It is critical, however, for those hunters who stalk backyard bucks to establish hard-core backyard hunting ethics, particularly regarding safety. It is also important to keep in mind that hunting backyard bucks is not all about killing. There should be elements of the hunt involved, as well. For those who want to increase their chances of shooting a larger-racked buck, especially in the Northeast, hunting backyard bucks may be the best tactic to use.

It is also important to understand that adult bucks in farm country or other more traditional hunting areas live and hide from hunters by using small patches of cover to conceal themselves during heavy hunting pressure. Many times, rural bucks seek out this type of cover only days into the season. During the 1990s, I use to bow hunt on a friend's five-hundred-acre farm in Hope, New Jersey. I'd rarely see another archer, as my friend kept his land well posted. Throughout the bow season, the bucks showed no indication of being affected by hunting pressure. They even entered the fields to feed long before dusk.

Bucks in farm country often bed in open woods just short distances from agricultural fields. Most times they'll select beds slightly higher than their surroundings. Photo Credit: CanStock Photo.

During New Jersey's shotgun season, however, the adult bucks encountered many more hunters, as my friend's entire family gun hunts. By the third or fourth day of the season, seeing a deer, never mind a buck, in the fields or woods on this farm was all but over. They had moved off to less-pressured areas; they did not go nocturnal.

Directly across the road from my friend's place was a large swamp that ran to the base of a steep mountain. Both the swamp and the mountain were surrounded by open overgrown fields dotted with small pockets of cover. While everybody else climbed their way up the steep ledges of the mountain or splashed through the swamp, I had success by posting in semi-open ground in small patches of thickets, cattails, and quarter- to half-acre woodlots of second growth. Many of the woodlots were only fifty to one hundred yards from the road. I consistently scored on good bucks when hunting that farm and using that tactic. Hunting pressured bucks means treating them as if they were cottontail rabbits. Always expect a buck to be hiding in the slightest bit of cover, especially after the firearm season is a week old or more. A word of advice about hunting small, often passed up, patches of cover: Never hunt them half-heartedly. I have seen friends check out small patches of cover by kicking logs and shaking brush while their rifles were hung over their shoulders or held unready in their hands. I'm never surprised when they're left dumbfounded as a buck explodes from cover and safely disappears in seconds. Always check this type of cover with your gun or bow at the ready and with the attitude that a buck is hiding there. He may well be!

Lastly, even after kicking or walking through a small patch of cover, don't walk off and continue hunting if nothing breaks out immediately. Instead, after you have gone through the cover, walk off ten or so yards to where you have a good vantage point and watch the patch of cover carefully at the ready for at least ten to fifteen minutes. Adult bucks can curl themselves up into small packages and have the uncanny ability to let hunters walk within feet of them without getting nervous enough to run. They have

When hunting suburban bucks find a deer trail crossing from food sources to bedding areas. It won't take long to locate a good buck. Photo Credit: CanStock Photo.

learned most times the danger will pass by using this technique. When you stand by and wait several minutes, however, even the craftiest buck's nerves begin to fray, and he'll eventually get nervous enough to get up to escape.

Okay let's get back to hunting tactics for backyard bucks. This is a tactic that will put you where the deer are just by paying a little attention to their signs. For instance, find an area where deer leave their bedding areas from behind houses, etc. Then locate where the deer cross the road from the backyard or other small patch of cover they are using. Next, find where they enter the woods or fields on the opposite side of the road to reach their feeding areas. Once you discover exactly where the deer leave from one side of the road and enter on the other side, you have a prime location to set up a ground or tree blind within fifty yards off the entry point to where the deer are going to feed. However, check your local game laws first. Even though this tactic doesn't provide the usual aesthetics of a hunt, it will provide the element of surprise to your hunt. Mature bucks and adult does have learned not to expect danger this close to the road. Once deer get twenty or thirty yards into the woods, they often stop to regroup, and this behavior can lead to good shooting opportunities at close ranges!

Through experience, I have learned to let the first several deer pass by unmolested. They are likely to be females and immature bucks. The lead doe will usually run the group across the road. She will then allow them time to regroup before moving on. Generally, only minutes later, an older buck will cross and enter the woodlot behind the does. Interestingly enough, an adult buck will often hang up for several minutes only fifty or so yards into the woods. Over my years of hunting I have observed many mature bucks exhibit this milling about behavior. In fact, sometimes they will mill about for nearly twenty or thirty minutes before they decide to leave.

Since most of the suburban bucks I've been talking about usually reside on small patches of private land, it becomes critical for the

When hunting in suburban areas, let does and young bucks pass unmolested. Adult bucks tend to slowly bring up the rear, and often pause before moving again. Photo Credit: Depositphotos.

hunter to obtain permission long before the deer season begins. Start now by introducing yourself to property owners so you may gain their confidence and trust. Let them know you are a safe, dedicated hunter. Assure them you'll be careful of pets, property, and people. Guarantee them that you will be inconspicuous to the neighbors. Explain that you will treat their land as if it were your own. Assure them that you will take only the most ethical of shots with bow or gun. Promise you will not make a pest of yourself, and you will always hunt their land alone. Offer to provide them with a notarized hold harmless release. And, if they like game, offer to share your deer meat with them. Only then will you greatly improve your chances of having their property available for you to hunt.

Unbelievable hunting opportunities can be realized when you are hunting what has come to be known as backyard deer. Suburban deer are extremely predictable. They live and hide close to houses in small patches of cover. This behavior compels deer, especially adult bucks, to follow defined pattern routes. In some cases, many cases in fact, backyard bucks have little choice about how they get from point A to point B. Varying from prescribed trails only brings them closer to encounters with danger and the unknown. Therefore, come heck or high water, backyard bucks do not allow themselves the luxury of roaming their range, particularly during shooting light. They are the vulnerable, predictable adult trophy-class whitetails of suburbia! Cash in by hunting big bucks in small places!

Chapter Fifteen

How to Create Buck Beds

Over the past several years of owning and managing our 192 acres of land, we have come to learn a lot about one particular type of deer management strategy. It is a method known as half-cutting, or what is more commonly referred to as hinge-cutting. Hinge-cutting is the primary component in helping hunters to create secure buck beds. The offshoot to hinge-cutting trees to create buck beds also allows hunters to provide another type of food plot for their deer, albeit an unorthodox food source. The creation of buck beds is a technique that will help you attract more deer to your land. It is designed to draw adult bucks that find the newly created areas to be sheltered and safe bedding spots that also provide additional sources of deer browse. This tactic unfortunately goes mostly unnoticed by hunters.

I often refer to creating buck beds through hinge-cutting trees as multipronged strategic plots. Why? Because I have discovered when I have maneuvered the landscape and finessed it to look more attractive and gnarly, it has worked extraordinarily well to lure adult bucks to regularly use my hinge-cut zones as prime bedding areas. I dis-covered the strategy of hinge-cutting as an outcome of bulldozing a trail through the middle of a one-hundred-acre section of our land fourteen years ago.

As the project got underway, the hired dozer operator asked where I wanted to put all the large trees and other brush he

When hunters create buck beds, they quickly discover that does will also use them. Photo Credit: CanStock Photo/RonRowan.

Photo Credit: CanStock Photo/RonRowan.

was pushing down. I saw it as an opportunity to use the trees and other material to create additional wildlife cover. I asked him to scatter the larger trunks and their branches in a few different sections along the trail that already had secondary growth, heavy brush, and other thick natural vegetation. I also requested that he make sure the trunks of each tree were laid in haphazard piles on top of one another. By the end of the project, we had numerous entanglements of large trees piled up in several different areas on both sides of the newly made trail.

After a few years, however, branches of the trees rotted, which made the areas more visible again. I decided to cut down some junk trees and have them topple onto the bare tree trunks. Coincidently, I hired a forester to evaluate the lumber on our land. On the day I was cutting the junk trees, the forester was doing his survey. As he passed me, he stopped to ask what I was doing. After a brief discussion he said, "You know, instead of cutting down the trees, why not hinge-cut them? That way they will continue to live and not only form terrific piles of cover from their trunks and branches, they will also make available an ongoing source of food for deer." The moment he finished his thought, I thanked him for his advice and told him from now on I would hinge-cut trees instead of cutting them down entirely. He smiled and continued on his way.

The forester had turned on a light in my head and had given me the missing pieces to a puzzle. Although I was familiar with hinge-cutting, I hadn't tied it to creating wildlife cover. I sat on a log for a while eating lunch and thinking of what the forester had just told me. That day my multipronged strategic hinge-cutting tactic was born.

I have since spent a lot of time hinge-cutting trees on different areas of our land to act as prime cover, attractive buck bedding areas, and long-term food sources for the deer on our property. As time passed, I fine-tuned our hinge-cutting

Forester Mark Decker, spraying "junk trees" to be cut down. They laid on top of each other and we hinge-cut several of the small trees surrounding them to create cover for buck beds. Photo Credit: Fiduccia Enterprises.

to include not only some of the smaller junk trees but also some apple trees, maple trees, and oaks—all about two to four inches in diameter. Over the next couple of years, we saw how our hinge-cutting strategy began to attract more and more deer, especially mature bucks.

The following fall while we were riding my Arctic Cat Prowler down the bull-dozed trail, my son Cody, my cousin Leo, and I saw three different bucks bedding in three different spots where I had created the buck beds using the hinge-cut tactic. It was obvious that the key to attracting those three particular bucks, as well as many others bucks over the last dozen years, was hinge-cutting trees to create more attractive bedding areas.

What is Hinge-Cut?

The goal of hinge-cutting a tree is to topple it to the ground without cutting through the entire trunk. The end purpose is that the tree remains alive and therefore provides deer browse for many years even though it has been felled. A hinge-cut tree must be cut about two thirds of the way through the trunk of the tree—a reason why hinge-cutting

trees is dangerous—to enable the tree to fall to the ground. When cutting, you must be careful not sever the cambium layer, the heavy soft tissue directly under the bark, on the opposite side of the tree to keep it intact. The trees that are the best candidates to survive being hinge-cut are maple, hickory, cedar, and elm.

This modified cutting technique requires a downward cut at a 45- to 50-degree angle, which is difficult to start but offers good results. As mentioned, a good hinge-cut usually cuts at least two thirds of the way through the tree at knee to waist height. It is always helpful to cut just enough holding wood to allow you or a helper to push the tree to the ground.

The falling tree in this photo is obviously way too large to consider using as a hinged-cut tree. Photo Credit: Fiduccia Enterprises.

A Warning

As a caveat here, I must include an urgent warning about hinge-cutting trees. Hinge-cutting is an extremely dangerous, life-threatening procedure. This is especially true if attempting to hinge-cut mature, older trees. Never attempt to hinge-cut mature trees. It is highly recommended that anyone not experienced in using a chainsaw to fell trees should absolutely not, under any circumstance, try to hinge-cut trees by themselves. It's best to hire a professional forester to either teach you how to safely perform hinge-cuts or actually do the work for you.

Hinge-cut trees should be about six inches in diameter. If you are inexperienced using a chain saw, a hand saw is the safest way to hinge-cut trees. Photo Credit: CanStock Photo/nevem.

When first learning to hinge-cut trees, select trees as small as two inches in diameter to start. Once you gain some experience, slowly graduate to three-inch diameter trees and eventually work your way up to trees about six inches in diameter. It is unwise to hinge-cut trees larger than eight inches in diameter because larger trees tend to not survive hinge-cutting for very long. Most importantly, large trees represent a real and present danger to the hinge-cutter. When large trees fall, they tend to get hung up on other trees. These are referred to as leaners. Leaning trees are also called widow makers for good reasons. Many people, including professional loggers, have been seriously injured or killed by leaning trees that fell on them. Even though it's the smaller trees that are mostly hinge-cut, they can still present a serious element of danger if you don't pay total attention when hinge-cutting them. Finally, it is never wise to hinge-cut trees alone. An extra person can alert the cutter to potential dangers he or she sees. Be extra careful to avoid hinge-cutting trees with large dead or live limbs.

Hinge-Cutting Purposes

For the deer hunter, the primary purpose behind hinge-cutting trees is to create thick cover that bucks find attractive and safe to bed or hide in. Thus, this tactic encourages

This young buck is about to bed down behind the large downed log. By creating hinge-cuts around this log, we created an ideal buck bedding area. Photo Credit: DepositPhotos.

bucks to remain on a property more regularly. A secondary but equally important reason is to provide a food source in an area of thick cover so deer feel safe enough to bed and eat there throughout the day. Thirdly, hinge-cut sites are excellent locations at which hunters can ambush mature bucks. Hinge-cutting techniques do more than simply create buck bedding areas and provide increased deer browse. There are hinge-cut techniques that restrict deer movement, encourage more movement, force deer movement to certain areas, improve timber, and create visual barriers.

Selecting Areas to Build Deer Beds

Adult bucks usually prefer to bed down on high ground, but not all high ground is at the top of a mountain. On some properties, high ground can be an area that is only a few feet higher than the surrounding terrain. When building a buck bed, select a general spot that provides a bulge, knob or two, or a protuberance on the ground even if it is only slightly higher than the surrounding area. Any hump or protrusion is a prime spot to create a single buck bed.

I generally keep each single buck bed area I create small because after bachelor herds break up, an adult buck likes to bed alone or with one doe. I keep the area to about twenty-four by fifteen feet (360 square feet) or eight by five yards. That is plenty of area for two adult deer to bed down in. When I make doe beds, I make them at least seventy-five by one-hundred

Be it a natural buck bed or a man-made bed, bucks prefer to be on highest point in the area. Even if it is only several inches higher in elevation than the surrounding land. Photo Credit: CanStock Photo/brm1949.

twenty feet (9,000 square feet) or twenty-five by forty yards because does tend to bed with yearlings and fawns, so additional room is mandatory. By keeping my single buck beds small, I can create several of them in different key areas on our land.

The area you select should contain a least some of the types of trees that are good for being hinge-cut. Once you have decided on the exact spot to locate the buck bed, hinge-cut as many trees as is practical within the area. Begin by toppling several hinge-cut trees onto one another. Next, hinge-cut several trees to lie within the area close to each other—but not on top or over one another. When you find the exact spot for a buck bed, preferably a high point, cut a few trees down completely. Make sure at least one or two trunks of the trees lie flat on the ground parallel to each other, and provide enough space between them for a large deer to lie comfortably in. The next step is to hinge-cut several trees around the two felled trees in order for them to completely hide the two tree trunks lying flat on the forest floor. When you

Felling several large trunked trees that are surrounded by small trees is an ideal way to start a buck bed. Next, hinge-cut close by trees (six inches or so in diameter) to create cover and food. Photo Credit: CanStock Photo/blinow61.

are done, step back and look at the entire area. It should look like a heavy windstorm blew down lots of trees and brush. Pay particular attention to the exact spot of the buck bed. It should appear tangled-looking enough for a person to want to avoid walking through it. That will ensure that it looks snarled or gnarly enough for an adult buck to bed down in.

Finally, while a majority of the hinge-cut trees in a buck bed are low enough to provide a buck easy and secure access to the food, they also have to provide good concealment from predators. I make sure to hinge-cut several trees so they are leaning higher—about four to five feet off the ground—so a buck can stand in the bed and still feel he is screened enough to check for danger before leaving.

When I turned fifty years old, my dad, bless his soul, told me, "Son, from now on, things on your body will start to hurt or break." Dad wasn't exaggerating. Ever since I turned fifty, I seem to wake up each morning with some body part that either hurts or isn't working properly. This summer I will turn sixty-nine. I've got a lot of body

When possible, I hinge-cut crab apple or other old orchard fruit trees near the intended buck bed area. The tree will provide extra cover and will be within easy reach for the buck to reach food. Photo Credit: Fiduccia Enterprises.

parts that hurt, are discombobulated, or are near broken. Each year it has steadily become more challenging for me to manage our land without pain. Whether it is planting food plots, mowing trails, putting up stands, or planting nut and fruit trees, it takes a toll physically. No matter if you are twenty or sixty-nine, you'll discover that creating buck beds is hard work. Wrestling with dozens of trees is difficult at best and dangerous at all times. But it is well worth every second of effort, as it will improve your buck hunting by leaps and bounds.

Chapter Sixteen

The Buck Grunt: Often Misused and Misunderstood

The use of deer calls has gotten a lot of attention in print and on television over the past couple of decades. Unfortunately, many deer hunting authorities contend that using deer calls is a surefire trophy-producing strategy. It would be absolutely incorrect to believe that is the case. Anyone who plans to use deer calls should resolve to understand that calls can be effective, but only as part of an overall deer hunting plan. Hunters shouldn't rely on calls to be their only tactic but rather should consider them one of many methods that they can include in their arsenal of hunting strategies.

With that said, it is important to emphasize deer calls can and do produce reliable responses by deer. But like a majority of deer hunting techniques, calling only works well when used correctly—during the proper

During my 48 years of using deer calls, I have discovered through trial and error that buck grunts that imitate the natural low-guttural sounds of a buck are more effective than using aggressive loud grunt vocalizations. Have you ever heard a buck "roar"? With more than fifty years of hunting—I haven't. Photo Credit: Fiduccia Enterprises.

Photo Credit Ted Rose.

time of year and under the appropriate conditions. For me, the prime time for getting action from my calls is usually from mid-October to mid-December. During that particular time of year, I'm never in the woods without my deer calls—a snort, blat, bleat, and grunt. I carry a set of rattling antlers, too, as they can actually be considered a deer calling tool.

One of the most used deer calls that is often misused and misunderstood by hunters is the buck grunt—mostly because there is so much puffery propaganda about grunt calls. Over the past several years, some deer hunting authorities have written stories about using grunt vocalizations to imitate a buck roar, bark, or growl sounds. The reality, at least for me, is that in my five decades of hunting whitetails across North America, I have never heard any free-range buck make any of these hyper-vocalizations, particularly a growl or roar.

The different grunt sounds are the deer vocalizations most often imitated by hunters. Unfortunately, they are also the most confounding calls because the grunts' success can vary widely. I will attempt to correct that situation in this chapter and demonstrate to you how you can make the grunt one of the most effective deer calls. But first, let me set the stage about deer calling in general.

During my forty-eight years of deer calling experience, I have discovered through trial and error—mostly error—how to be consistently successful when I use deer calls.

I can attribute most of my success to being a low-impact deer caller. In other words, I have learned to imitate deer vocalizations as I have heard deer make them in the wild. I emulate their communications as closely as I possibly can. Trust me when I tell you that any hunter can achieve a high degree of deer calling success. The key to being a good caller is to pay meticulous attention to the volume, length, and pitch of the vocalizations deer make and duplicate them as closely as possible. For instance, top-notch Las Vegas impressionists study their subjects' voices closely before trying to reproduce their vocal

A buck I called in using a subdued trail grunt. He was fifteen yards from me when I released my arrow. It's very rare occurrence for me not to have my grunt and other calls afield when I'm hunting. Photo Credit: Fiduccia Enterprises.

sounds. Once they feel comfortable they have the tone correct, they can reproduce it with uncanny accuracy. Therefore, the best deer callers in the nation are those who can accurately reproduce deer vocalizations to sound as natural as possible. Basically, that means staying away from making your calls sound too aggressive, too loud, and, most importantly, unnaturally long in length. It also helps to avoid sounds such as the bark, growl, and roar.

A Research Study

There have been innumerable research studies done on whitetail vocalizations. Some differ when it comes to categorizing the whitetail's language, but a majority of studies are in agreement about the list of sounds whitetails make. The most celebrated study was conducted at the University of Georgia in 1988 by eminent researchers Larry Marchinton, Karl Miller, and Tom Atkinson. The team identified ninety different deer vocalizations. Eventually they grouped them into eleven primary communications that are most commonly vocalized by whitetails. They include:

1. Maternal Grunt (a doe grunt)
2. Contact Grunt
3. Low Grunt
4. Tending Grunt
5. Grunt-Snort-Wheeze
6. Flehmen Sniff
7. Snort
8. Mew
9. Bleat
10. Bawl
11. Nursing Whine

Overview of Deer Calls

I began using deer calls to attract deer in the mid–1960s. Through my myriad of failures and subsequent successes, I have been fortunate to have gained considerable knowledge and an intuitive understanding about using deer vocalizations to draw, reveal, hold, stop, or intentionally spook deer from cover. I also did a significant amount of field research

My son Peter Cody with a mature 10-point, heavy bodied Canadian buck he grunted in using a contact grunt vocalization. Photo Credit: Fiduccia Enterprises.

on deer sounds. Of all the different whitetail strategies I use, deer calling is among my favorite tactics. It is by far the number one subject I am most interested in when it comes to studying whitetails.

Over the years, I have developed my own simple list of deer sounds. I categorized the eleven vocalizations classified by the researchers mentioned previously to a more manageable list. They include four primary sounds, including the grunt, adult-blat, fawn-bleat, and snort. At this point, I should clarify that many researchers classify the bleat as one primary sound. I don't. Like any animal, young creatures, including humans, have a much higher-pitched voice. As all young animals mature, their voices change to a deeper tone. Therefore, I separate the category that researchers have combined into mew, bleat, and bawl into two different groupings.

Immature deer make bleats and bawls, while adult deer make deeper sounding blats and bawls. When it comes to recreating deer vocalizations, it is crucial to imitate sounds as they naturally exist in the wild. If you were trying to imitate a fawn bleating for the doe to feed it and you made the call even slightly deeper than the high-pitched bleat of a fawn, you would not get the response you intended.

Again, through repeated trial and error, I have ascertained that each of the four primary vocalizations deer make have several variations

Kate took this mule buck using a burp grunt vocalization as the buck followed close behind a doe. Mule deer respond well to many deer calls, including grunt vocalizations. Photo Credit: Fiduccia Enterprises.

I rattled-in this Georgia buck. He hung up in brush about seventy-five yards from my stand. To encourage him to step out, I made a contact grunt vocalization. Photo Credit: Fiduccia Enterprises.

to them. For instance, the primary grunt has eight cadences or variations that I refer to as the contact grunt, ticking grunt, tending grunt, trail grunt, grunt-wheeze, grunt-snort, grunt-snort-wheeze, and the rolling grunt. So, too, has each of the other primary vocalizations—adult blat, fawn bleat, and snort. Learning any of the four primary deer vocalizations and each of their sub-cadences isn't difficult.

Every hunter who wants to be a consistently successful deer caller must understand what each primary and sub-cadence vocalization means to deer. Otherwise he or she will inevitably use the wrong sound at an inopportune time. This is especially true when it comes to the primary grunt. Because the primary grunt so often has times when it is effective and other times when it is totally ineffective, the grunt frequently perplexes a lot of hunters. The secret to being a successful caller—other than extreme confidence—whether using a grunt or any other deer vocalization is to always know the right times to use a call, what the sound should naturally sound like, and exactly what you want your call to express or communicate to another deer. Once you achieve that goal, you will become fluent in what I call deerneaze, the language of deer conversation.

Inflection is Crucial

As I have said, the three most important components about deer calling are the call's volume, tone or inflection, and intent. Consider this: If your wife or husband calls you and says, "Honey, would you please come here?" You would most likely react by immediately responding to the query. But if he or she said to you, "Hey you, get the heck over here right now!" you would most likely not respond at all, or if you did, you would do so cautiously. Although the statement is basically the same, the volume, tonality, and intent they convey are utterly different. Needless to say, each vocalization a deer utters and how they are conveyed can either make a deer react positively or negatively to the sound.

Volume

The most problematic issue preventing hunters from becoming top-notch, consistently successful deer callers is that they often apply too high a volume to their calls. This usually happens for two chief reasons. First, most hunters don't realize how far the sound of a call will travel and be heard by deer. Studies on this subject have concluded that in low to mild wind conditions, low-pitched deer calls can be detected by deer for a few hundred feet. Think about that for a moment. If you have ever heard a natural grunt, you know that it is not a loud sound, yet you can hear the buck making it from a considerable distance. The same applies to the bleat and blat. Only the snort is naturally made by deer to sound loud, and the reason for that is the vocalization is meant to alert other deer to imminent danger. It is made loud enough not only to quickly alert nearby deer, but for deer several hundred feet away to hear it, as well. All other deer vocalizations should be made in a low and natural tone. If they are not, they will suggest aggression to deer, or worse yet, the call will sound unnatural. Callers who insist on making loud deer calls will be lonely callers; callers who keep the volume of the deer calls to a low level will always have more action.

Length

The length of time a call is made can either make it sound natural to deer or incredibly unrealistic. Each individual cadence of the four primary vocalizations can be regarded as short rather than long. In other words, when in doubt about how long you should make

a call for, opt for calling a shorter period of time rather than a longer interlude. Even the alarm-distress snort, which is one of the only vocalizations that can be termed long, isn't really that lengthy—perhaps each alarm-distress vocalization is a few intervals of five seconds each. An alarm-distress sounds like *whew, whew, whew, whew, whew, whew, whew.* The deer might even repeat the sequence a few times. Although the entire sequence is long, each individual whew is short. If a caller made each whew into a

I never go deer hunting without my grunt call. When used correctly, it can be the chief element to having a successful hunt. Photo Credit: Fiduccia Enterprises.

wwwhhheeewww, it would not only sound unrealistic to the deer, it would guarantee total failure to the caller. The same holds true for a grunt. The cadences of the primary grunt are among the shortest in length of the deer sounds.

The Confounding Grunt Call

If you are like a majority of deer hunters, you have a drawer chock full of a variety of knives and another drawer jammed full of different types of grunt calls. Most hunters are hopelessly obsessed with owning and using a wide variety of commercial grunt calls. Do you know why? Because at one time or another, almost every hunter has used a grunt call to successfully attract a buck. The grunt will coax bucks of all age classes into responding. It can be used effectively when blind calling, or using a call to attract deer that the hunter has not seen, or to lure in a buck that has been spotted. I view a grunt as a key tool in my arsenal of deer calls.

However, every hunter who uses a grunt call has experienced an identical problem. Sometimes hunters will see a buck, grunt at it, and the buck will respond immediately to the sound and either walk briskly, trot, or even run into the area with his guard totally out of action. Other times hunters will grunt to a buck they see, and the buck will totally ignore the call and walk away as if he never heard it. Anyone who has ever used a grunt call can relate to both scenarios.

My experience has taught me the chief reason a buck ignores a grunt call is that what the caller is sending is a combination of wrong messages. Often a grunt is made more loudly than it should be. This is through no fault of most hunters, as some deer hunting authorities over-tout the virtues of the grunt call as a surefire tactic and compound the problem by recommending that grunts should be made loudly and aggressively. Despite what most hunters read or are told about the merits of using a grunt call in this fashion, the information is flawed. Combine that with the fact that the grunt's effectiveness has a smaller window of usefulness than the other deer vocalizations, and you can see how it can be problematic.

A buck hot on the trail of an estrus doe. He would be making a low-pitched trail grunt as he searches for the estrus doe. Photo Credit: CanStock Photos.

The window for the grunt call's **peak opportunity** occurs during the chase period of breeding season. If you hunt within the latitudes and longitudes of 40° to 50° North and 50° to 120° East/West within the United States, and most of you reading this probably do, the zenith period of the **big chase** phase which takes place only days before the primary rut will take place between October 31 and November 10, allowing a few days on either end. The pinnacle of the **primary rut**, however, will take place between November 10 and November 20, give or take a few days before or after the dates provided. This is the best time frame to capitalize on using a grunt call. This window of opportunity will provide the most occasions for grunting success. Employing a grunt call before and after these dates is a hit-and-miss proposition, regardless of what you have heard or read.

For the record, both does and bucks make grunt vocalizations. I'm going to address the grunts made by bucks. Although there are several sub-cadences to the primary buck grunt, there are only four that you need to know when, where, why, and how to use. They include the contact grunt, click grunt, trail grunt, and tending grunt. I believe three of the other four grunt vocalizations, the grunt-wheeze, grunt-snort, and grunt-snort-wheeze, are received by other bucks, even adult bucks high on the pecking order threatening communications. Many other deer authorities claim they are **aggressive** vocalizations. There is a **slight** but meaningful difference between the two interpretations. An aggressive vocalization might invite a conflict between male deer. A threatening vocalization will frighten more bucks than it will attract. In either case, the sounds are often used incorrectly by hunters, and deer will react negatively to these grunt vocalizations when they aren't made to sound natural.

In my forty-eight years of using a grunt call, I have never called in a buck using a grunt-snort or grunt-wheeze. I did call in one buck using the grunt-snort-wheeze, but I am positive that was an oddity. I will explain the incident later in the chapter. That doesn't mean using any of these grunt vocalizations won't work; they might. All it implies is that I have never had success when using these highly threatening vocalizations. The last of the remaining four grunts is the so-called rolling grunt, a sound that is yet to be proven by me. I will discuss more about this vocalization later in this chapter.

Contact Grunt

This is a vocalization that is made throughout the entire year by both male and female deer. It is also referred to as the contact social grunt because it is basically a social

This is a classic example of a contact grunt. It usually takes place as two bucks enter a feeding location where does are. Photo Credit: Ted Rose.

greeting vocalization. Adult does make it to stay in contact, especially when they are out of sight from their unit group. They also use it as a maternal grunt to call to hidden fawns to let them know it is time to nurse or be fed. When used by a doe in this manner, the sound is made slightly longer and with a touch more intensity.

Researchers claim only does make the contact grunt vocalization. I have to respectfully disagree, as I have heard bucks make it, as well. Often bucks use it as they enter feeding locations to greet other bucks and does within those areas, such as acorn-filled woods, agricultural fields, food plots, orchards, and even staging areas. It is not an assertive or aggressive vocalization. Bucks make it as a social greeting, and they usually start to make it during early fall prior to the beginning of the breeding season. It is a single subdued grunt that is so low it is difficult to hear, and therefore it is often unnoticed by deer hunters.

This vocalization is a terrific call during the early archery season and through the transition period into the pre-rut—a time when both bucks and does are traveling together with members of the same gender. It should be made as a single brief, low-intensity grunt that is barely audible and carries for only a short distance. Bucks express this vocalization for no apparent reason, although many, including me, feel it represents a hello.

A hunter can use this vocalization to draw a buck toward his or her stand. When a buck hears a contact grunt, he will often wander over to check out the buck that made it. In my mind's eye, this call could be classified more accurately as a curiosity call rather than a social call. It is definitely worth using to draw a buck in to your stand during the early fall season before the rut begins. For the best results, keep the grunt short and low in volume. It should sound like *uurrp*. It is best to use on a buck that is within sight but out of range.

The Trailing Grunt

The trail grunt or trailing grunt is the one deer vocalization hunters hear and recognize the most, as it is definitely among one of the most identified sexual sounds

A majority of times, a buck making a trail grunt is alone as he quickly moves along a trail while burping softly. A buck that is accompanying a doe in estrus makes a tending grunt. Photo Credit: CanStock Photos.

bucks make during the rut. Novice hunters will sometimes confuse the trailing grunt with the tending grunt—understandably so. Except for a couple of slight nuances, they sound similar. Therefore, it is prudent for hunters to learn how to differentiate between the two. The trailing grunt, as the name indicates, is a vocalization a buck makes in two different situations. One is when he is trailing an estrus doe he can see. More commonly, however, it is used when a buck is trotting along with his nose planted firmly to the ground as he scent trails an estrus doe that he hasn't seen yet.

Although this vocalization is short in duration, it is louder and more repetitive than the contact grunt. The passion of the sound clearly indicates that the buck is highly stimulated. While some bucks will grunt each time their front hooves hit the ground, others may only make a few grunts every twenty to fifty yards. This is one of the few deer vocalizations where there is no correct or incorrect way to imitate it; deer can tolerate differences in how it is mimicked by the hunter. The key point to remember when making a trail grunt is to try and impersonate a buck that is sexually excited. The call's volume has to be somewhat greater than the contact grunt but not too loud.

When blind calling to a buck using the trail grunt, a sequence might sound like *uurrp, uurp, uurp, uurrp, uurp, uurp, uurrp, uurp, uurp, uurrp.* I will often make ten to fifteen or more grunts in quick succession. Then I will wait several minutes and make another sequence but in a different direction. Like with all my strategies, I try to create the entire illusion. A buck making a trailing grunt is on the move. So when I'm making a trail grunt, I slowly turn my head from left to right or vice versa to mimic more realistically a buck that is moving. However, when you spot a buck and want to make a trail grunt to him, only call until you get his attention. Once he reacts, stop calling and let his instinctive curious behavior weave its magic.

The Tending Grunt

This is a guttural grunt of moderate intensity with a low pitch made by bucks during the rut. It is most commonly heard when a buck has actually caught up with an estrus doe and he is accompanying, or tending, her. It can also be made by bucks zigzagging along a trail in search of an estrus doe. Tending grunts seem to be made by bucks two and a half years old and older. The tending grunt is of longer duration than any of the other grunts, which is something to keep in mind when trying to imitate this call.

Bucks following close behind a doe are said to be "tending" her as they wait for the doe to be receptive to their sexual advances. Photo Credit: Ted Rose.

I can tell you from experience that at times—not many but some—the differences between a trailing grunt and a tending grunt are nearly negligible, but they are indeed different. Other times, the differences between the two vocalizations are more obvious. This is the grunt that is made with more volume than other grunts. I have heard some bucks make tending grunts that sounded more like a burp from Barney, an animated cartoon character on *The Simpsons*, than a natural grunt from a buck. That is why I often refer to the tending grunt as the burp-o-matic or burp grunt. I have also described it to sound like a wild pig with his nose stuck under leaves as he roots around for food. I truly believe a buck that makes this sound is stimulated by an estrus doe. I have heard this burp-like vocalization many times when I have seen the buck with his nose squarely pressed under a doe's tail.

The key to this calling sequence is to keep the sound low, guttural, and slightly louder than the trailing grunt. To give you a reference for just how loud this grunt should sound, it should be loud enough for a person to hear it that is no more than forty or fifty yards away. But it should definitely not be made so loud that it transforms from sounding excited to an aggressive vocalization.

The tending grunt sequence can be made with a dozen or more quick and short guttural grunts—*brp, brp, brp, brp, brp brp, brp, brp, brp, brp.* I generally make ten to twenty of them in a row. Avoid the temptation to make them louder than they need to be. You'll have the best results by keeping the volume slightly higher but remembering to keep it low enough to sound natural, short, quick, repetitive, and guttural.

It can be said of the tending grunt, that bucks make it with more volume than other grunts. However, they don't make it aggressively loud. It is sometimes accompanied by what can be best described a brief woofing sound. Photo Credit: Depositphotos.

Bucks making tending grunts are the most vocal bucks. This sound can sometimes have uncanny variations, as well. It is most likely what hunters describe when they hear a woofing dog-like sound. The woofing noise is caused by the air the buck expels from his mouth and nostrils as both are planted tightly on or under the hair of the doe's tail. In all my experiences with deer calling, the tending grunt has initiated many odd grunt vocalizations. With that said, I don't want to allude by any stretch of the imagination that the odd sounding tending grunts I have heard created growls, barks, or roars. But it is hard to go wrong when making a tending grunt because there are so many variations of it, and bucks tend to be tolerant of them. One last tip: Sometimes I mix a few ticking clicks in with my tending grunt vocalizations. You'll understand why shortly.

The Ticking Grunt

The ticking grunt is also known as the clicking grunt. The first time I heard a buck clicking was about twenty years ago, and I didn't know exactly what to make of it. Since my first encounter with this vocalization, each time I witnessed a buck making the sound, a doe was either close to him or within his sight. On a few occasions, I observed the bucks were making tending grunt vocalizations prior to the ticking grunts. So from what I observed, I would suspect that when another buck hears the ticking grunt, he knows there is not only another buck close by, but there is also an estrus doe. That makes this call well worth including in your deer calling bag of tricks.

The clicking or ticking grunt is not a common sound. Even some experienced hunters I know have never heard it. In fact, I haven't heard it anywhere as often as

I have heard other buck grunting vocalizations. Researchers have suggested that the ticking grunt may be used to impart potential aggression. They also claim that depending on the age class of a buck, the volume of the ticking vocalizations will vary.

What I have discovered about this version of the grunt is that bucks make it using a short series of ticking sounds that are perhaps several seconds in overall length. However, the sound generally has a low tone, is guttural, and is repetitive. Immature bucks two and a half years and younger make a higher-pitched version of the ticking grunt. I have coaxed bucks into range using ticking grunts mostly during the primary chase period of the breeding season—October 31 through November 10, allowing a few days on either end. On windless days, the sound travels well, and I'm sure a buck can hear it from hundreds of feet away. The exciting aspect of the ticking grunt is that, from my experience, it draws in an older age class of bucks.

My grunt call, "The Deer Doctor's RealTone E-Z Grunt," mimics the ticking grunt. (My apologies for the obvious sales pitch, my wife *made* me do it.) If you can make this sound with your mouth, there are many grunt calls on the market that can replicate the clicking grunt. Simply put any grunt call to your lips and say *tick, tick, tick.* Produce a series of short singular repetitive sounds—*tick, tick, tick, tick, tick.* I generally make about ten to fifteen of them in a row. To imitate the natural sound of a ticking grunt, make a dozen or more ticks quickly in a row. To make them sound even more natural, alternate between a short series of about ten ticks and then a longer series of perhaps twenty.

To duplicate this sound almost identically, place your tongue over your top front teeth and quickly and repeatedly open and close your mouth. It will be problematic making this sound if your mouth is dry. As I do with all my deer calls and when I am rattling, make your calls sound as if they are coming from several directions. This will help immensely to fool a buck into thinking another buck is moving about.

While my encounters with this call have been with mature bucks, that doesn't mean it won't attract immature

I have discovered that immature bucks like the one seen here, are just as apt to respond to a ticking grunt as mature bucks are. Photo Credit: Depositphotos.

bucks, as well. The conundrum about alluding to mature bucks is that the term mature buck is relative. In New York, a mature buck can be less than three and a half years old and still be a valid contender to breed does. So the bottom line is the ticking grunt vocalization should be used confidently to try to coax a buck in, either used alone or in conjunction with a tending grunt sound.

The Rolling Grunt

I have not had a lot of experience with the rolling grunt. In fact, I have never called in a buck using it. To be frank, I accidently discovered it being made by bucks in 2012. I'm not even absolutely sure it can be classified as an actual buck vocalization. But before you decide to pay no attention to reading this further, let me share what I have discovered about this interesting and mystifying buck sound.

We've owned our land for fifteen years. During that time, we have painstakingly created a carefully managed property and deer herd. Over the last several years, our adult buck population has increased noticeably. It is not uncommon for us to see several mature bucks using our land regularly. Every summer for the past five years, I've spent at least three to four evenings a week in a blind overlooking our food plots. I have documented on video the vocal and body language of bucks and does in the fields from mid-June through the end of December.

What I have absolutely established on our land is that starting as early as October, the vocal behavior of bucks within all age classes slowly begins to change. I have heard bucks making blats and contact grunts more often from this time frame on. I'm more than reasonably sure this is the same time frame bucks change their vocal behavior elsewhere, too.

Intriguingly, from Halloween on, bucks' vocal behaviors on our land grow exponentially. As they enter a field filled with twenty-five to thirty-five deer, including adult does, yearlings, fawns, and young one-and-a-half-year-old bucks, they

Two mature bucks taken on our New York property in 2009. Photo Credit: Fiduccia Enterprises.

use a wider variety of vocalizations—more contact grunts, guttural adult blats, and some occasional low grunts accompanied by a single low snort. This is a sound I believe is used to establish where a particular buck presently sits within the pecking order.

From Halloween on, does also become slightly more upset each time a buck enters the field. By the first couple of days of November, they go from slightly upset to being distraught when a buck exits the woods and enters the fields—particularly if the buck has a set of antlers. By November 5, bucks become increasingly more belligerent with other bucks and also more persistent at harassing does.

For three consecutive years, by November 10, I would begin to hear an unusual and almost inaudible grunt sound from adult bucks. As usual for this time of year, as soon as bucks enter our fields they instantly begin to approach the does by either walking briskly or trotting quickly toward them. As they approach, the adult does become tense and stare directly at the approaching bucks with eye-to-eye contact. Their body language clearly demonstrates that they are ready to run off if need be.

Now here is the most intriguing part of what I have witnessed. If a buck approaches a doe and vocalizes the unusual grunt sound I'm referring to, the doe instantaneously runs off about fifty yards and stops. If, as the buck approaches, he vocalizes any of the routine grunt sounds, the doe still exhibits nervousness, but once the buck gets too close, she will only trot a short distance from him and stop. This may happen several times, but she doesn't leave the field.

I have named the vocalization I have heard the rolling grunt. Its sound can best be described as a rolling sound, *bthrrrrrrrr, bthrrrrr.* As the buck approaches a doe, the sound lasts for several seconds. This vocalization is barely audible, which may account for why no one else has made mention of this deer sound. It took me forty-eight years of hunting whitetails to hear it. I can duplicate the sound by placing my tongue on the roof of my mouth and blowing air over it. But although I can mimic the sound, it comes out much louder than the rolling grunts I have heard bucks make.

I've observed when a buck approaches a doe while making a 'rolling-grunt,' she will quickly run off a short distance and stop only when she puts sufficient space between them. Photo Credit: Ted Rose.

I intend to test this vocalization over the next few deer seasons. In the meantime, I also intend to share what I have heard with some well-known deer biologists for their valued input. If it turns out to be a valid deer vocalization that can be used effectively to provide hunting opportunities, you will be reading about it in a magazine and hearing about it on our television program. For now, it remains an interesting theory that must be proven about a possible deer vocalization that has gone mostly unnoticed. There is another possibility as well: The sound may be nothing more than a variation of the ticking grunt.

The remaining grunt communications include the grunt-snort and grunt-snort-wheeze. In spite of the fact that many pros endorse using these vocalizations, I don't. Why? Almost every time I have used them to hunt whitetails in North America, I have found these two vocalizations have frightened many more bucks away than they lured to my stand.

The Grunt-Snort and the Grunt-Wheeze

The grunt-snort and the grunt-wheeze are made mostly by bucks, especially during the rut, although female deer use them occasionally throughout the year. The grunt-snort is a low guttural grunt accompanied by a short sharp snort. The grunt-wheeze is a deep grunt accompanied by what sounds like a wheeze that a person with a serious cough would make after a fit. Higher-ranking deer use this threatening communication almost entirely toward subordinate deer. As I mentioned earlier, while I believe the grunt-snort and the grunt-wheeze may be seen by other deer pros as being aggressive vocalizations, I feel they are used as a severe a warning or reprimand rather than being belligerent sounds. In the end, I don't advocate using either of these two sounds to lure in bucks. While there may be an unusual combination of elements that come together one day to allow the grunt-snort or grunt-wheeze to attract a buck, my use of them suggests otherwise. I have found the risk of using these two vocalizations simply too high for me to recommend them.

Grunt-Snort-Wheeze

This is the vocalization I said I would explain later—another vocalization I have consistently found will do more harm than good when used to attract a buck. I field tested the grunt-snort-wheeze in states and provinces across North America and all tests resulted in negative responses. On one occasion I tested the grunt-snort-wheeze while hunting in Saskatchewan, Canada. The buck that responded, however, turned out to be a yearling four point. He ran in, stopped briefly, and bolted off as quickly as he appeared. I think he responded out of total curiosity, or he may have heard the sound and it scared the snot out of him.

Some seasoned outdoor professional hunters swear this call will attract what is collectively known as dominant bucks. In the times I have tested this variation of the primary grunt in Saskatchewan, Canada, and several other places where giant bucks roam, I have had bad luck with it. On a trophy deer hunt in Lamar, Colorado, in the early nineties, I was watching a buck milling about in a staging area waiting for the light to fade before heading into a field of wheat one hundred yards behind the blind. The hunt was during the peak of the primary rut. The outfitter invited me with the caveat that I shoot only one particular buck whose antlers the outfitter estimated would score 190-plus Boone & Crocket inches. So the buck I was watching was quite safe, albeit I would have killed him in an instant if I weren't hunting the other buck. He was huge with a heavy ten-point set of antlers that would have easily scored 155 to 160-plus Boone & Crocket inches. I watched him for about twenty minutes as he made a scrape and rubbed a sizeable tree. The buck emitted several deep grunts as he pawed up the earth to make his scrape. I decided that since I wasn't going to shoot this buck, he would join the exclusive club with the other nine adult bucks I test-called using the grunt-snort-wheeze.

The other eight, unfortunately for me, were all bucks I would have shot. One was a giant buck I was bow hunting in Buffalo County, Wisconsin. Even today I can see his heavy antlers when I close my eyes and think of him. After hearing me make a grunt-snort-wheeze, he turned himself inside out and ran across a never-ending field of soybeans. I watched him as he ran, ran, and ran some more before soaring in the air over a barbwire fence and into the woods.

So I took out my grunt and made another test of the grunt-snort-wheeze as the Colorado buck was urinating near his scrape. I barely finished the vocalization when I could see the buck's neck hair stand

Over the many years I have tested the grunt-snort-wheeze, all-sized-antlered even a buck with antlers this large could flee from hearing the sound of a grunt-snort-wheeze! Photo Credit: Ted Rose.

straight up. In the next instant, he ran off as if a bolt of lightning had hit him in his nuts! That was the last buck I ever used a grunt-snort-wheeze on. He convinced me that the grunt-snort-wheeze sucks for attracting bucks!

In all my experiences using the grunt-snort-wheeze, grunt-wheeze, and grunt-snort, I found that adult bucks, even those who had large antlers and heavy bodies, instantly acted negatively upon hearing these three particular grunt variations. In each instance, the calls were used during the peak phase of the primary rut, and my evaluation of each of the three grunts is that they imply incompatible and threatening vocalizations. The message these sub-cadences of the primary grunt sends is, "Hey, you. Do you want me to rip your head off and stuff your antlers down your throat?" Apparently, that message is taken seriously by 99.9999 percent of other bucks, no matter how high they rank in the pecking order. In other words, don't use these variations if you want to kill the buck you are calling. That might be a controversial statement and one that isn't particularly popular with some call makers, but it is what I have found to be true over forty-eight years of using deer calls. End of story.

Grunt Vocalizations

While variations of the grunt call can cause a buck to respond immediately, they can also discourage a buck from responding equally as fast, especially if any of the primary grunt's sub-cadences are used at the wrong time and under the wrong circumstances. In the overall method of deer calling, a hunter must be aware that the window of opportunity for using a grunt call successfully is somewhat small when compared to the other primary sounds, such as the adult blat, fawn bleat, and snort. That's because bucks don't grunt nearly as often as hunters are led to believe. As I mentioned, there are probably fewer than ten to fifteen days during the entire deer season, including all three phases of the rut, that bucks actually engage in making a wide variation of low-pitched grunt vocalizations.

But I definitely assure you that during that time frame, you absolutely don't want to be caught in the woods without having a quality grunt call in your daypack. While the grunt's window of opportunity may be small, it is among the most effective deer vocalizations. No other call has the ability to attract a buck as quickly or enthusiastically as the grunt call. When used correctly, the primary grunt and its sub-cadences are without question unmatched as deer calls. One last thought here: When I say that the grunt has a small window of opportunity, I am not suggesting that a grunt call can't be used successfully to call in a buck in mid-October. It can. But don't expect a buck to display the same type of excitement and eagerness when responding to a grunt vocalization before or after the dates I mentioned. In the end, the primary grunt and its variations are a foolproof tactic when used correctly.

Grunt Calling Tips:

- To increase your calling success, never call to a buck that is walking directly toward you or looking at you. The odds are much greater that in these two scenarios, the deer will see you. Wait until the deer is angled away or not looking at you. By keeping a deer guessing where the vocalization is coming from, it will eventually get close enough to offer a shot.

- One of the most common and costly calling mistakes made is to make a grunt call too loudly. In a deer's world, a high-volume communication sound suggests threatening behavior or the potential for physical aggression. Trying to make your calls sound like they are being made by the toughest buck in the woods will end up working against you. Loud, intensive grunts only serve to intimidate an overwhelming number of other bucks, including adult bucks that occupy a high position in the pecking order.

- By keeping the volume of grunt calls low, the sound will be interpreted as if it is coming from a buck that can be intimidated by using aggressive body language or that can be easily defeated in the unlikely event of a fight.

- If you grunt at a buck and he pays no attention to it, stop using the grunt call and use an estrus adult doe blat instead. Many times this one tactic will be all that is needed to get the buck interested enough to respond.

- When using a grunt or any other deer call and you see the buck approaching but he eventually hangs up, stop calling. Let the deer's natural curiosity work in your favor. Be patient. The buck will either start circling toward you or he will become uninterested and slowly walk off. At that moment, either a soft tending or trail grunt will work to pique his interest again. I often include a low estrus blat, as well.

- Bucks generally don't respond well to any type of grunts that the caller makes repeatedly. It doesn't seem natural to them. What I mean by repeatedly is blowing a particular grunt over and over for minutes at a time. Even when you make trail or tending grunt vocalizations, take short 90- to 120-second breaks to make them sound right.

- When using a grunt call or rattling, the most important part of the tactic includes paying strict attention with your eyes, ears, and even nose. Research has proven that about 75 to 80 percent of game that is called, respond without ever being seen by the hunter. A whitetail buck's instinctive behavior almost always necessitates that he respond cautiously. Therefore, he will slip silently into the area, take advantage of all available cover, and remain hidden until he is sure it is safe to proceed. After each call, scrutinize the surrounding cover in all directions. Look for pieces of the deer rather than the entire deer. Pay close attention to nearby saplings, and look for movement from them. Bucks that respond to grunts will sometimes stop and get into a mock battle with a sapling to release tension or frustration before moving into more open areas. Many times I have heard a soft guttural grunt from nearby cover before ever spotting the buck. Don't underestimate the value of using your sense of smell. During the rut, bucks can smell of tarsal scent. The odor is easily detected but only if you set your brain to the task of actually reacting to it. Over the years, I have killed several bucks by smelling them before actually seeing them.

- A terrific decoy tactic that includes a grunt call is what I term my Big Four. Set up two decoy bucks with small antlers facing one another closely. If the decoys' ears are moveable, turn them backward so the bucks look aggressive toward each other. Spray one buck's back legs with tarsal scent and the other buck's back legs with buck urine. Begin by rattling—not overaggressively but enough for the clicking and ticking of the antlers to be heard for one hundred yards or so in all directions. Rattle for about ninety seconds, stop for about two minutes, make a few short burp grunts, and rattle again for another ninety seconds. Then make several tending grunts quickly followed by a couple of stutter estrus blats. Set everything down and start looking, listening, and smelling. If there is a buck in the area, your tactic should have gotten his utmost attention. Remember, he may not rush out to investigate what is going on. So be patient. I have had to wait an hour or longer on more than one occasion for a buck to respond to this strategy—several times even after I saw the buck come in only a short time after ending the estrus blats!

Chapter Seventeen

Impractical Expectations

I'm going to start this chapter the same way I have started my deer tactic seminars over the past thirty-plus years. Most hunters secretly don't acknowledge or give themselves enough recognition for being what they actually are—effective and efficient buck hunters. They add to that drawback by also setting pie-in-the-sky goals regarding taking an adult whitetail buck with trophy-sized antlers. The second part of my statement stems from most hunters throughout North America having impractical expectations of killing trophy-class bucks.

The truth is there are scores of average hunters who are much better deer hunters than they will allow themselves to believe. This is particularly the case when it comes to hunters who stalk mature bucks in states within New England and the Northeast. Why, you ask? The simple truth is that deer throughout several of the states that make up New England and the Northeast (Massachusetts, Connecticut, Rhode Island, New York, New Jersey, and Pennsylvania), especially adult bucks, undergo the heaviest hunting pressure of all deer found throughout North America. Therefore, they are more difficult prey to hunt with consistent success than bucks in

A majority of hunters in New England and the Northeast would consider this eight-point buck a trophy and rightfully so. Any buck in these areas that lives long enough to grow antlers like this, is an elusive, wily, and expert survivor. Photo Credit: CanstockPhoto Inc/brm1949.

Photo Credit Ted Rose.

other states and provinces. Before anyone retorts that there are more hunters and consequently more hunting pressure in the Midwest and in places such as Texas, consider this: These areas are not as heavily populated, nor are they as urbanized, or developed, as New England and Northeast states.

Hence, the deer residing in these heavily hunted areas have evolved to be the most challenging, elusive, cunning, and crafty of all the whitetail deer. It is hard to deny that the excessive hunting pressure in most areas of New England and the Northeast is the prime reason it is difficult for hunters to consistently take the types of adult bucks often seen killed by a number of hunting-program hosts on the outdoor television networks.

Unfortunately, too many hunters are overimpressed by the outrageously large-antlered bucks killed on those TV shows. Week after week, the hosts—you all know who they are—slay one trophy-class buck after another. The unrelenting taking of these huge-antlered bucks sends a subliminal and negative message to hunters watching the show: See me hunt; see me kill these trophy bucks; don't you wish you could? These hosts unknowingly (hopefully) leave countless deer hunters across North America feeling enormously frustrated and that they are inept as buck hunters. That is absolutely unacceptable to me and should be to you, as well.

You're not any less skilled a deer hunter than they are, and I include myself as part of "they." Most of you simply don't have the type of exceptional ongoing opportunities to hunt that a vast majority of television hosts do, including myself. If you were

able to hunt whitetails in Minnesota, Michigan, Wisconsin, Iowa, Missouri, Illinois, Indiana, Ohio, Texas, Montana, Saskatchewan, Alberta, and beyond, you, too, would more than likely be consistently killing trophy-class bucks with enormous antlers!

Unfortunately, some of these TV hosts would lead you to believe that they bag trophy after trophy because they have superpowers that give them exceptional skills most other hunters don't have or

A fourteen-point a buck taken on the famed Kennedy Ranch in Sarita, Texas. Clearly the opportunity I had to hunt on a four-hundred-thousand-acre ranch owned by the Catholic Church afforded me the opportunity to kill this deer. It net scored 169 5/8". Photo Credit: Fiduccia Enterprises.

can't acquire. They act as if that's what accounts for them being able to kill trophy bucks with antlers that measure 150 to 200 Boone & Crockett inches each and every week. If you were hunting on a farm or ranch that had all the prime naturally found **Alpha** minerals, (like calcium, phosphorous and sodium–see Side Bar), that help to grow enormous antlers and property with little hunting pressure, you would take the same types of massive antlered bucks. There are no superpower skills.

A lot of the hosts who adorn the front covers of hunting magazines own gigantic tracts of land they hunt on. Take, for instance, Lee and Tiffany Lakosky. They originally had a three-hundred-acre farm in Iowa, the mecca of big-antlered bucks. On a *Realtree Outdoors* TV segment, Lee said they "maintained one hundred food plots on a total of around six hundred acres." Yes, you read that correctly. He then went on to say they now have "several farms totaling six thousand acres." Do you think you'd be able to kill the same types of adult bucks that Lee and Tiffany do if you had six thousand private acres with Alpha minerals along with one hundred food plots on severely under-hunted land? I do.

And this story is similar to that of many other TV hosts, including Pat and Nicole Reeve, the Drury brothers, etc. I'm not criticizing these folks; they are all dedicated, skilled, and ethical hunters. However, there should be no doubt that they have the bull by the horns or the buck by the antlers, so to speak, when it comes to the type of land they hunt and the genetics of the bucks that live there. Now, are you starting to follow why not all hunters are destined to take the type of trophy bucks seen in magazines and on outdoor television shows?

I don't want to leave myself out of this group, either. I, too, hunt my 192-acre private farm that is not heavily hunted, and I have about five acres of food plots. However, my soil is not blessed with the types of minerals that help bucks grow huge antlers, so I have realistic expectations about the size antlers my bucks can achieve. At this point, if you're still comparing your deer hunting success to that of television hosts of outdoor shows, consider this: How come most, if not all, of the hosts who consistently kill huge-antler bucks rarely, if ever, hunt in New York, New Jersey, Pennsylvania, or other heavily hunted areas of the Northeast and some New England states? The answer is as plain as the antlers on a trophy-class buck's head—the majority of New England and the Northeast states simply don't have the ingredients—Alpha minerals, highly nutritious food sources, superior genetics, and under-hunted lands—necessary for a majority of mature bucks in these areas to consistently grow antlers that measure 160 to 200 or more inches. In addition to that, hunting pressured bucks in these areas isn't easy for most hosts. It wouldn't surprise me in the least if most of them were unable to even take a buck within a week's time frame in these areas. See, it isn't you or your supposed lack of buck hunting skills.

Hopefully by now I have helped anyone reading this, especially those of you who live in the heavily hunted areas described, to believe that your hunting skills are comparable to any host, including me, on television. Now, here's the real kicker. There are those hosts who genuinely use tactics or strategies that the average buck hunter may not utilize. Therein is something important to consider. Using a variety of different tactics—my favorites are those that can be termed proactive strategies—will help any hunter increase his or her current level of deer hunting skills noticeably.

Equally as important is that every average, above-average, and even highly skilled buck hunter in North America must be cognizant of and realistic about the potential size of antlers bucks can achieve in the areas they hunt. In other words, don't set your antler goals or expectations so high that they are not realistically matched to the genetics, minerals, food sources, and hunting pressure of the land hunted. If you leave these factors out of the equation when setting the antler expectations of your next buck, you are potentially setting yourself up for a letdown.

Instead, to avoid disappointment from antler ground shrinkage, set practical goals that realistically correspond to your hunting styles, the strategies used, herd genetics, available minerals, overall habitat, the potential nutritious food sources, and the hunting pressure. Decide what your priorities actually are when it comes to killing a mature buck. As is often is the case for those who live or hunt in Maine, people are most interested in the live and dressed weights of a buck instead of his headgear. Some hunters are most impressed by the number of points a buck's antlers have. Some

For hunters in heavily hunted states, seeing a buck like this during hunting season would be considered a rare event. Setting antler goals this high is simply not practical in most areas throughout New England and the Northeast. With that said, however, let's all keep the dream alive! Photo Credit: Ted Rose.

are captivated by the width of a set of antlers. Still others are enamored by the age class of an adult buck. Most buck hunters, whom I affectionately refer to as boneheads, however, are entirely fascinated by a buck that sports a set of antlers containing all the above elements (width, spread, points, etc.).

Once you make the decision of what type of antler priorities you adhere to, the next step is to discover if they are actually practical for the area you are hunting. For instance, one of our yearly goals on our farm is to discover, by use of trail cameras and actual sightings, if our farm holds a couple of bucks with antlers that will net score 130 to 145 inches or more. Such antlers would be large enough for me to focus on hunting for them. In New York, that is considered a terrific buck, indeed.

Many outdoor television hosts would scoff at killing a buck whose antlers would score within that bracket. However, my expectations are set to match the growth that my land's minerals, herd genetics, food sources, surrounding hunting pressure, etc. will realistically provide for bucks three and a half years or older. Once I select a target buck and a backup buck, I focus on killing one or the other—or, if the opportunity presents itself, one larger. If I don't get the chance to take any within my goals, I stick to the decision and won't shoot any other buck with smaller antlers. If this is a goal you might consider, remember this important point—you must be satisfied with your decision. If by the end of the season, you haven't killed the target buck, your tag will go unused. If you are totally satisfied with that potentially happening, this tactic may be a good plan for you to abide by.

This two-and-a-half-year-old buck's antlers are typical on our land. Periodically we have been fortunate to take older bucks with larger antlers that were above the goals we set (see the photo montage at the end of this chapter). Every few years we have taken older bucks that have scored 134, 143, 148, and 151 inches. Photo Credit: Fiduccia Enterprises.

It is a practical strategy to first discover what the average antler size of mature three-and-a-half-year-old or older buck is for your area. Once you have determined that, you can set pragmatic expectations for the type of antlered bucks you want to take.

What I have discovered is that in areas with soils that are not rich in Alpha minerals and that lack superior genetics, it pays to make sure the other elements that help grow large antlers are present. This often contributes to one common equation: providing high-quality, nutritious food sources. If practical, that can be achieved by planting a variety of high-protein food plots or fruit trees and chestnut trees. If that is not possible, the natural vegetation can be fertilized and enhanced to encourage better antler growth on the land you hunt. Top-quality food will enable you to target the largest antlered adult bucks—the ones whose antlers meet your realistic expectations. Without being able to provide such food sources, it may be necessary and practical to widen your choice of bucks even though some may have slightly smaller antlers than expected.

Remember what I have always articulated and written in many of my deer hunting books, magazine articles, TV shows, and outdoor newspaper columns. The taking of a buck should be fun. Hunting should not be entirely about the size of a buck's antlers. It should also be about the overall experience and satisfaction of any hunt. I especially adhere to this philosophy when it comes to first-time deer hunters, young and old, those who have hunted many years but have never taken a buck, and those hunters who simply don't subscribe to having to shoot only large-racked bucks.

To these equally ardent deer hunters, I say this: Sometimes the aesthetic value of a particular deer hunt is so memorable that the taking of a buck with antlers smaller than dreamed about or hoped for far outweighs the desire or commitment made to take a larger antlered buck. This choice should not be influenced by anyone other than you. Let your heart and your conscience guide your decision about what buck to shoot. If the buck you are looking at makes your heart beat out of your chest but his antlers aren't the size your friends would shoot, it doesn't mean you have to pass him up. The only sidebar here is that a hunter who decides to kill a buck with bragging-sized antlers should remember that he or she should make no false excuses about why they shot the buck. Relate the taking of the buck to friends and family as it was inspired when you saw the deer, and nothing else needs to be said.

With that said, however, when you take smaller-antlered deer, you should never complain about how you never get to see adult bucks with big antlers. In order to kill a mature buck with impressive antlers, you have to allow the smaller antlerd bucks to go by your stand unharmed.

Chapter Eighteen

Hunt Like You Mean It

As I mentioned numerous times, the key to successful deer hunting is to unquestionably believe you are a good deer hunter and that you have good deer hunting skills. Many hunters lose quality buck-killing opportunities because they doubt themselves and their deer hunting tactic choices.

Each and every day a hunter goes afield, he or she must know—not ponder or wish—that they will see a buck. Bear in mind, if hunters don't devote their entire attention to the job at hand, hunting, they critically reduce their odds of killing a buck. A simple fact about life is that no matter what a person does in his or her profession, family life, or sport he or she enjoys, to do any of it well, that person must be totally focused on the job at hand. In other words, be in the game!

Successful businessmen, athletes, entrepreneurs, and yes, even deer hunters all have a few common elements they share. They are confident in their abilities and in themselves. Equally important, no matter what field they are in, they concentrate totally on what they are currently doing.

When it comes to being confident and focusing at the job at hand, baseball Hall of Famer Wade Boggs is the consummate example, whether in professional baseball or deer hunting. Photo Credit: Fiduccia Enterprises.

Photo Credit: Ted Rose.

Let's say you have been sitting in a tree stand or blind for a few hours, and you are becoming bored. If you allow your mind to drift on the things that have to be accomplished on your next day off or, much worse, start texting or calling hunting companions on the two-way radios, you have opened a Pandora's Box that is filled with failure. If you're not paying attention during the time you're on stand, you may not hear the subtle grunt of a buck passing through the cover, see the slight movement of antlers glistening in the sunlight, or see and hear a small tree rocking back and forth as a buck rubs it. The fact is it only takes seconds for a mature buck to sneak by your stand without being detected. I have tested this theory countless times in our fields during and after deer season (mostly after). I text messages, sometimes long ones some times short ones. On countless occasions, I have lifted my head to either see a deer that weren't there only a minute or so before, or see one as it is only seconds from disappearing from the field into nearby cover.

If you're thinking about work-related issues, the unfinished chores to be done at home, the credit card bills, or even daydreaming about killing a trophy buck, you're potentially missing opportunities to see and shoot a buck or doe. Instead, if you commit to totally concentrating on deer hunting, you increase your odds of killing a buck. Pay total attention to the sights, sounds, and even the odors around your stand. If you have ever attended one of my deer hunting seminars, you have heard this analogy: If a football player goes into any game thinking of something other than playing football, he runs a high risk of having a lousy game, getting pulled by the coach, or, in the worst case scenario, getting absolutely hammered by a lineman. The same principle holds true for deer hunters. If you get to your stand and spend the next two hours doubting the stand selection you made is the right one, you might as well have stayed home. When you doubt your ability and the effectiveness of using deer calls, rattling, decoying, or simply ambushing a passing deer, you have thrown a spoke into the wheel of good fortune. If you are skeptical about what I'm sharing with you, take this advice the next time you go deer hunting. Talk to yourself. Promise that you will not doubt your stand selection. Instead, firmly believe the site you chose is just not a good selection, it is the top selection. While you are on stand, remain totally focused and filled with confidence that you will see a buck. By following what you're about to read, I can assure you that this method will help you to see and bag more deer the next time you go afield.

Pay attention to every natural sound you hear while posted in your stand. You'll be surprised that when you are actually listening carefully for natural sounds, you will hear them. A lot of hunters have never heard a buck grunt or a doe blat in the wild for

Being entirely attentive on stand allows the brain to process ambient forest sounds. A single crack of a dry branch, a sapling being snapped back and forth, the clacking of rocks and subtle splashing in a creek, and other forest settings can all be the catalyst to alert a hunter of an oncoming deer. Photo Credit: Depositphotos.

two reasons. First, they don't know what to listen for. Second, even if they know what a grunt sounds like, they're not paying enough attention to pick up the subtle grunt or blat of a passing buck or doe! The human brain actually prevents you from hearing ambient sounds if it is concentrating on another issue you have to think about. There's some food for thought. Or perhaps it would be better stated as some food that got away because of frivolous thoughts you occupied your brain with!

For the sake of any novice who is reading this, I want to include some advice that every veteran deer hunter already knows. When you hear a turkey purr or if a crow or squirrel cries out a warning, concentrate on the surrounding cover with intensity. It you think you hear a snap of a branch or a slight kicking up of leaves, assume it is an approaching buck (not a doe) and focus all your senses on that area so you are absolutely ready to react should a buck try to slip by through a shooting lane unnoticed. If you spot what looks like the ear, nose, eye, or other body part of a deer, don't question yourself. Instead, assume it is a deer and study it carefully in your binoculars. You will be surprised to discover that many times it will turn out to be part of a deer you're looking at! Of course, you must absolutely identify it as such.

I have never put the following information in print before. for over 50 years of hunting deer. I always assume every unidentifiable deer, sound, movement, musk odor, or gut-feeling is made by a buck approaching my stand. If I see a deer run across the road, I instantly proclaim in my mind that it is a buck. If I jump a deer and it runs off I react as if it is a buck getting away. Until I can absolutely confirm that what I saw, heard, smelled, or anticipated it isn't a buck, all deer to me are bucks. Crazy you say, I think not. It keeps my anticipation high, it allows me to be totally focused, and I'm always excited. Remember you're as good a deer hunter as the guy who consistently bags his buck. You just have to learn to believe that you are.

Chapter Nineteen

Is Five Days Enough Time to Kill a Trophy Buck?

For many hunters, booking an out-of-state hunt is all the rage, particularly for hunts to take a trophy-class whitetail buck. Since the economy has improved somewhat over the past few years, it has once again become more a reality than a dream for a nonprofessional hunter to book the deer hunt of a lifetime. If you have dreamed of or are planning an out-of-state whitetail hunt, there are several points to consider realistically before contacting an outfitter who will help you fulfill your ambition and increase your success.

The first item on the agenda is to set a budget and be candid with yourself about what you can comfortably afford to spend. Next is to commit to

This Canadian bruiser of a buck has a set of antlers that dreams are made of. Finding an out-of-state and/or country outfitter that can turn your dream of killing a buck like this into a reality requires a lot of homework. Photo Credit: Ted Rose.

Photo Credit: Fiduccia Enterprises.

booking a hunt with an experienced, reliable, and licensed outfitter who is a member a state or province Professional Outfitters Association. It is also wise to be realistic about the number of days most outfitters provide their clients. Generally speaking, free-range hunts average about seven days long. Two of those days are dedicated to traveling. So in essence, the hunt is usually five days long.

In the thirty-two years I have produced our television program, *Woods N' Water Big Game Adventures*, I have been fortunate to have hunted whitetail deer in many states and Canadian provinces, so I say the following from years of experience. Five days of hunting for a mature whitetail buck is sometimes not enough time. That is an important point worth considering prior to booking a hunt. It may be wise to seek out an outfitter who is flexible about extending the hunt for a few days if need be. Most outfitters who will consider this option do so by calculating the daily cost of the trip and charging that rate for the extra days. For instance, if the total cost of the five-day hunt is $5,000, every extra day will cost an additional $1,000.

Over the years, I have been on many five-day hunts that ended without taking a buck. In some instances, I never even got to see a buck with the size of antlers I was hunting for because of unexpected weather conditions—mostly above-average warm or even hot temperatures. In fact, you must remember there are an endless number of variables that can affect the outcome of a hunt. With that said, careful—no, make that meticulous—planning and down-to-earth expectations can help eliminate a lot of the components that can lead to an unsuccessful hunt. One of the more important factors is exploring the option of additional days in written contract form with your intended outfitter.

In 1991, a year I would like to delete from my memory, I was on a five-day

Always inquire about the types of blinds and/or tree stands an outfitter uses. A comfortable, warm blind, or safe, secure tree stand results in more hours of hunting and will increase your success factor immensely. Photo Credit: Darkwoods Blinds.

whitetail hunt with an outfitter in Lamar, Colorado. By week's end, I had several bucks, but none were the Boone & Crockett class buck that the outfitter assured me was roaming the river bottom of the farm I was hunting. The entire week was clear but extremely cold, as the temperatures never climbed above single digits.

On the evening of the next-to-last day, while shivering uncontrollably, I was glassing the edge of the riverbank from the frigid metal-enclosed blind that had been our home over the past few days.

(Changing the subject momentarily, it is always wise to ask outfitters to describe the types and quality of the blinds or stands you will be spending many hours in before booking. They need not only to be safe but also provide warmth and comfort. That may seem trivial now, but it won't be when you're sitting in a flimsy blind or stand in temperatures in the teens for hours each day. Remember, the more comfortable you are, the more likely you will be focused on hunting rather than keeping warm.)

While scanning the riverbank, I saw a doe climb up the embarkment from the river below. Behind her was a ten-point buck. As the buck chased the doe in circles through the waist-high brush, I contemplated shooting him. He would have easily scored in the 150-inch range. But I had committed from day one to hunt for a larger-antlered buck, so I let the ten-pointer pass. I watched both of them, along with about fifty other deer, including bucks of various antler sizes, feed in an alfalfa field as the last flickers of shooting light began to fade along with my hopes of seeing the big buck.

The last day of the hunt brought our usual 3:30 a.m. wake-up call. While eating breakfast, the outfitter suggested I stay a few extra days with the expectation that the time would allow me the chance to get a glimpse of the giant buck. Unfortunately, I was already booked for an elk hunt in New Mexico, and I was scheduled to arrive there the next day to begin another five-day hunt. I reluctantly left without taking a buck or filming a television program. As Lady Luck would have it, an industry peer and friend of mine, Craig Boddington, who is one of the nation's most respected journalists and prominent big-game hunters, arrived at the lodge the afternoon I left. According to the outfitter Boddington killed a 180-inch class Boone & Crockett buck from the metal blind the next morning!

During what was to be a five-day deer hunt in Saskatchewan in 2001, I killed the largest buck I have taken to date. The buck green-scored 208 1/8 Boone & Crockett inches, and he ended up netting 207 3/8 Boone & Crockett inches. I saw the buck within the first two hours of the first day of my hunt, but the buck escaped our first

If I didn't extend my five-day hunt by remaining three extra days, I wouldn't have killed this giant buck. He is the largest buck I have taken to date. Photo Credit: Fiduccia Enterprises.

encounter unscathed. On the last day of the hunt, the outfitter asked if I could stay another couple of days. Remembering the Colorado hunt mentioned above, I quickly accepted the outfitter's offer. Although I didn't have another hunt lined up, I would have stayed even if I did. One lesson was all I needed to avoid making the same mistake twice.

Despite my enthusiasm and anticipation, two days later I had seen neither hide nor hair—nor antler—of the giant buck. My flight back to New York was scheduled to depart early the next morning. When we got up, the weather was bone-chilling cold. The thermometer read -32° F, but there wasn't a hint of wind. It was still two hours before light, and we were about to start packing up our gear when the outfitter said, "If you change your flight until tomorrow morning and hunt today, I'll pay the extra change fees the airline charges you. I have a gut feeling today's the day that buck will show himself again."

We hunted the edges of three different field locations in the morning. By 11 a.m., we were

Fortunately, my decision to extend my hunt prevented years of second-guessing myself about what might have been if I had left at the end of my five-day hunt. Photo Credit: Fiduccia Enterprises.

cold and needed to warm up by walking to another large alfalfa field. Only minutes after we settled in, we saw a doe flagging her tail some three hundred yards away. I used an adult estrus blat and called the doe in to our location. She overshot us and disappeared over a small knob. The instant the doe vanished from the field, the huge buck busted out of the woods like someone had stuck a hot iron up his backside and ran across the field faster than I have ever seen a deer run. I shot him on the dead run—the first time I had ever shot at a deer moving anywhere close to the speed he was moving. An hour later, we found him piled up in a ravine. The fast, flat-shooting .270 130-grain bullet caught him farther back than I was aiming, but it managed to hit his liver. Had I not had the extra few days to hunt, this story would have ended much differently, eh?

There is one other element about booking a seven- to ten-day (actual hunting time) deer hunt. It substantially reduces the stress often associated with three- to five-day hunts. Although planning out-of-state or Canadian hunts that are seven to ten days long is difficult on the budget and the time away from home, it can definitely make the difference in taking a buck or not filling your tag.

Here are some tips to make sure the hunt you book will provide the most options for a good time and success.

- Your first decision is your budget. Once you have this, you must live within that budget and remain practical about what the money you are spending will actually buy you.
- Next, decide on what state or province you want to hunt. Then narrow down where the best areas are. Only then should you start your search for reliable outfitters.
- Once you contact a potential outfitter, ask as many detailed questions of him or her as possible. If the outfitter becomes annoyed, move on to the next outfitter on your list.
- Keep your questions in person or on the phone to the point. Don't bore him or her to death with your expertise, stories of past hunts, etc. If you do, he or she will begin to lose interest, and your hunt will suffer in the end.

- Talk turkey. Ask if there is a possibility of booking a longer hunt rather than the standard five days. If he or she is agreeable, ask the price and make sure to get it in writing.
- Know all you can about the success rates, which should be realistic, what is offered in field care, and preparing the deer for transport. This is a crucial question when hunting in Canada.
- Ask about the details of lodging, food, transportation, and other services provided.
- Question whether you will be accompanied by a guide at all times. If the answer is no, choose another outfitter.
- If an outfitter places hunters on stands or blinds all day and picks them up at night, it should be a major red flag.
- Generally, an outfitter is the owner and operator, and the guides are usually responsible for taking clients afield. Ask who will be guiding you and how long they have worked for the outfitter.
- It is not unacceptable to ask about gratuities and what the average tip is.
- Discuss how the outfitter hunts: stands, still hunting, drives, etc.
- Always be frank about your style of hunting and your physical condition.
- Don't be too shy to ask about the hunting conditions. How physically tough are they?
- Don't allow guides to push you too hard or walk you too fast.
- Ask if you will be picked up and dropped off at the airport at no extra cost.

I always recommend going to consumer sport shows to book hunts. While the web is useful, nothing beats talking face-to-face with the outfitter. Recognizing a good deal when it comes along also helps. But it should be a red flag if the outfitter's price is much less than the cost of other outfitters from his area who are offering the same type of hunt.

Always take the references given by the outfitter with a grain of salt. The best way to get information from his references is to congratulate them on taking a nice animal early on in the conversation. When you talk to a successful hunter, ask him if he went on the hunt with friends who didn't score, then ask for their phone numbers and call them. It is most helpful to talk to the hunters who did not wind up getting their deer. They're the folks who can give you the best information.

Once you have settled on an outfitter, make sure he is willing to put everything he told you in a formal agreement. Having a contract is good business for both the outfitter and you. He should be as interested in providing you with an agreement as you are in getting one from him. If he isn't, move on to the next outfitter. You have already encountered your first problem with this one, and it will only get worse from that point on. I promise you that! When you get the agreement, read the entire document carefully from start to finish. Make sure it includes everything you discussed with the outfitter and coincides with the notes you took during your talks with him.

Most states require a contract between hunter and outfitter. Licensed and permitted outfitters are held accountable to far more regulatory agencies than you would think. If the outfitter you choose doesn't offer a contract, it may be due to the fact that he or she is either not a legal outfitter or is one that has had problems. Check all outfitters out with the state or province's official outfitter's association to be sure they have not had complaints filed against them.

If you take the above advice, it still doesn't guarantee a successful or fun hunt, but it does help. If you don't do your homework carefully, you're in store for a hunt destined to go badly.

Many times the outfitter will not be the one to guide you. He will have an established group of seasoned hunters who know the land and the game. The outfitter will assign guides to his hunters. Over my fifty years of hunting, I have learned some very important things about guides. While most are excellent at what they do, others are less than excellent. Not all guides are created equally.

- If you and your guide fail to hit it off after a day, the number one rule to follow is to **immediately** make the outfitter aware of any problems you are having with your guide. If things don't change quickly, approach the outfitter again in a direct way and ask him to provide you with another guide. When you talk with outfitter, be frank, firm, and brief. Whatever you do, don't be longwinded and come off sounding like a crybaby.

- For the most part, remember the guide is there to help you bag your deer. So basically he is in charge. With that said, however, don't hesitate to share your ideas about tactics. A seasoned guide will be open to hearing your suggestions. If he insists on a particular strategy, go with his plan. Generally, I'll follow a guide's lead for the first few days of a hunt. If things aren't progressing as I expect them to, I then politely suggest we try one of my plans.

- Even a long-time hunter can learn tactics from most guides. Don't be shy about asking questions of your guide. Why he used a particular strategy? Why did he select a certain stand site? Most guides are open to such queries, but not all of them are.

- I recently read that in order for a hunter to gain respect from a guide, they get involved and help the guide field dress their game, hang stands, even at night, split wood, and in general pitch in. While it is not a bad idea to help out, I don't endorse overdoing it. Most hunters pay the outfitter a hefty price for the hunt, and they are expected to leave a substantial tip for the guide. The guide gets paid to field dress your animal. I read that by field dressing your own animal, the guide will realize you are not there to be "pampered" and he feel you are a "real hunter." That's total nonsense. If you want to dress out your game go right ahead and do so. But don't be forced into it thinking he won't respect your ability as a hunter if you don't.

- One last tip of advice, if things are slow and you aren't seeing deer, don't complain, or get in a huff and sulk around. This is the number one reason guides become annoyed. It's hunting —sometimes things just don't go the way they were planned.

Chapter Twenty

Buck Fever: How to Beat It

My earliest recollection of when the phenomenon commonly known as buck fever struck me was in 1964. It was my first deer hunt and the only one I would participate in that fall after my experience. My single encounter with buck fever forced me to reevaluate my aspirations about the sport of deer hunting. I wanted to determine if my primal urge to be a hunter was as genuine a quest as I thought it was before going on another deer hunt.

My first deer hunt was only forty-five minutes from the heart of New York City, and it took place between the small hamlets of Cold Spring and Beacon. At that time, they were two tiny communities that straddled the boundaries of Putnam and Dutchess counties in southern New York. After getting a recommendation and doing some research about the area, I chose to hunt Breakneck Ridge (see left), which is part of the Hudson Highland mountain range—a rugged piece of real estate along the Hudson River. Breakneck Ridge was indeed a fitting name for the mountain. The ascent from the railroad tracks was exceedingly steep and treacherous. When I reached the peak, I glanced down and spied only a black dot that was my 1957 black Chevy—Blackie as I called her—nearly 1,300 feet below. Blackie was comfortably parked to the right of the tunnel opening that trains and vehicles drove through at the base of the mountain.

Breakneck Ridge was brought to my attention by the owner of a local hunting and fishing store in Brooklyn, New York, that I regularly spent time at. The owner assured me that the mountain offered good deer hunting opportunities, and because the access

Photo of Breakneck Ridge. Photo Credit: iStockphoto.

was so difficult, it was lightly hunted. At eighteen years old, I was a solid 188 pounds and in top-notch physical condition, so I wasn't concerned about ascending the steep slopes. On the morning of my hunt, the climb went quickly and without much incident. That wasn't the way the rest of the day was destined to go, however.

When I finally reached the pinnacle of Breakneck Ridge, I checked my watch. It was 11:30 a.m. I decided I still had plenty of time to find a good location for the hunt. After a short fifteen-minute walk, I found what I felt was an ideal spot to post for the afternoon. I decided to sit on a large flat rock that was a few feet off the ground. It overlooked a stand of mixed oak trees just below me. At the back end of the trees was a huge swamp.

After an hour or so, I grabbed my lunch and took a Brooklyn-man-sized bite from my Italian hero, filled with Capicola and Basilicata Provolone imported from southern Italy. Without being embarrassed to say so, the hero was also brimming with spicy Italian olives and sweet peppers. As you might have already guessed, I bought the mouthwatering hoagie at an Italian deli—Giovanni's on Eighty-Sixth Street in Bay Ridge, Brooklyn. What? You wanna make somthin' of dat?!

I don't know if what followed next was due to the lip-smacking vocalizations I was expressing from the combined zesty flavors in each bite of my culinary chef d'oeuvre hero or the wonderful odors the hero emitted that slowly permeated throughout the woods. But either one, or both, caused an extraordinary happening of the deer kind. The next time I looked up from my hero, I was staring at a buck whose head was adorned with a beautiful set of antlers not fifty yards from me. He may have been a dandy eight- or ten-point buck—I frankly don't remember counting his points. But at the time, I knew I wanted to take him!

This is where the principal details of the story remain fuzzy for me. From the exact moment I saw the buck's antlers, I don't recall even now exactly how the rest of the sequence of events unraveled. I do remember that the buck was so preoccupied eating acorns that he hadn't seen me, at least not at the precise point

Breakneck Ridge highest peak is about 1,260 feet and lies within the Hudson Highlands State Park. The steep cliffs are a result of years of quarrying. The Metro North Railroad runs right by the base of the ridge along Route 9.

in time that I saw him. Without any further ado, my next hunting strategy was to take another bite out of my hero! What, you ask? Yes, without any thought, I took another bite out of my Italian hero. That fact is burned into my memory.

While my teeth held tightly to the sandwich, I picked up my shotgun, which was leaning on a small log next to me. Without any apparent awareness, even before aiming at the buck, I began to eject each shell from the shotgun. Each and every dang one of them! As the slugs fell to the ledge, they dinged just loud enough to catch the buck's attention. That fact momentarily brought me back to reality, which lasted about a tenth of a second before I heard myself saying in a quite normal voice level, "What ★&^$# is happening here?!"

My next memory is of being light-headed and nauseous. I don't know for sure, but I assume the buck did not like hearing my profanity. In what I think was an instant—it could very well not have been—the buck started to move off. Now that the shotgun was totally empty, I obviously felt it was the perfect opportunity for me to place the crosshairs of the scope on the buck and pull the ★&★%^$% trigger before he vanished into the swamp. Click! I think I may have fired and chambered several more imaginary slugs into the empty chamber of the shotgun. I did so even though I don't recall if the buck was still in my sight after I pulled the trigger the first time.

Now here comes the most worrisome part about the event. After an incomprehensible time frame passed, my next recollection of the hunt was of me eating my hero again. I guess I thought the flavors of the sandwich would snap me back into making sense of what just took place. While continuing to devour the hero, I noticed several shotgun slugs scattered in a demented arrangement on the ledge. My shotgun, however, was not in my hand nor was it in sight. I would later find it beneath the ledge and charmingly marked with a nick to the stock, as well as a scratch delightfully complimenting the barrel of my Redfield 3x9 wide-angle scope. Nice, eh? More disturbing to me at the time was that I also noticed the contents of some of my expensive and delicious Italian hero strewn about the ledge.

Without any hesitation, I gathered up my fugitive Capicola, Basilicata Provolone, and some peppers—I left the olives where they landed—and placed them neatly back into the hero. I'm a Virgo. This is a true and under-exaggerated account of that day. Until this writing, it is an incident I had only shared with a hunting companion of that era, Tony Hidalgo, bless his soul.

To top off my fuzzy recollections, I'm still not certain how the hunt ended. I do recall gathering up my binoculars, shells, and other belongings and walking away from the ledge. Sometime after that, I must have safely made my way down Breakneck Ridge

I bagged this terrific 10-point buck on Breakneck Ridge in 1968, four years after my bout with Buck Fever on same mountain. It is rock solid proof Buck Fever is indeed curable (behind me is my cousin Steven Peter Somma with my dog Briar).

and fortunately reached the bottom unscathed. I opened the car door, started Blackie, and drove her home.

It wasn't until few years later when I read about a condition called buck fever in one of the big three magazines of the time that I realized what I had gone through had a name. The article mentioned that deer hunters who get buck fever do strange things when they see a buck. It went on to say that some hunters with the fever go through a variety of bizarre and unintelligible actions. Only after reading that article did I put two and two together. During my first-ever deer hunt, seeing my first buck ever had caused me so much stress that it resulted in me having an acute attack of buck fever!

Over the following years, I have read many more articles about buck fever. One article that stands out in my mind was about a study done at the 69 annual Scientific Session of the American Heart Association. It asserted that buck fever could put men, especially if they had clogged arteries, at high risk for heart attacks. Researchers went on to question whether severe physical and high emotional levels of stress caused by a hunter seeing a buck could trigger dangerous variations in hunters' heart-rate levels.

The research data revealed that the mere event of seeing a buck during deer season put rigorous demands on the cardiovascular system of the hunters monitored during the study. For the hunters who participated in the study, the dangers of having a buck fever episode that could result in a heart attack were real. For some of the hunters, adrenaline surges occurred simply after they saw a buck, as on my first deer hunt. The data shows that hunters' heart rates soared from 78 beats per minute to 168 beats per minute. That's a major heart-rate increase—twice the normal heart-rate prior to seeing the buck.

Over the past five decades since I had my bout with buck fever, the research studies that have been done and the data they have compiled further document that buck fever can cause radical physiological reactions when hunters confront game. It went on to give the term buck fever a more medically accurate term—anxiety disorder. One such study by collaborators Tom Heberlein and Rich Steadman revealed that a hunter:

"… must initiate a series of actions (i.e., positioning the weapon and timing the shot to his target). Such functions are preceded with activation of the sympathetic nervous system, beginning with the orienting response. This response is activated when the game is first perceived as a change in the environment and becomes the focus of attention.

"Sensory thresholds are lowered, brain activity is increased, blood flow to the limbs is altered, and the heart rate and respiration change in preparation to act. A second source of response comes from the action itself (i.e. the effects of movement). Physical exercise demands increase oxygen flow to the muscles, requiring an increase in heart rate. Emotion and arousal also heighten the physiological response. Most hunters refer to the entire event as 'Buck Fever,' which is the hunter's high that can get out of control, spoil success, and lead to injury."

Many other physicians, scientists, and experts in this particular field concur that buck fever is a realistic form of "hysteria in which the cerebrum and cerebellum shut down simultaneously and victims of buck fever are left either temporarily mentally paralyzed." Sometimes they are unable to react effectively enough that they can cycle a whole magazine of ammo through the rifle without pulling the trigger, as I did.

Research has also confirmed that some hunters are immune to buck fever, while others only encounter episodes of it once or twice in their hunting lives. Some hunters, however, are unfortunate enough to come down with buck fever all the time. While some get the condition with one species and not another, other hunters become afflicted no matter what type of game they are hunting.

Some hunters who are plagued with the disorder learn how not to have reoccurring cases, but it takes concentration and practice to achieve that goal. I have been extremely fortunate that I have not had another buck fever incident since my encounter with it fifty-one years ago. As I have mentioned previously, it only takes once for me to realize I can't repeat a hunting mistake if I want to be a consistently successful deer stalker.

Thankfully, for gun or bow hunters who consistently face buck fever, there are ways to substantially reduce the number of episodes and perhaps even cure them permanently. Both require a commitment to developing a routine that works specifically for each hunter. If they are practiced, they will help any hunter reduce or even eliminate their affliction. The first and most crucial step is to recognize buck fever for what it is: a serious medical condition that has been both documented and acknowledged by the medical community, who have categorized buck fever as acute anxiety disorder. This is a valid condition that should not be scoffed at by others or dismissed by those who are afflicted by it. Once a hunter admits buck fever is an accepted medical condition and understands it can be treated, a cure can be achievable.

There are countless solutions on the Internet, in magazines and books, and on television that assert their therapies will limit, control, or totally prevent episodes of buck fever. The varied remedies range from being practical to being outright hogwash. With that in mind, allow me to share what has worked for me. Remember, each case of acute anxiety disorder affects hunters differently. Cases can range from mild to severe, so no one remedy can be applied as a cure-all for everyone, but my advice should help you. I have shared my methods with other hunters with buck fever, and it has helped a majority of them to either substantially reduce or eliminate future encounters of the condition. Still, keep in mind that it is virtually impossible to help everyone. To prove that point, I will share some anecdotes about two hunters who have had consistent battles with buck fever. One of them admitted he was stricken with anxiety disorder

At the time Outdoor Life magazine was considered one of the "big-three" outdoor periodicals. The story about buck fever appeared in an Outdoor Life magazine of that period.

many times but accepted it as a medical condition. The other hunter denied he ever had a case of buck fever or that it was a verified medical condition.

The first hunter is a close friend. In fact, he works in the outdoor industry. He is a longtime hunter who has had many successful hunts during his lifetime. There are times, however, that he suffers from severe anxiety attacks that cause him to miss or wound game, particularly whitetail bucks. I have actually seen him be overwrought by cases of buck fever that were accompanied by severe heebie-jeebies and acute loss of concentration—all of which caused him to shoot at game numerous times before it escaped unharmed or, worse yet, wounded. I have witnessed this same hunter, when shooting at paper targets at a range, consistently place shots in the bull's-eye at distances of one hundred yards and farther. When he hunts other types of game, including birds, small game, or predators, he is a deadly shot. Yet when he sees a mature buck or other big game animal with antlers, he begins falling apart at the sight of the animal—a classic symptom of acute anxiety disorder.

I have been on hunts with this person when I was directly beside him as game approached. During these instances, I helped calm him down long enough for him to kill the animal even though it may have taken him more than one shot to dispatch it. Other times, I came onto the scene shortly after he had wounded game, and we had to trail it. During these occasions, I had to talk to him in a reassuring tone, which prompted him to calm down. When we finally located the animals, I would encourage him about what to do next, all of which ended in taking the game successfully. This hunter not only accepts advice, he is open to it, and he shares it in his outdoor writings. I have not had the pleasure of hunting with him over the past few years, but he tells me that he has fewer bouts of buck fever than ever before. Because he recognizes the problem, he is progressing nicely and is working toward eliminating this condition completely.

The second hunter's tale of woe with buck fever is completely opposite. He, too, is a seasoned big-game hunter that I have witnessed becoming distraught when a variety of antlered big game approached him. Similarly to the first hunter, he is also deadly accurate at the range with a gun or bow. Coincidentally, as with the first hunter, I had many opportunities to hunt closely alongside him. Both hunters have appeared on my television program, *Woods N' Water*. The first hunter was a backup cameraman, and the second hunter was a special guest.

This hunter didn't exhibit outward signs of anxiety or a visible loss of concentration. But I could always notice a widening of his eyes and a quickening of his breath after he saw antlered game and was preparing to shoot it. On countless occasions, this

It is important to practice something as mundane as smoothly placing the safety to the firing position. It ensures basic shooting techniques are achieved at a subconscious level rather than having to think to long about them. Photo Credit: Fiduccia Enterprises.

hunter ended up either having to shoot at a buck or other big game animal several times before even hitting it once, if at all. Other times, if he was fortunate enough to hit the animal, it escaped, albeit wounded. Most times, the game was recovered, but a couple of times it wasn't, which was the catalyst for me to stop hunting with him. Until this day, he continues to have bouts of buck fever that consistently end up with him shooting at animals multiple times.

This hunter will not accept any advice on the matter, nor does his type A personality allow him to admit he is affected by repeated cases of acute anxiety disorder. In fact, when I used to hunt with him, he often referred to buck fever as being an old wives' tale rather than acknowledging that it is actually a certifiable medical ailment. For this hunter, there is no hope of helping him to reduce—never mind eliminate—his buck fever as long as he continues to believe he doesn't have the condition.

How, then, can hunters affected by buck fever lessen or eradicate the condition? First and foremost, they must admit it is medically accepted as an anxiety disorder. Equally important, they must acknowledge that they have endured attacks of buck fever. Once these two elements are recognized, recovery is already well underway.

So what are the methods to win, or at least fight, the battle of reducing or remedying buck fever? While each case will require different analysis that is specific to each hunter, there are general guidelines that can be followed.

Pre-Hunt Steps

Experience: There is no doubt that performing the same act over and over again builds experience and confidence. Both are important elements toward ending bouts with buck fever. The more a person practices his or her shooting skills, builds familiarity

Cody practices shooting from sticks a lot during the off season. Repeated practice will let any hunter set them up quickly, securely, and provide the confidence to make a clean one-shot kill. Photo Credit: Fiduccia Enterprises.

with a firearm, and other important components related to accurate shot placement, the more confidence he or she will have in making an accurate kill shot when antlered game appears. The repetitious act of using proper shooting methods will become the norm instead of the unusual. Doing so lessens the likelihood that any man or woman—though women hunters rarely suffer from buck fever—will encounter future bouts of anxiety disorder associated with hunting antlered game.

Embrace Your Firearm: Being totally comfortable, familiar, and confident in your firearm or bow is a crucial first step to relieving future bouts of buck fever. When a hunter's firearm becomes a natural, automatic extension of his or her arm, it is another positive step toward getting the condition under control.

Practice Accurate Shooting Skills: One of the most important factors about shooting antlered game is to make consistently accurate shots. This component is often overlooked. However, it is essential to getting a handle on an anxiety disorder condition. Knowing with self-assurance where to place the bullet to make a precise one-shot kill under rapid sight acquisition will launch a hunter light-years ahead in eliminating future bouts of buck fever.

To finely hone your shot-placement skills, when sighting in at a range it is important to use deer targets that include both skeletal and organ images. Pick different locations on the target,

To consistently place a bullet where you want it to hit the game your hunting, it is important to practice with a target of the animal you intend to hunt. Photo Credit: Fiduccia Enterprises.

including high shoulder, mid-shoulder, heart, lungs, kidney, ears, nose, etc., and place two or three shots in each of the areas selected. Don't be concerned about shooting tight groups—that's not your purpose here. All you want to do is place one shot at a time in the same picture area.

Real-World Target Procurement

After you have achieved the above steps, repeat them, but this time, add another element—quick target acquisition, or QTA. Select part of the deer on the target that is one of the larger organs, such as the lungs. Now comes the more crucial part of this practice. Take any stance you are comfortable with. I like to do this type of practice from a chair in my shooting house at our range. It simulates sitting in a tree stand or shooting blind. I add an additional component of difficulty, too. To ensure safety, I place one bullet in the clip—not the chamber of the rifle—and confirm the safety is set in the "on" position. I put the rifle across my lap as I would when I'm hunting.

Then I imagine the buck target is a buck that just walked into my view. I pick up the rifle with controlled rapidity and quietness, and I bolt the shell into the chamber. Again with controlled swiftness, I raise the rifle and acquire the entire deer in my scope. This is instantly followed by placing the crosshairs on the selected body

part of the deer. I almost always select the shoulder because that's where I shoot 95 percent of my game. By constantly practicing placing my shot in the shoulder on targets at the range, when I shoot an animal, it feels natural to me to instantly place the crosshairs. Then I flip the safety to the "off" position. I take a deep breath in, exhale halfway out, and compress the trigger. This all takes place in five to seven seconds.

When you achieve consistent hits in the larger target areas, you can begin practicing on smaller

If you shoot free-hand when hunting, practice free-hand shooting in the off-season. It will increase your in-filed shooting success significantly. Photo Credit: Fiduccia Enterprises.

areas, such as the mid- or high shoulder. This practice will increase your in-field hunting shooting skills tenfold. It will also provide you much more confidence in the field. Once this is practiced and accomplished with consistent success, it will play a major part in elevating your confidence.

You might find it helpful to go to YouTube and search Peter Fiduccia's *Woods N' Water* "One Shot Kills"—not *Southern Woods n' Water*, that's not us. After reviewing the nearly dozen or more one-shot kills, remember that shot placement is the chief component for Kate, Cody, and me to learn how to confidently and consistently make accurate shots to the vital areas we aimed at. Once you master the art of precise shot placement, you will be able to instantly focus on picking a spot on the game, firing your rifle, and hitting the exact spot you aimed at. Instead of worrying about whether you are going to make an accurate shot, you will know you can. Becoming a maestro at shot placement will help your shooting become an automatic behavior, which enables you to take more control over buck fever.

Shooting Rests: Using a shooting rest when it is practical and possible is a key element to placing a projectile precisely where you want it to impact. Purchase a shooting rest and practice shooting with it long before season begins. It will steady your aim by a factor of ten, which aids in building your self-confidence even further. Use any durable, reliable shooting rest you feel comfortable with as long as it steadies your aim.

The YPOD gun rest provides the proper elevation for hunters and shooters, is lightweight and can easily be slipped in a cargo pants pocket. It is useful both at the shooting range and in the deer stand. Photo Credit: www.theypod.com.

Breathing Techniques: Using the proper breathing method for shooting is also an important part of improving your accuracy. For hunters to consistently deliver accurate shots, they must learn how to inhale and exhale properly using a quick, smooth rhythm. Basically, take in a deep breath, exhale halfway, hold your aim on the game, and compress the trigger. Sometimes I take in a deep breath, exhale completely, and shoot the game when my lungs are empty. Try both at the range and see what provides you with more accuracy. Breathing techniques vary depending on several factors, including whether you are shooting game at close

Dry firing practice creates excellent trigger control and improves shooting skills. More importantly it assures dead-on accuracy when shooting at game. Photo Credit: Fiduccia Enterprises.

or far distances. Search the Internet for more detailed instruction on breathing techniques. However, I keep my breathing methods short in duration to make them more natural and practical for my hunting styles. The old adage time is of the essence holds true when you are trying to get your shot off at game. If you delay taking your shot, you run a few considerable risks: your aim may wander, your arm may begin to shake, and the animal may wander off. Therefore, your breathing techniques must match the way you hunt.

Trigger Control Methods: Dry firing is the process of operating your empty hunting rifle as if you were shooting it. Dry firing is safe to do and will not harm today's technically advanced rifles. Before dry firing any firearm, it must be triple checked to make sure it is empty. Dry firing is a highly effective practice to improve your shooting skills. Learning how to control compressing a trigger takes practice. The key principle in dry firing is to develop muscle memory through repetition. Dry fire your rifle at a range target, and squeeze the trigger like normal. This allows you to analyze your form without worrying about the recoil. It also helps you get comfortable with the trigger on the rifle you will be hunting with. Dry fire practice also helps keep you from flinching. Old wisdom claims a shooter should squeeze the trigger until it goes off and the shot surprises him. Top-notch shooters know exactly when the rifle is going to fire, and they are ready for the recoil, but they don't flinch in expectation of it. Training your trigger finger will unquestionably make you a better shooter. Again, this will provide you confidence of being able to hit your game exactly where you aim.

Get Familiar: There are some experts who claim that to reduce buck fever, hunters should get out in the field and get used to seeing bucks in the wild. They also recommend looking at videos and pictures of bucks. Seriously, they do. I find this type of information ridiculously inept. No matter how much time a hunter who experiences buck fever spends in the field or looking at images of bucks outside of hunting season, it doesn't conform to reality. Buck fever comes on when a hunter realizes he or she is about to send an arrow or bullet on its way to kill a buck. Seeing bucks outside of when they are being hunted to condition one's self is unrealistic advice.

The Actual Hunt

There He Is: When a buck first appears, many hunters who endure the rigors of buck fever instantly become captivated by the antlers and may even try to count the number of points on the buck's rack. The first step to follow in the field to alleviate an anxiety disorder is to not stare at the rack longer than it takes for you to decide whether you want to shoot the buck. From the moment you decide you want to take the buck, the antlers should no longer be of further interest to you. I swear, this single recommendation will help fight a dreaded case of heebie-jeebies. You must learn to take your mind totally off the antlers. You can admire them when the buck is lying dead at your feet. That may sound a bit insensitive, but trust me, it is important.

Any hunter's heart would beat more quickly seeing a buck like this. Hunters stricken with chronic bouts of buck fever, however, endure more severe reactions including a dramatic rise in heart rates, increased blood pressure, body shakes, labored breathing, and other debilitating symptoms. Photo Credit: CanStock Photos/EEI_Tony.

It's Time to Focus: Once you have decided to take the buck, it's time to walk yourself through the steps to ensure you will make a surefire kill shot. For the fifty-plus years I have been hunting big game, I have talked myself through a bow or firearm shot each and every time. Sometimes this is to myself, other times it is in the lowest of whispers—when I am hunting from a blind. My steadfast firearm routine goes like this: rifle up, steady, put him in the scope, pick a spot, flip the safety, breathe in, exhale, shoot. My bow hunting sequence is: check posture, set release, bow up, relax bow hand, draw, anchor point, pick a spot, place pin, breathe in, exhale, release, and follow through. This may sound like I'm a mental case of some sort, but it has provided me with the consistent ability to drop 98 percent of my firearm game dead in their tracks. That is not a boast; it's a fact. This happens only through the commitment to practice what I advise to others.

RECAP

1. See the buck
2. Confirm you want to shoot it
3. Stop looking at the antlers
4. Raise the rifle
5. Put the buck in the scope
6. Pick the spot to shoot
7. Flip the safety off
8. Take a deep breath in
9. Exhale halfway or all the way
10. Compress the trigger and shoot

Conscious Mind: Use this list as an internal chant to keep the routine of preparing to shoot consistent and, more importantly, to keep the conscious mind from straying from the job at hand, which is making an accurate shot at a buck. It also prevents the mind from looking at the buck's antlers because you are concentrating on doing this one task well. When your conscious mind is focused on activating mind and body in the taking the shot, anxiety disorder becomes nonexistent. You have physically eliminated your mind's ability to stray to other things, such as the buck's antlers.

I liken this analysis to several occasions when I was a light-heavyweight boxer when I lived in Brooklyn, while I was in the army, and much later in life

I'm a passionate boxing fan. One of my favorite boxers is former heavyweight Jerry Cooney. We're at the VIP "Gala" Cocktail Reception during the 2015 Hall of Fame Induction weekend. Photo Credit: Peter Cody Fiduccia.

Michael Lee Moorer is one of only four men to win one or more versions of the world heavyweight championship on three separate occasions! He was also the former world lightweight champ. Moorer ranks high on my list of all-time favorite boxers. Photo Credit: Peter Cody Fiduccia.

when I lived in Vail, Colorado. Whenever I entered the ring, I didn't allow myself to look at the opponent—even when the referee took us through the prefight rules. I concentrated instead on what my first round routine would be for each individual fight, and while the ref talked, I lipped my routine to myself. When the bell rang, I consciously talked myself through the fight. Most times it went something like this: jab, jab, jab, uppercut, jab, jab, uppercut, right cross, step back. Set, jab, jab, body shot, jab, jab, jab, uppercut, body shot. This continued throughout the fight. Rarely did I stare at the opponent between rounds. I needed my conscious mind to focus on the fight and not the fact that my adversary might be taller, more muscular, or may look more fearsome than I wanted him to appear.

Out of the fifty-two fights that I accumulated over more than a dozen years, I only lost two. The two losses were both categorically due to a lapse in my routine. One was with a boxer reported to have exceptional hand speed and knockout power. Both were qualities I supposedly had. Other boxers' information intimidated me so much that during the first round I looked at his impressive body size and sculptured physique, and I never saw his foot movement set me up for the

Kate shares a humorous moment with former two-time world heavyweight champ Riddick Bowe. Bowe won the WBA, WBC, and IBF titles and became the undisputed heavyweight champ in 1992. Kate and I, along with our friend Fred Greer (Food Safety Inspector for New York Custom Processing and former USDA inspector), annually attend this Gala reception together. Photo Credit: Peter Cody Fiduccia.

knockout blow he delivered. My conscious mind couldn't cope with doing more than one job well.

The second loss was due to overconfidence. My adversary was smaller, and he reportedly wasn't as fast as I was. My nickname was The Rabbit. My coach apparently detected my egotism early on. In the corner after the first round, he said, and I'm paraphrasing here, "Hey you, pay ★&^#$@ attention to his footwork. This kid is setting you up for a big right hand." I never saw the big right hand coming, but I sure as hell felt it. I was too busy silently concentrating on how this guy could never beat me, and this conscious lapse left me with a huge bulbous knot on my temple and a severely deflated ego.

No matter what sport you are involved in, you must be consciously involved in what you are doing at the moment it counts most. If it requires talking to yourself to get the job done effectively, so be it. Therein lies one of the problems that can hinder hunters afflicted with buck fever. Many are too embarrassed to admit to themselves and their hunting companions that they get overexcited when they see game.

To conquer buck fever, you have to admit you have the problem. So here, too, you must talk to yourself and say: "I don't have any reason to be ashamed that I have bouts of buck fever. I know I have a problem. I get too excited when I see a buck I want to shoot. It's affecting my hunting abilities, and I want that to stop." Share the confession with your hunting buddies. If they ridicule you, ignore them. Do you really care what they think, anyway? Is it that big of a deal that you get excited and nervous when you see a buck? If it is, it shouldn't be. Hunters get overexcited because they basically care too much about making a good shot. Being concerned about something often throws a wrench in our conscious mind. It disrupts the attentiveness of what is happening at any given moment, and bam, you don't see the big right hand coming!

So there you have it. If you have struggled with buck fever or any of the terms related to it—anxiety disorder, severe nervousness syndrome, or acute hyperventilation—now you know it is a qualified and recognized medical condition that has been unnecessarily endured by millions of hunters throughout North America for way too long. With determination, conviction, and practice, you can stop overreacting to antlered game. Instead, you can become a Cool-Hand Luke-type hunter who will not fall apart with overexcitement when antlered game approaches, which will help you put meat in the freezer and mounts in your trophy room. More importantly, you will have more fun when you hunt by eliminating bad hunts.

One Last Thought on Buck Fever: The only time to contract a case of buck fever is when you walk up to your buck and he's lying deader than snot on the ground. Now you can do the heebie-jeebies dance of success. It no longer matters if you get over-excited because you're supposed to be that happy now—unless you have high blood pressure problems. In that case, stay relaxed, Cool-Hand Luke!

Chapter Twenty-One

Don't Get Patterned, Keep Deer Guessing

Are deer catching on to your pattern because you repeatedly use the same tree stand? Sometimes deer will sense this, and other times they simply don't. But the concept that a hunter can use the same stand repeatedly and still see deer from it is not something a majority of professional or experienced hunters believe. Most pros and veteran hunters will tell you that deer will unconditionally begin to pattern a hunter who uses the same stand day in and day out. Moreover, they highly recommend that hunters avoid using the same stand routinely and often add that overuse of a stand will prevent a hunter from killing a buck, especially an adult buck.

Admittedly their advice is, to a degree, spot on. But as I have said for many years, nothing about deer hunting tactics—and, friends, I mean nothing—is written in stone!

There are no absolutes or guarantees that abiding by or using certain strategies, mine included, will assure you of always getting your buck. Not by a long shot. Thanks to Lady Luck and her alter ego, Murphy's Law, a hunter can have incredible deer hunting successes or heart-wrenching failures without doing anything at all to cause either.

This buck has spotted something he is not comfortable with. Avoid this look by a buck simply by not over using a stand location day after day. Photo Credit: Ted Rose.

Photo Credit Ted Rose.

So while there are times deer can pattern hunters, there are other times deer don't pattern hunters. The key is for hunters to evaluate and recognize when deer catch on and when they don't. By doing so, you allow Lady Luck to shine more often on your hunting excursions and avoid Murphy's Law. This hypothesis is especially applicable to the question asked in the beginning of this chapter: Are deer patterning you?

On opening day of the November 2014 firearm season, I saw four bucks and more than a dozen does from a blind called Big View, one of my two favorite blinds on our farm. By 2 p.m., I was loading an eight-point buck into my Arctic Cat Prowler 550 XT. With my tag filled, I decided to use the blind over the next several days for exploratory reconnaissance missions to see if other bucks were still coming into our fields in search of estrus does or food. Even deep into the firearm season and into the late December muzzleloader season, it isn't unusual for us to see twenty to forty deer as they feed, on and off, during the entire day in the food plots that Big View overlooks. Over the next week, I consistently saw no fewer than twenty deer feeding in the fields below the blind. Their behavior was a clear indication to me that they were not overly pressured, and they hadn't been able to pattern my approach even though I was using the blind repeatedly.

Big View, which is an enclosed, raised blind, sits at the end of a row of mature trees at the highest elevation on our land. The view from it includes 24.49 acres of plantable fields. One large seven-acre field planted in a variety of food plots is sectioned off by rows of pines. It helps make the entire field appear as four smaller and more secluded fields to our deer. Of those 24.49 acres, about ten acres are planted in food plots, including traditional types of small grains, brassicas, clovers, sugar beets, and chicory, and more than an acre is planted in fruit and chestnut trees. All the plots act to draw deer into them throughout the entire year, especially during the hunting season.

The remaining 14.49 acres are left in standing hay. By late fall, the uncut hay can reach heights of

An image taken from Big View. While the photo only captured the buck and four does, there were several more deer scattered in the field just out of view. By 4:30 p.m., thirty-one deer and thirty-one turkeys could be seen in the field. Photo Credit: Fiduccia Enterprises.

several feet, and it provides deer with excellent fawning grounds, bedding areas, and escape cover. Throughout the summer and early fall, I mow more than a dozen narrow, zigzag trails through the hay to help us reach Big View and all the other blinds and tree stands along the edges of the fields. No matter what direction the wind is blowing, the trails allow us to reach any of several blinds without being seen or scented by the deer approaching or feeding in food plots.

On the second Monday of New York's firearm season, my cousin Leo and I began to walk up one of the several cleared trails used to reach Big View. While we walked, we stopped a few times to poke our heads over the standing hay to see if there were deer in the fields below the blind. When we got within sixty yards of Big View, we paused to look again, and this time we saw several does in a food plot at the end of the last sectioned-off field named Finger Field, a long rectangular field that is 315 yards below Big View.

We ducked back onto the trail and continued carefully toward the blind. I was totally focused on the deer below us when I heard Leo whisper, "Buck!" I turned just in time to see a six-point buck standing along our border seventy-five yards from where we stood on the trail. He had plainly just crossed the barbed-wire fence onto our land from the neighbor's property. We were about twenty-five yards from reaching Big View. Although the deer that regularly used the lower field had not yet patterned my daily scouting approach, the buck was now aware of human pressure, and I suspected he would use the information to approach the fields from a different way in order to avoid any further close calls. over the remainder of the hunting season.

Although at this particular encounter, the six-point buck had not connected my advance to the blind with him patterning me, if I had bumped him just a time or two more, he would have without a doubt started to buttonhole my approach to this blind. When a hunter uses a stand routinely, it doesn't take long for deer, especially a savvy adult buck or doe, to catch on to the hunter's approach.

I learned this lesson very early in my deer hunting exploits. Throughout the seventies, opening day of deer season would find me hunting a 125-acre farm located a few miles from the hamlet of Grahamsville in Sullivan County, New York. I had exclusive permission to hunt the property and had built a few permanent tree stands on it. I would go to my favorite stand most often throughout the entire season.

The first couple of days, I would see a considerable number of deer. By the end of the week, however, the number dropped exponentially. By the end of the second weekend of the season, my sightings were few and far between. Hunting from a favorite stand was something that I saw other hunters do regularly, so I thought nothing of using the same tactic. I frequently used the same two or three stands for two more seasons before the light finally came on and I realized deer were anticipating or, worse yet, recognizing my routine. They knew when I would approach in the morning, when I would leave for lunch or change stands, and when I would return. It became apparent to me that the deer knew when it was safe to pass through the block of hardwoods I was hunting and when it wasn't. Once I understood what I was doing wrong, I made the adjustment.

For many years after that, I avoided using the same stand more than twice in a row. In some instances, I would hunt a stand once and then not return to hunt it again for at least a few days. There are about fifteen million deer hunters in the United States. My bet is that an unpredictable number of them routinely go to either their favorite stand or the same few stands over the entire deer season—a habit that becomes so routine it likely goes unnoticed or realized by hunters for countless years. Worse yet, a hunter's habits often become obvious to deer. The reality is, deer recognize a hunter's repeated patterns quicker and better than most hunters ever get to know the deer's habits.

It doesn't take long for deer to associate footfalls, human scent, human voices, and time patterns that generally go along with humans entering and exiting their home grounds. Biologists claim many research studies have documented that deer watch hunters as they approach their stands without the hunters ever seeing or realizing the deer are watching them. This behavior is part of the reason deer sightings drop so dramatically after the first week of hunting season. Deer quickly identify the presence of humans and adjust their movement patterns. Again, thanks to countless deer research studies that have been done over the past three decades, we have learned from these findings that deer don't move from their home range and hightail it to the next county to avoid

I can only imagine how many hunters, including me, have been walked by a buck like this as we move to our stands. No hunter, no matter how skilled, escapes this scenario. Photo Credit: CanStock Photos.

hunting season human pressure; they simply tweak their behavior slightly and find much more secure places to hide.

To demonstrate and support this point, consider this study. Dr. Michael Chamberlain and one of his former graduate students, Justin Thayer, who at the time of the study were both at Louisiana State University, found deer actually keep track of hunter movements. The duo performed a radio telemetry collar study on a forty-thousand-acre section of hardwoods in Louisiana by putting collars on twenty-two bucks and monitoring their movements. The land was hunted by members of several hunting clubs each fall, which created a substantial amount of human presence and hunting pressure. Not surprisingly, a considerable percentage of adult bucks were able to avoid being killed by the hunters even though the research determined the bucks were often close by.

Even more interestingly, Thayer said, "Time and time again hunters would tell us that they knew bucks were around, but they never saw them. Many times I would take a reading and know a buck was within fifty yards of a deer blind, but the hunter never saw it."

So what is the countermove to avoid this problem? My answer has been to keep deer I hunt guessing about when I'm going to a particular stand. I also realized I had to keep my hunting strategies, such as rattling, calling, and using decoys, from becoming routine, as well. So I altered my tactics by including deviations to my rattling sequences and changed the pitch of my deer calls—but not the volume so much.

I also started to play the shell game with my deer stands, but only after certain components became obvious. For instance, when I'm hunting on our 192 acres of land, I can immediately detect when there is a sudden decline in deer movement. Once I determine that deer numbers are lessening, I know it is time for me to change my stand locations to keep deer guessing as to where I will show up. If I'm hunting stands near my fields, sanctuary, and woods—a ninety-five-acre section—on the west side of my land and notice a drop in deer sightings, I quickly switch over to the ninety-seven entirely wooded acres on the east side of my property and hunt from different stands there for a few days and vice versa.

But not all hunters have the options to make switches to different stands and areas. If your options are limited, then what are the alternatives to limit deer from patterning you? One solution is to keep deer guessing. Whether that entails entering and exiting stands by a few different routes, leaving an ATV or vehicle parked in a different area, or using different rhythms when rattling or using deer calls, the

During the peak of the breeding season, an adult buck can cover miles while trying to locate a receptive doe. In doing so, he may not return to his original starting point for two to three days. Photo Credit: Depositphotos.

key is to keep deer guessing as to exactly what they can expect from you. Another effective tactic to keep them guessing is to use one of my chief recommended strategies, which is to hunt a stand from 10 a.m. to 1 p.m.—a time when many hunters have left the woods for a lunch break etc. As I have written since 1988, this is one surefire tactic to kill an adult buck—at least as surefire as any strategy can be. Now that you're thinking I have made a case for why you should never hunt the same stand day after day, let me throw a wrench into that assessment. As I asked earlier, is it remotely possible to hunt from the same stand repeatedly? And is it possible to see deer consistently from it, including mature bucks, ah, hmm, eh? You can go to the deer hunting bank that it is most definitely possible. However, there's a caveat. It can absolutely be done but only under certain conditions. If the right conditions exist and specific strategies are followed, it is certainly possible to hunt the same stand for several days in a row without having deer pattern you and alter their movements.

One of the scenarios that I firmly believe allows hunters to go to the same stands repeatedly without being patterned occurs during the primary rut. It's not groundbreaking news that during the rut, bucks, especially adult bucks, hardly ever stick to a regular mode of travel. Instead, they cover as much ground as possible in search of estrus does. Often a buck does not return to the same ground he scoured the prior day looking for receptive does, thus he avoids checking the same area two days in a row.

This breeding behavior vastly reduces the chances of a hunter being patterned by a particular buck—mostly since the odds of the buck being in the same area the following day are diminished. Furthermore, the primary rut also helps attract transient bucks into a new area to search for does to breed. When this happens, the odds of seeing a buck that hasn't been in the area before and hasn't been alerted to you using your stand previously are dramatically increased—even if you have hunted the same stand a few days in a row.

Some deer authorities advocate that it can be beneficial during the primary rut to play the shell game. They recommend hunters should move from one stand to another every day. However, I feel strongly that stand jumping, particularly during the primary rut, may indeed lessen a hunter's chances to kill a good buck rather than increase them. Why? If the stand you are about to give up on happens to be in a good location that naturally attracts does and bucks during the rut, it should be hunted, not abandoned, even if that means hunting the stand several times in a row. The probability of taking a buck from that stand far outweighs the risk of jumping from one stand to another. This is practical only when you have been paying attention to a few crucial common-sense components, such as keeping human scent to a bare minimum and arriving and leaving at different times.

The next scenario in which I believe a stand can be hunted several times in a row is when hunters can alter their entry and exit routes to the stand to evade deer detection. As I described in the start of this chapter, Leo and I spooked a buck from its bed on the way to my Big View stand that overlooked a large section of fields planted in a variety of food plots. Even though we jumped the buck on the way in, I knew the odds were high that we would still use the stand and get an opportunity to see another buck or two while posted there.

The food plots were already choked with does, yearlings, and fawns, and the chances of one or more of them being in estrus were more than reasonable. So now all we had to do was get into Big View without busting the deer from the fields below. We slowly walked the last dozen or so yards hunched over to make our outlines look less human and more like four-footed animals to the deer feeding a couple of hundred yards below us. We reached the stand without alerting a single deer, climbed in, and waited. By 4:30 p.m., we had seen twenty-eight deer, including a few small-racked bucks. Leo chose to wait to hunt the stand the following day rather than take one of the smaller-antlered bucks we were watching. We left the stand without being detected by the deer. We just quietly moved off the hill using a different trail from the one we walked in on.

You're not committing deer-hunting hari-kiri by using a stand regularly, despite what most experienced hunters and deer

By moving slowly and using stealth-type skills, it is possible to get to a stand that overlooks fields even when deer are there. Photo Credit: Ted Rose.

experts preach about not overhunting a stand. I assure you that under the right circumstances it can be done. A few of my industry friends also support this hypothesis.
Among them are Greg Miller and Tom Indebro. Both are acclaimed long-time deer
hunting authorities, and both hold to the belief that under certain circumstances deer
stands can be hunted more often than previously thought without fear of having
bucks or does pattern a hunter.

For instance, it is common knowledge to most hunters that deer are highly adaptable creatures. The proof is how deer have evolved to successfully live in metropoli-
tan and suburban areas where human occurrences are ongoing. When deer undergo
repeated non-harmful exposure to humans, they become more accepting of human
presence. Under these particular circumstances, a deer stand can be used more often,
and deer will tolerate the repeated use more.

Tom Indebro owns and operates one of the nation's most successful deer hunting
lodges, Bluff Country Outfitters in Buffalo County, Wisconsin. Tom is a deer guru. He
eats, sleeps, and talks about deer incessantly. I have hunted at his place a few times, and
each time I have come away learning something from him about deer. Tom feels that
deer become jaded to human presence. He said, "Buffalo County has many areas that
see a lot of human activities to begin with. With all the farming, logging, and ATV use,
there are spots where deer see humans a couple of times each day. When that happens, it
gets to the point where they stop caring. I know that is the case here on my home farm."

Indebro typically has several hunters stalking deer on his land during any one week.
Sometimes he tries to convince a hunter to switch stands, as he did with me when I
was there. While I was open to Tom's suggestions, many of his hunters refused to switch
stands. Even though they are hunting the same stands more than is normally recommended, Tom said, "They are seeing mature bucks almost every sit, so why change
their stand?"

While this may sound a bit extreme, I can assure you I have experienced similar
deer behavior on our farm. During the deer season, I can walk by an area we call future
pond, which is at the far west end of our refuge and about seventy-five yards from our
food plots. On several occasions during the firearm season, I have seen both does and
bucks watch me from their beds as I walk past the area. Once deer get used to seeing
and hearing humans within their home range, they become somewhat jaded to human
presence. This doesn't mean an adult buck won't head for the hills if you casually walk
into this bedroom. But it does mean you can carefully enter and exit the same stand
more often than you would imagine without over alarming resident deer.

Conclusion

The fundamental point is that deer can pattern hunters if the hunters are careless and show no regard for entering and exiting their stands or if they fail to change their hunting tactics and use the same strategies time and time again. Deer will also start to pattern hunters who are complacent about what time they arrive, leave, and return to their stands or those who fail to keep human scent to a minimum. Deer will be quick to pick up human scent, and when they do, it is a safe bet that they will swiftly move from the area.

On the flip side of the coin, under certain conditions, stands can be hunted in succession when the right tactics are used. Each circumstance is specific and requires a common-sense analysis to determine if a stand you are hunting will allow the deer to tolerate repeated use. But it can be done if the conditions mentioned previously exist and the correct methods are abided by.

One of the most important components about being able to hunt a stand numerous times without having a buck pattern you is to remember that bucks move in and out of different areas repeatedly during the rut. Therefore, spooking one buck doesn't inevitably mean you have ruined your chances to hunt that stand the next day. In fact, if the buck you spooked was either with a receptive doe or his olfactory senses told him one was definitely in the area, he will likely show up again in the area the following day.

Do your homework to prevent getting patterned by deer. If you decide that you can hunt a stand much more often, stick to the plans included here, particularly about how to get to and leave that stand from different places each day. You may end up discovering those simple tactics will allow you to hunt your favorite stand without concern about being patterned by your deer, which gives you the outdoorsmen's edge.

Chapter Twenty-Two

The Surefire Way to Hold Bucks: Create a Refuge

One of the most important elements in creating better deer and other wildlife hunting opportunities on land that is owned or leased is to create a wildlife refuge or sanctuary. Spring is the best time to put that plan into motion.

The primary rule for creating a refuge is that it must be treated exactly as the word is defined in dictionaries: **"A condition of being sheltered from pursuit; an area of safety, free of danger, trespass, or trouble; a place where no harm can come to its occupants; any place safe accommodations; a place of total immunity."** Merely setting aside a section of acreage and calling it a refuge but not treating it as such will not work as it is intended to and therefore is not worth the effort.

The prerequisite for making a refuge is to create a secure area for deer that remains absolutely undisturbed from any type of human intrusion forever!

We intentionally bought sanctuary signs that are worded bluntly. The capped words KEEP OUT are meant mostly to be terse toward ourselves. They are forceful reminders that the definition and purpose of a refuge means to STAY OUT! Photo Credit: Peter Cody Fiduccia.

Photo Credit: CanStock Photo/EEI_Tony.

This is the only way a refuge, sanctuary, safe haven, or whatever word you choose will allow deer and other wildlife to feel categorically safe and secure. Once they do, they will use it consistently to seek protection from human predation.

Whether a refuge is created on land totaling fifty acres, one thousand acres, or more, that area must never undergo human trespass again. I drum that point home because it often ignored. If you set aside a portion of land as a refuge, stay the heck out of it if you want it to actually attract and hold deer, including mature bucks.

The total amount of land dedicated to a refuge should be about 5 to 15 percent of the total acreage of the property. Additionally, for a refuge to be an attractive safe haven to deer, it must be planned carefully. A sanctuary should include the thickest overgrown cover on the property, a thick stand of mature evergreens if possible, a wet area, and some high knobs even if they are only slightly higher than the rest of the land. Most importantly, it should have a small natural water source—even a couple of tiny man-made potholes that collect rain and runoff will do. If possible, it should have some natural forage within its borders, perhaps a few apple and pear trees, and a couple of mature oaks for acorns would be a bonus. The most functional refuges include other nutritious food sources just outside their borders, such as food plots and Dunstan chestnut trees. It is also highly recommended that a refuge be set up as close to the center of the property as possible.

Some of the fastest growing shrubs to include are bayberry, which grows to six- to nine-foot heights; high brush cranberry, which reaches ten to fifteen feet tall; sandbar willows, which grow up to twenty feet and are excellent deer forage; sumac; and dogwood. Deer will eat and bed in all these plantings. You can also hinge-cut existing trees to provide more reachable natural food sources. The trunks of the trees will create cover off the ground, which decreases visibility. If the site is a first-rate location but lacks some of the important elements mentioned, take time to create them before dedicating the area as a sanctuary. This also provides the opportunity to put in plants for coverage, a pothole or two for water, fifty or more white pine seedlings, and some hard and soft mast trees if need be. It won't be beneficial to do these things after the refuge is established. The end goal for creating a sanctuary is to provide abundant cover that will eventually be hard to see and walk through, full of edible plants and browse, with a source of water, and, most crucially, complete privacy and safety for wildlife.

When a refuge is created properly, deer learn quickly to retreat to it in order to feel secure within its boundaries. Once that happens, they seldom need or desire to leave the refuge to seek other properties. The only time a doe or buck will forsake the security

Once adult bucks like this find a refuge that remains entirely free of human trespass—they're prompt to hang a "home-sweet-home" sign up within its borders. Photo Credit: CanStock Photo/ brm1949.

of a sanctuary is during the rut, but even then it will only be for short periods of time.

Creating a refuge on our land that includes the elements I've mentioned has helped tremendously in attracting and holding deer on our 192 acres. In fact, creating a total nonhunting, no-trespass refuge zone has been the single most effective strategy to increase our daylight deer sightings, including adult bucks. We were fortunate that the location of our twenty-six-acre refuge, which occupies 14 percent of our total acreage, had sufficient cover and almost all the other elements within it. More beneficially, it is located almost in the middle of the land. Three sides of our sanctuary lay adjacent to our planted fields. The other side borders an area with dozens of apple trees and thick second growth. After posting the sanctuary in 2001, we never entered it again for any reason. While I am certainly curious about what the interior area looks like, the benefits of creating a complete year-round safe haven far outweighs trespassing into our refuge to satisfy my inquisitiveness.

At seminars and other events, I get the opportunity to talk with hundreds, if not thousands, of hunters and deer managers every year. They often relate stories about their sanctuaries. The conversation inevitably gets to a point where they mention a variety of reasons why they "had to" enter their sanctuary. One of the prime justifications is to look for shed antlers. The second most popular excuse is to check out the number of scrapes and rubs. A wide array of other justifications range from looking for tracks and other deer signs to logging the area to planting food plots or fruit trees. Unbelievably, some

At my seminars over the years I have heard uncountable stories about why hunters entered their sanctuaries. I can count the acceptable reasons on less than the fingers of one hand. Photo Credit: Fiduccia Enterprises.

people have told me they entered their sanctuary to count the number of deer they see while walking through it! This is the most ridiculous of all reasons to enter a refuge!

The only reasonable and ethical reason for anyone to enter their refuge is to retrieve a wounded deer. Even then, specific rules must be established and followed without exception.

If a wounded deer enters our sanctuary—luckily it hasn't happened since it was established—we don't allow anyone to search for it during daylight hours. Searching for a wounded deer after dark accomplishes two goals. First, it prevents spooking the wounded deer out of the sanctuary and perhaps onto a neighbor's property. Second, it doesn't disturb the deer within the refuge, which is the key element for creating the sanctuary in the first place.

Spook an adult buck from a sanctuary just one time and he may not return to it again—at least not for a while. Entering the refuge after dark reduces the possibility of kicking up deer because a majority will have left the refuge to feed. This can be a difficult rule to follow, but it will go a long way to help keep the area secure for deer.

Develop specific guidelines on how to go about retrieving the wounded deer from the sanctuary. First, it must firmly be established that the deer is actually in the sanctuary. Soon after the wounded deer is suspected of entering the refuge, set hunters in stands nearby and let things settle down for an hour if enough daylight is available.

Then have the hunter who wounded the deer walk slowly along the refuge's borders to carefully look for blood with a high-powered flashlight if necessary. If no blood is found, the deer is most likely still in the refuge. However, if blood is found outside the borders, it obviously left the sanctuary and can be tracked without entering the refuge.

This rule prevents an unnecessary trespass through the refuge. If it is determined, however, that the deer is in the refuge and may be alive and suffering, the only ethical option left is to enter the refuge to retrieve it. No more than two hunters should be allowed into the sanctuary to look for and recover the animal after it gets dark.

Over the past fourteen years, our refuge has developed into a high-traffic deer area. Throughout the year, countless deer trails lead in and out of it. Deer are often seen in the sanctuary either bedding or standing watching us while we work or plant nearby fields. They have come to realize over time that no matter what is happening outside the protected area, they are completely safe, as they are left totally undisturbed while they remain inside. As soon as the neighbors begin shooting, deer pour into our refuge knowing it is the safe place. By the second day of firearm season, the number of deer in our refuges swell noticeably.

Once deer recognize where a refuge is, they will use it for security and cover throughout all four seasons of the year. Photo Credit: Ted Rose.

When a refuge is created, it will offer a haven to several groups of does, who rapidly learn it is a place of year-round safety. It is not unusual for us to sit in one of our deer blinds in late summer or early fall and watch up to forty deer in our food plots. Of that number, we have established that at least half of them enter the food plots from different points in our refuge.

Once a sanctuary attracts adult female deer, they will come to call it home. Inherently, they will attract adult bucks, particularly throughout all the phases of the rut. We have also documented that some bucks we have shot have never been seen while scouting from our blinds in summer or captured in photos by our trail cameras in fall. Again, the key for our refuge's success is entirely attributed to the fact that we absolutely enforce our strict off-limits policies. For the past fourteen years we have never stepped foot in our refuge—not to look for deer signs, rubs, scrapes, shed antlers, or to count the deer. We can't call it a refuge if it's penetrated for any reason other than to recover a wounded deer.

I assure you that you can take everything I mentioned to the deer hunting bank for immediate success. Create a refuge, and you will see the difference in the number of deer on your land in one season. The excitement and anticipation of creating a refuge result in better odds to be in the right stand at the right time when an estrus doe unknowingly coerces a buck from the security of the sanctuary and lures him past your stand! Then, and only then, will you realize the importance and practicality of creating a place of total safety that is never disturbed for any reason whatsoever.

Our sanctuary signs read, "Keep Out... Sanctuary!" I bought them not only to warn others, but also to remind Kate, Cody, and me about the absolute importance of never penetrating our refuge!

Sanctuary signs are inexpensive. Buy enough to post your refuge copiously enough to discourage anyone from entering it. Photo Credit: Fiduccia Enterprises.

Chapter Twenty-Three

No Fields to Plant?
No Problem!

There is no doubt that planting wildlife food plots is all the rage for hunters who either own or lease lands. However, not all hunters who have property or rent hunting lands have either the availability of fields to plant or have the time, money, and equipment to plant food plots. So what is a hunter to do? Well the fact is, while planting food plots definitely helps provide a tremendous amount of nutritious food for deer and other wildlife, it isn't the only way to provide quality forage for wildlife.

Back in 1984, when I gave my first deer hunting seminar at a sport show at the World Hunting & Fishing Outdoor Expo in Rockland County, New York, I talked about fertilizing natural vegetation to improve both the habitat and deer hunting on any given property. I discussed how fertilizing oak trees would improve the mast harvest and how hunters could attract wildlife by fertilizing shrubs and other vegetation on their lands.

Although traditional food plots like this winter-hardy marathon red clover provide quality nutrition for deer, many naturally available shrubs also provide highly nutritious vegetation, particularly when they are regularly fertilized, pruned, and otherwise cared for by landowners. Photo Credit: Fiduccia Enterprises.

Photo Credit: Fiduccia Enterprises.

There are some key benefits to fertilizing natural vegetation as opposed to planting food plots. It is a project that doesn't require clearing and preparing plots to plant seeds. It is also a less expensive undertaking when compared to planting food plots. Basically, all that is needed is a quality fertilizer—T-19 fertilizer works on a majority of shrubs and other natural vegetation—and possibly lime.

An important factor about fertilizing shrubs and other vegetation is to define what plants deer prefer eating. Then locate plants established in the areas that receive at least five to six hours of sunlight per day. They will be the best plants to fertilize because sunlight is the prime ingredient in growing healthy browse. Once that is accomplished, the next step is to take soil samples for each shrub or browse that is going to be fertilized. If you skip this step, you are wasting time, effort, and money. Send the soil samples in to your local conservation resource offices for analysis. Once the pH level is determined, you will have the correct information about how to get the pH factor to where it should be. A good pH level usually falls from 6.0 to 6.9. A reading of 7.0 is considered neutral. A reading of 5.9 or lower demonstrates the soil is acidic—the lower the pH, the more acidic the soil.

After a season of fertilizing and possibly liming shrubs and vegetation, you will begin to see a few changes. The leaves will be darker green in color, they will sprout more shoots, each overall plant will look larger and healthier, and they will produce a higher volume of berries, etc.

In this chapter, I have named some shrubs and other plants that will respond well to fertilizer. Of course, enhance your deer foods according to what types of shrubs and plants are native to your property. For the food plotter who only plants and grows clovers, legumes, grains, brassicas, grasses, and other seeds, enhancing the natural vegetation on your land will help round out your food plot program nicely.

As an added benefit to fertilizing naturally growing browse, deer and other wildlife utilize many of these indigenous plants, trees, shrubs, and bushes as bedding areas and shelter from inclement weather, as well as places to have and keep fawns safe. Other wildlife use the browse to nest, rear their young, and provide safe travel corridors and runways.

There is an extensive assortment of wild growing shrubs and browse on the white-tail deer's list of preferred food items, including a variety of wildflowers, woody plants, forbs, shrubs, bushes, groundcover, leaves, and other plants, such as mushrooms and even poison ivy, which ranks high on their list of favored items. Regrettably, there are too many to include in this chapter. Therefore, I have listed some of the natural shrubs and other plants that will benefit you to fertilize. The plants listed are also good choices to plant on your property to increase naturally occurring vegetation for deer to eat. When I fertilize my shrubs, I use either an NPK of 15-3-3 or 15-5-10.

Natural Growing Vegetation to Fertilize, Lime, or Plant

An American holly's fruit is consumed by big game animals, birds, and small mammals. Photo Credit: Depositphotos.

American Holly: American holly is found from central Florida to northeastern Massachusetts, and southern Missouri to south-central Texas. It prefers moist, slightly acidic but well-drained soils, but it is intolerant of extended flooding, saturated soils, or dry conditions. American holly is found in a variety of hardwood forest habitats, most often as an understory tree. It is shade tolerant and slow growing. Its flowers and fruit are consumed by game birds, songbirds, big game, and other animals. This plant makes good protective shelter for deer and other animals. The branches are short and slender, the roots are thick and fleshy, and the flowers are pollinated by bees and other insects, including wasps, ants, and night-flying moths. The berries are reported to be poisonous to humans but are an important survival food for game birds and songbirds that eat them after other food sources are exhausted. The tree also forms a thick canopy, which offers birds protection from predators and storms.

American Plum: The American plum can be described accurately as either a shrub or small tree. It does well in sun or partial shade, and it prefers moist soil that is well drained. It grows as a small understory tree in open forests, but it also grows in open areas and spreads by root suckers. The flowers are white, about one inch across, and fragrant. Deer quickly detect their odor, which attracts them to the shrub. The fruit is about one inch in diameter and grows in clusters that are yellow to red when ripe. The ripe fruit becomes soft and succulent and has a scrumptious flavor to wildlife. The American plum is an important pollen source for native bees. It is heavily relied on by deer and other wildlife for food, browse, and cover.

Arrowwood: Arrowwood prefers full sun or light shade, and it is found growing on open sites ranging from dry hillsides to wetlands among cattails. Its color in fall ranges from purples, reds, and pinks to shades of orange, peach, and yellow. Its flowers are small and creamy white. The berries are dark blue to black, form in flat-topped clusters, and are tiny—only about one fourth of an inch. The fruit is held far longer than on most shrubs, usually well into winter, which makes this a high priority plant to fertilize and lime for winter deer food. Arrowwood is an outstanding shrub for wildlife.

The mature height of the bayberry is 6'-9'. It is a very aromatic plant. The fruit will persist through the winter, providing food for deer and game birds. I plant bayberry. Photo Credit: Depositphotos.

Bayberry: This plant is one of the few naturally growing shrubs that can fix nitrogen back into the soil, which makes it an important plant to fertilize and lime. More interestingly, it is said that bayberry is extraordinarily versatile and will grow well in even the poorest of sandy soils. The mature height of the bayberry is six to nine feet. It is aromatic and will grow in a wide variety of site conditions, from sandy, poor soils to heavy clay soils. Because this plant tolerates extremes, it also thrives in bogs, marshland, and wet woodlands. It grows in areas along roadsides, on sand dunes near mid-Atlantic beaches, and in old abandoned fields. The fruit will persist through the winter, which provides food for deer and game birds. Bayberry bushes are tough, hardy plants that have pleasantly scented foliage and berries. They are native to the continental United States and grow vigorously along the East Coast and throughout the South. Bayberry shrubs are also known as candleberry, tallow shrub, waxberry, and tallow berry.

Beach Plum: A native shrub of the Atlantic coastal region, the beach plum is a round, dense bush that grows four to ten feet tall. It prefers sandy, well-drained soils and full sun, and it has edible fruit that grows one to one and a half inches long. It is a good cover plant. Beautiful white blossoms cover the branches of this shrub-like tree in the spring. The blossoms develop into colorful fruits that all wildlife will eat, including deer, bear, turkey, and game birds. The fruit is popular among people who make it into delicious jams and jellies. The fruit may be bluish purple, red, or even yellow when it ripens in September. It actually flourishes in the poorest acidic soils imaginable. It is so hardy that it tolerates long droughts, subzero cold, and most plant diseases. It's a plant that will work well in any wildlife management fertilizing program. Beach plum usually bears its fruit the year following planting. When fertilized regularly, it will bear abundant fruit almost every year. Beach plum is ranked as a top wildlife food item.

Blackberry and Raspberry: These shrubs are among the more profuse deer forage. They grow and flourish everywhere. They prefer to establish along the edges of fields, along fencerows, in overgrown fields, orchards, and in open or mostly open areas where they can receive full sunlight for most of the day. The fruits they provide are highly sought out by deer and other wildlife, including deer, bear, turkey, grouse, songbirds, and even humans. Large thick stands of these shrubs make excellent deer cover and beds. Blackberry, raspberry, and other species of wild berries make excellent places for game birds to build nests and rear their young. When lands do not have a variety of naturally occurring berry shrubs, it is practical to plant them in both open and some wooded areas, so long as they get at least six hours of sunlight per day.

Each year I order and plant several varieties of wild berries on our lands. All varieties of the berries are highly prized by all big and small game as well as nonhunted species of animals and birds. Photo Credit: Depositphotos.

Bristly Locust: This plant is a deciduous running shrub that likes full sun and medium to dry soils. Because it is among the few nitrogen-fixing species, it can grow in poor soils. It has been grown in acidic soils with pH levels as low as 3.5 and alkaline, or basic, soils with a pH level as high as 8! It will spread naturally by root sprouts into extensive thickets. Anyone looking to create deer cover should put this shrub on their list to fertilize or plant. It is a medium-sized, fast-growing shrub that can reach ten to twelve feet tall. Bristly locust is excellent for erosion control, mine reclamation, or roadside banks. Its seedpods are two to five feet long, and it has a purplish flower. The bristly branches and pods make great cover that is hard to penetrate and create an excellent barrier to prevent prying eyes from seeing into areas along roads, etc. It is not a top plant that wildlife eat, but they seek it for cover, which makes it a worthwhile plant to fertilize.

Common Buttonbush: This is a large deciduous shrub that reaches six to twelve feet tall. It has a flower that forms a ball-like seed cluster approximately one inch in diameter, which is readily eaten by waterfowl. Buttonbush, which prefers wetter areas, is a good shrub to fertilize. It can be found growing along stream banks, cattail marshes, along pond shorelines, and in swampy lands. The leaves are in pairs or threes with blades up to eight inches long. It has glossy dark green leaves that lack significant fall color. The common buttonbush flowers are small, distinctive, dense, spherical clusters with a fringe of pistils protruding beyond the white corollas. Common buttonbush is a long-lasting bush. Its unusual blossoms are white or pale pink one-inch globes. Subsequent rounded masses of nuts persist through the winter. The trunks of this bush are often twisted and gnarly looking, which makes them perfect cover for deer and other wildlife. The branches spread out, which make it look like a small tree. The white flowers resemble pincushions, and the button-like balls of fruit are eaten by deer and other wildlife.

Grey Dogwood: This is a valuable deciduous spreading shrub for wildlife because its high calcium and fat contents make it palatable. In May, the copious white flowers are stunningly attractive. Grey dogwood is a hardy species. It can succeed in any soil of good or moderate fertility and can withstand temperatures down to -13° F (-25° C). The wood is heavy, strong, and extremely shock resistant. The fruits, seeds, flowers, and twigs of this tree are a food source to many species of wildlife, including deer, black bear, turkey, grouse, pheasants, rabbits, beavers, squirrels, and many other nonhunted species of birds and wildlife. However, the seeds of this tree are poisonous to humans. Dogwood provides excellent shelter and habitat for deer and other game. Grey dogwood was once considered a weed because of its ability to spread in disturbed areas. It is one of the few native shrubs that can persist along roadsides invaded by buckthorn and shrub honeysuckle.

Eastern Red Cedar: This is a columnar tree that, when grown in groups, can reach heights of thirty to fifty feet. Eastern red cedar prefers open, well-drained sites. Its twigs are readily browsed by all species of deer. The female tree bears a small blue berry, which provides food for all types of game and nonhunted animals. Male trees bear a tiny cone. Cedar provides important nesting and secure cover for deer and other wildlife, particularly in winter when the dense foliage protects game from foul weather and cold temperatures. It also helps them escape detection from predators, especially in large stands. The berries serve as an important winter food for birds. Deer will seek out eastern red cedar in winter to eat its berries and to use it as a source of cover from the elements. Male deer often rub their antlers on cedar.

Elderberry is a native shrub of North America that grows up to fifteen feet in height. It prefers moist, organic soils. Photo Credit: Depositphotos.

Elderberry: This is a native deciduous shrub of North America that grows up to fifteen feet in height. Elderberry prefers moist, organic soil. The fruit is dark purple to black and about one eighth of an inch in size. Elderberries are relished by many game birds, deer, bear, and other mammals. Deer also eat the twigs and leaves. Elderberry is a fast grower and aggressive competitor with weeds and herbaceous species. Individual plants don't live long, however root masses produce new shoots quickly. Fertilizing elderberry can extend its lifespan. Elderberry as a wildlife plant should not be pruned or cut. Pruning will prevent it from growing wild and gnarly, which creates the type of cover deer and other wildlife use for security. This forest species will grow in full sun if the soil is well tilled and watered. It can be planted as a hedge or alone. Elderberry provides effective erosion control on moist sites. The berries grow in clusters, and along with its large flat-topped white flowers, they are edible to humans and used for making jams, pies, or wine. Deer and other wildlife seek this plant out for both food and cover. Native Americans made whistles and flutes from the stems.

Highbush Cranberry: This is a deciduous shrub that is actually not a cranberry at all, though its fruit strongly resembles cranberries in both appearance and taste. Highbush cranberry is a member of the honeysuckle family. Deer

The fruit of this plant is eaten by deer, bear, turkey, rabbits, grouse, pheasants, squirrels, and many other nonhunted animals. Photo Credit: Depositphotos.

seek it out as a food source, bedding area, and cover. It is a spreading, upright shrub of ten to fifteen feet tall. It makes large flower clusters in spring of four to five inches and bears a bright red edible fruit in the fall that lasts well into winter. It is noted for attracting wildlife, such as deer, bear, turkey, rabbits, grouse, pheasants, squirrels, and many other nonhunted animals that eat the fruit that time of year. When seeking highbush cranberry to fertilize, look in semi-open areas with moist, well-drained soils.

Juneberry: This shrub is a small, suckering, white-flowering shrub that will grow from three to eighteen feet. It produces an abundance of succulent bluish-purple berries in July that all wildlife eat, especially deer. Juneberry will tolerate the harsh climates of the north and alkaline soil, which makes it an easy shrub to plant and grow.

Prairie Willow: This plant is a deciduous shrub that can form dense thickets. It is medium-sized and grows three to nine feet tall. It prefers sandy, well-drained, open sites and grows well on drier sites in full sun but will tolerate partial shade. The best aspect of this plant is that it grows in thick clusters that make good visual barriers from the neighbor's property or along roads. It is also an excellent choice to create bedding areas for deer and other wildlife to use as a cover and to escape from inclement weather. Like all willows, it is a valuable food source, as its leaves, bark, buds, and catkins are eaten by various wildlife.

Pussy Willow: This thin-branched, medium-sized deciduous shrub will grow up to twenty feet tall! Locate pussy willow in wet areas, including marshes, stream banks, flooded ditches, or wet bottomlands. Grown in thick, heavy stands, deer will use it for cover. It is also an important browse species for all types of wildlife.

Red-Osier Dogwood: This is a medium-sized deciduous shrub with numerous stems that reach three to nineteen feet in height. The fruit is preferred mostly by ruffed grouse but will be eaten by deer and turkey, as well. It can be located in wet open areas. Wildlife also use this shrub as a windbreak and will seek out dense stands to escape from winter weather. Deer eat the stems and leaves of red-osier dogwood.

Rhododendron: Thick stands of rhododendron make good cover for deer. It will be found near streams and moist woods and is a favorite deer browse plant in winter.

Sumac: Commonly found in old fields and forest openings, this shrub can grow to twenty feet high. Sumac has heavy, stiff, brown twigs and branches. The leaves are twelve to sixteen inches long, and they exude a white sticky sap. In fall, sumac leaves turn bright red. The bark of the mature sumac is grayish brown and has roughened, raised pores, while it is smooth on young sumac plants. Sumac flowers from May to July. The male and female flowers are found in dense bunches among branched clusters mostly at the end of new growth. Sumac's fruit usually ripens in August or September. Many types of birds and small mammals use young sumac shrubs to nest in or to hide their young. Sumac fruit is eaten by songbirds, as well as game birds. Deer and cottontail rabbits eat the bark and twigs. Deer use dense patches of sumac to seek shelter from inclement weather and to hide from predators.

Most hunters find it hard to believe that deer and other game eat both sumac and poison ivy. Photo Credit: Fiduccia Enterprises.

Wild Grape: The wild grape is a deciduous woody vine. While it prefers to be planted in rich woods and along stream banks, wild grape will grow almost anywhere it can get decent soil and at least a half day of sunlight. The more sun the better. Its vine will rapidly grow up tree trunks to reach full sunlight. I like to make thick stands of this plant in overgrown fields and second growth stands of woods. The fruit is favored by most wildlife, including deer, wild turkey, bear, grouse, etc. Thickets of wild grape are used regularly by deer for cover, fawning, bedding, and as browse. It is one of the most valuable species for wildlife not only because of the fruit, but also because the vine stems provide secure nesting sites from a majority of predators. Wild grape is one of the naturally growing browse that I especially look for on our land. Once I locate it, I will heavily fertilize and lime it year in and year out. Birds, squirrels, and other small animals will eat the grapes as they ripen on the vine. Inevitably, not all the fruit is eaten by small game. Eventually, some of it ends up falling to the forest floor. When it does, deer smell the aroma and travel great distances to eat the fallen grapes.

If your land has a variety of common wild berries, like raspberry, make them a priority to fertilize. Deer consume all types of wild berries. Photo Credit: Depositphotos.

More Shrubs to Consider to Fertilize, Lime, or Plant

American cranberry, American elderberry, American hazelnut, black chokeberry, common chokeberry, Eastern redbud, flowering dogwood, ninebark, silky dogwood, Washington hawthorn, lespedeza serviceberry, wild rose, blueberry coralberry, wild rose elderberry, red raspberry, blueberry, hawthorn, winterberry hollies, dewberry spicebush, common witch hazel, Virginia creeper, Virginia rose, teaberry, partridgeberry, pigeonberry, bunchplum, squirrelberry, wetland rose, white flowering dogwood, toringo crabapple, streamco willow, sandbar willow, dwarf sand cherry, and rugosa rose.

In this chapter (22) and in chapters 23 through 25 I discuss a lot about NPK. NPK is part of the macronutrient group that includes six elements (N, K, Ca, Mg, P, and S). The most common are Nitrogen (N), Phosphorus (P), and Potassium (K). The three are more commonly referred to as NPK. They are all nutrients that all plants require in greater quantities.

There is also a group of elements known as the micronutrient group. Plants need them in smaller quantities. hey include the following elements: Iron (Fe), Manganese (Mn), Copper (Cu), Zinc (Zn), Boron (B), Molybdenum (Mo), Nickel (Ni) and Chlorine (Cl).

The sidebar below lists elements from both the macronutrient group and the micronutrient group. Both groups are known as the "essential elements" needed for all types of healthy plant growth.

C Carbon
H Hydrogen
O Oxygen
P Phosphorous★
K Potassium★
N Nitrogen★
S Sulfur
Ca Calcium★
Fe Iron
Mg Magnesium
B Boron
Mn Manganese
Cu Copper
Zn Zinc
Mo Molybdenum
Cl Chlorine
Ni Nickel
Co Cobalt

Chapter Twenty-Four

Killer Tactic: Fertilize Your Mature Oak Trees

During the fall, acorn mast crop accounts for about 40 percent of a deer's diet when available. Acorns are an important source of fall and winter food. To ensure a good crop of acorns, I considered fertilizing oak trees and wrote an article on this subject in 1983. Until that time, no one else had addressed this overlooked subject in print or electronically. Today, many more hunters understand the importance of improving the nutrition of natural vegetation, which also includes fertilizing hard and soft mast trees—that is, oak and fruit trees.

Although this chapter is dedicated to fertilizing and liming mature oak trees that were more than likely not planted by you, the same fertilizing and liming strategy can be applied to older fruit trees, too. It can also be used on younger oak, chestnut, or fruit trees.

There are a few different mixes of fertilizers that can be used on various types of oak trees. Generally, fertilizer spikes or granular fertilizers will benefit white, red, pin, or sawtooth oak and other hard-mast trees. The fertilizer choices include 18-12-12,

The surefire way to nurse an old apple or other fruit tree that isn't producing a good soft mast crop is to fertilize it regularly. There are many types of fertilizers designed for fruit trees including 08-18-18, 7-4-2, and others. Photo Credit: Fiduccia Enterprises.

Photo Credit: Ted Rose.

This white oak has been regularly fertilized for a few years. It is easy to see the mast crop results of an oak that has been fertilized repeatedly with the proper fertilizer mix of NPK. Photo Credit: Depositphotos.

18-6-12, 10-20-10, or 10-10-10, but a general tree fertilizer will also work. Place the fertilizer slightly under the soil around the entire drip line of a tree. The drip line is located directly under the end of the longest branch growing away from the tree's main trunk.

The best trees to fertilize should have a trunk diameter of no less than twenty inches. The fertilizer will cause the tree to produce larger, sweeter, and more abundant acorns even when other nearby oak trees haven't produced a good crop or any acorns at all! By undertaking a yearly program to enhance the production of a few oak trees on the lands you hunt, you will not only provide a higher quality of forage for deer, you will also create deer hunting hot spots!

Fertilizing oak trees on the lands you hunt serves two functions. It will improve the overall health of the deer, and it becomes a highly effective decoy tactic. Most hunters are totally surprised by the amazing results they get from fertilizing oak trees. I'm often told the outcome was totally unexpected. The strategy to fertilize oak trees will work on private, leased, or public hunting lands. One of the key elements is not to get too greedy with the number of oak trees you fertilize, and particularly on public lands. No matter where you use this strategy, it is crucial to keep the trees you fertilize a secret. On land you own, you can share the information with other hunters in the family. On leased or public lands, it is wise to not share what trees you fertilized even with your closest hunting partner. Trust me on this point! I once told a friend about a tree I had fertilized. I asked to respect the fact that I invited him to hunt the piece of land under some conditions—one of which was prohibiting hunting near my fertilized oaks. This condition applied even if I wasn't hunting with him. I not only caught him hunting a fertilized oak, I discovered him as he was field dressing a dandy twelve-point buck! His apologies never ended. I forgave him but never allowed him to hunt the property again.

This is a white oak leaf and acorn. If white oaks are absent on your land, fertilizing any other oaks will work equally well. Photo Credit: Depositphotos.

On leased land that is shared with several hunting buddies, keep the location of at least one oak tree that you fertilized to yourself. Another potential problem about fertilizing oaks on leased lands is that once the other hunters discover how effective the tactic is, they will begin to fertilize their own oaks. Sooner or later, that will diminish the strategy's success rate, which I will explain later.

Basically, you want to select a mature white oak tree to fertilize per twenty-five acres. Fertilized trees should be located as far apart from one another as possible within the acreage. If you don't have white oaks on your land, any other oak tree that has traditionally produced acorns will work just as well. The only reason I suggest white oaks first is that deer prefer their acorns to all other types.

On our 192-acre property, I selected eight red oak trees, as we don't have any white oak. If fertilizing on public land, select a single oak tree that is not part of a dense group but is among other oaks that are spread out within a much larger area. If you select an oak close to other oaks, eventually other hunters will discover your tree accidentally. It won't take long for them to figure out deer are frequenting your tree more than other acorn-dropping trees in the area. There goes your hot spot! It is less likely that they will discover your single fertilized tree that is part of a larger area. Most hunters will be looking for a patch of acorn-bearing trees growing closely together because they think the more acorns that fall from the group of trees, the better it will attract deer. That is true only when they don't have a single tree that provides them with more abundant, sweeter, larger acorns that will fall later in the season! If,

Cody makes a hole for fertilizer spike with the pinch bar. Make the hole just deep enough to fit the entire spike. Place the holes directly beneath the ends of the branches that are furthest away from the tree's trunk. That is where the feeding roots of the tree are located. Photo Credit: Fiduccia Enterprises.

however, you are more concerned about improving the overall health of the oaks on your land, then by all means you should fertilize as many of your oak trees as you see fit.

But remember, if you fertilize too many trees, it will provide the deer, bear, and turkey with too many options. Instead of having one or two locations where you know deer and other game will be feeding, they could be at any number of trees with prime-tasting acorns, which will make it difficult for you to predict exactly what oak tree they are going to visit. Knowing where deer and other game will dependably show up puts you in an optimum position to see them and have shooting opportunities.

Once you have selected the tree or trees you want to fertilize, begin by making twelve to eighteen holes, each deep enough to cover the length of a fertilizer spike, around the entire tree trunk. Make the holes directly below the drip line of the tree's longest branches with a pinch bar or similar type of tool. Beneath the soil of the drip line is where the tree's feeding root system is located. If you fertilize too closely to the main trunk, the benefits of the fertilizer reduce substantially. Before placing the spike in the hole, break it in half, then place both halves in a single hole. Cover it with a few inches of soil, but don't pack the soil too tightly over the spikes. If this is done on public ground, throw some leaves in a random manner over the area

to disguise the newly made holes. I suggest fertilizing the trees once in the spring and again in the fall. When practical, I put my fertilizer spikes in when rain is predicted within a few days.

If you'd rather use granulated fertilizer, simply fill the hole within an inch or two of the top with the mix and cover the holes with some soil. Pat the soil down gently and smooth it out with a small leaf rake. Then cover it with leaves, a few small twigs, and other forest debris to disguise that the tree has just been fertilized.

There are many types of tree fertilizers that will work on oaks. Check with local agriculture extension offices for their recommendations. Photo Credit: Fiduccia Enterprises.

Fertilizing oak trees is a terrific tactic that will produce acorns that are not only bigger, sweeter, and more abundant, but they will also drop later in the hunting season than surrounding acorns. This happens because the fertilizer improves the general health of the tree and keeps the acorn stems stronger, which results in the acorns being held longer on the branches. The end effect is when most of the unfertilized acorns have fallen and been quickly consumed by deer, bear, and turkey, your fertilized tree will drop its mast later in the fall—usually during the times you will be bow or firearm hunting from mid-October to mid- or late November!

The first year you employ this strategy, the tree will respond by providing a better acorn crop. There will be a noticeable increase in the tree's acorn production in the second year, which the deer and other game will quickly focus on. In the second year, the acorns will begin to look bigger to you, as well. They will also be noticeably more abundant.

By the third year, however, your fertilized trees will be producing bumper crops of acorns that will be bigger, more abundant, and fall later than those on the trees that weren't fertilized. More importantly, the acorns will taste sweeter to deer than the acorns from non-fertilized trees. This is the key factor that the deer and other wildlife will zone in on and record to memory.

Here's how to prove how effective this tactic really is. At the end of the third year, select a fallen acorn from your fertilized tree. After biting the fruit of the acorn, you will notice it has a bitter taste, as all acorns do. Wait until the bitter flavor is gone, then bite into an acorn that has fallen from a tree that wasn't fertilized. You will instantly notice the acorn has a stronger bitter flavor! Deer and other game interpret the less bitter acorn as being sweeter and therefore more palatable. Again, they will record the experience to memory and visit that tree for years to enjoy its better-tasting fruit!

If you share the location of the trees you fertilize with hunting

This image was taken in late December 2013. The fruit of this regularly fertilized apple tree hung on the branches much longer than the fruit on unfertilized trees did. Deer were eating the apples until late January. Photo Credit: Fiduccia Enterprises.

companions other than your immediate family, you will discover what I did. Without a doubt, they will hunt the area when you're not there. If that is okay with you, then by all means let them know where it is. If you want to take a buck year in and year out at these secret locations, then keep as tight-lipped about the location of the oaks you fertilize as you can.

I use this fertilization strategy on a lot of other naturally growing vegetation that deer consume throughout the summer and fall. Find out what plants deer prefer, such as shrubs and fruit trees, then ask your local farm agency what the best mix of fertilizer is for those specific plants. It will increase production, nutrition, and volume of the plant and its fruit, which will bring the deer to it on a reliable basis.

We have more than one hundred wild apple trees on our farm and a few pear trees. I pruned and fertilized the pear trees and four apple trees in key hunting locations. Over time, the deer have realized exactly which trees bear larger, more abundant, and sweeter fruit. Sometimes they stand there as if they are waiting for the fruit to drop. It is such a simple plan that consistently provides success.

Sometimes pruning wild fruit trees, vines, shrubs, and bushes helps, too. Pruning

should only be done when a tree is asleep, or dormant. Some people prefer to prune in the winter, from January through March. If you prune any later than March, you could send the plant into shock. It will take a year or two to recover, and during that time it will not produce fruit, mast, grapes, or berries. Other pros swear the best time is soon after leaf drop in fall occurs. Choose one method and see what works best for your pruning plans.

The one constant I have discovered about regularly fertilizing oaks, fruit, and chestnut, trees and shrubs is that their fruit remain on their branches much longer than the fruit on unfertilized trees. This photo was taken in January 2013! While some foresters claim fertilizing oaks does nothing to improve the mast, my proof is in the pictures. Photo Credit: Fiduccia Enterprises.

Give the oak fertilizing strategy a try. Make it an important part of your food plot and wildlife management program. I promise you will see immediate results during the first fall. In each subsequent year, the acorn production will get better, as will any other vegetation or fruit from trees you fertilize. It is a simple strategy to employ that reaps huge benefits. Don't hesitate another season!

Chapter Twenty-Five

Nut and Fruit Trees: The Most Overlooked Food Plots

Hunters with lands that don't include any fields or open areas shouldn't think they can't plant food plots. Even on lands that are either entirely or predominately wooded, hunters can enjoy the satisfaction and benefit of planting food to attract deer. The only difference is that their plots will be made up of a wide assortment of soft- and hard-mast crops like fruit, nut, and berry trees, as well as fruit-bearing bushes—all of which can be planted in wooded areas. Another advantage to planting hard- and soft-mast trees and bushes is that once they are planted, they require much less year-to-year work than customary food plots.

As a long-time food-plot consultant, I have had many clients who are so fixated with planting the usual seeds, such as clovers, brassicas, and small grains, that they often over-look the importance of including fruit, nut, and berry trees as viable plots of food. Most food plot managers have been sold on the idea that the most important aspect of their plots is to include plants containing varied levels of protein. What

Apple trees are more adaptable to being planted in wooded areas than other fruit trees are. They will still need about six hours of sunlight per day. Photo Credit: Fiduccia Enterprises.

Photo Credit: Fiduccia Enterprises.

Deer love chestnuts. We planted over forty three-year old Dunstan chestnut trees. Within a year of planting they produced chestnuts! Visit www.chestnuthilloutdoors.com to find where to buy Dunstan Chestnut trees in your area. Photo Credit: Fiduccia Enterprises.

they don't pay attention to is also providing deer with food sources that supply them with digestible energy.

There is no argument that deer benefit greatly from eating high levels of protein that are contained in many of the usual varieties of food plot plants during spring and summer. But as their demand for energy increases in September and October in preparation for breeding, they require more high-energy types of foods. High-energy foods are converted into fat, which become stockpiles of energy for deer to fatten up on. They rely on the fat reserves to fuel them in winter.

Therefore, it should be standard operating procedure to include these types of high-energy plantings within all food plot management programs. They are sure to help deer build their fat reserves to a maximum amount. To provide your deer with high-energy foods for late fall and winter, you must include a variety of hard and soft mast trees, bushes, and shrubs that produce as much high-energy fruit as possible.

A well-managed one-hundred-acre piece of land can provide all the elements a deer needs to survive. Within that area, there should be a certain amount of land allocated to standard food plots, fruit trees or soft mast, nut trees or hard mast, native grasses, shrubs, browse, weeds, and water sources. For instance, a parcel of land this size should consist of at least two to three acres dedicated to food plots. If your land includes many acres of fields, you can double, triple, or quadruple the amount of acreage dedicated to food plots. At least 35 percent of the land should include ground cover, including stands of evergreens, second growth, and any other type of vegetation or grass that deer can use to escape foul weather or predators.

Fruit Trees

As part of our broad food plot management plan on our land, we set aside both field and wooded areas to plant a variety of fruit trees. We're fortunate to have about forty

This small hard and soft mast grove has a few varieties of pear and peach trees (left) and about thirty Dunstan Chestnut trees. Photo Credit: Fiduccia Enterprises.

acres of cultivated fields. About ten acres are used for traditional food plots, and about twenty-five acres are used to allow hay to grow as deer cover that we keep uncut all year. The remaining five acres are dedicated to fruit, nut, and berry trees and bushes. Some of our fruit trees are planted in orchard rows, and some are planted unsystematically. We also plant fruit and nut trees in woodland settings by making sure to remove enough junk trees to provide sunlight and less competition for the new plantings. If you have overgrown bushy areas that are not the best for planting traditional food plots, instead of leaving them dormant, consider them as choice spots to plant hard and soft fruit-bearing trees.

On our land, I have found that planting mast trees that aren't available to deer on bordering properties dramatically increases the number of deer that regularly visit our property. For instance, we have a considerable number of apple trees. Our neighbors also have a lot of apple trees. Therefore, our fruit and nut tree food plot management plan was to specifically plant a wide variety of chestnut, hickory, gobbler sawtooth nut, pear, cherry, plum, and peach trees.

It is important to remember when purchasing fruit trees to avoid buying hybrid types when practical, as they are more susceptible to disease. Heirloom types are a better choice. I prefer to buy varieties that produce late-dropping fruit. Many varieties of fruit-bearing trees need to be pollinated by either a male or female tree of the same species. It is advisable to plant the accompanying tree within thirty to seventy-five feet. Some varieties of fruit and nut trees are self-pollinating.

This two-year-old peach tree grew peaches only three months after we planted and fertilized it. Photo Credit: Fiduccia Enterprises.

The fruit—soft- and hard-mast—dropped by these trees quickly draws deer and other wildlife to their bounty, much like a magnet draws iron. Deer temporarily abandon most other food items, including high-protein clovers, when ripe pears, apples, and other fruit, nuts, and acorns begin to fall. In many cases, deer will eat the fruit and nuts within hours after they begin to hit the ground. The fruit will remain a priority food source until it is completely exhausted by wildlife. I have seen deer dig up rotten pears and apples beneath several inches of snow on our farm in late December.

Soft-Mast Fruit Trees: In order of my preference, my top three recommendations for soft-mast trees are pears, apples, and peaches. They are all varieties of fruit trees that grow well throughout the Great Lakes, Northeast, and New England. If your land already includes an abundance of any one of these fruits, make an adjustment. For instance, if you have too many apple trees, then plant plums or nectarines in their place. While some fruit trees are self-pollinating, it is safer to always buy two of the same trees to ensure pollination.

Here are some of my favorite varieties of late-season, cold-hardy trees.

Pear: Bartlett, Ayer, Atlantic Queen, and Blake's Harrow

Apple: Enterprise, Cortland, Honeygold, and Keepsake

Peach: Intrepid, Bell of Georgia, and Polar Peach Chill Hours: 800

The key to having hard- and soft-mast trees bear fruit early is to buy them from a reliable orchard like www.chestnuthilloutdoors.com. They also need to be planted properly and fertilized with a slow release type fertilizer (which should be used on hard- and soft-mast trees). Photo Credit: Fiduccia Enterprises.

Nut Trees: Again, in order of my preference, my top three selections of hard-mast trees are blight-resistant Dunstan Chestnuts, the American hazelnut, also known as filbert, and gobbler sawtooth oak. They are all fast-growing nut trees that will do well throughout northern climates. If your land already includes too many of one of these species, make an adjustment. For best results, always plant at least two trees to aid pollination. I recommend the following varieties and sources:

Chestnut: Dunstan Chestnuts (www.chestnuthilloutdoors.com)

Hazelnut: The American Hazelnut (www.gurneys.com)

Gobbler Sawtooth: (www.tytyga.com)

All fruit and nut trees require particular care when being planted. Follow the directions carefully. Like most trees, the hole must be at least twice as wide as the root ball and slightly deeper. As long as the tree is not very young, lay an inch of slow-release 10-10-10 fertilizer at the bottom of the hole. If the tree is a year or more old use Osmocote 18-6-12 fertilizer at planting; it provides excellent nutrition but, since it is a slow-release fertilizer, it won't burn the roots.

Shrubs, Bushes, and Vines

Planting a variety of fruit-bearing shrubs and vines will enhance any food plot program. Some shrubs, such as the Allegheny chinquapin, which is a medium-sized bush that produces an abundance of edible, small, sweet nuts, are relished by a wide variety of game and other wildlife. Like hardwood trees, the mast crop produced by shrubs will attract and hold deer, turkey, and other wildlife on your land until the mast is totally eaten.

Other nontraditional shrubs that benefit from a well-managed food plot program include American beautyberry, which produces purple berries and grows to about six feet tall. Its berries are enjoyed by a wide variety of game and nonhunted species. The red mulberry grows to a height of sixty feet and is attractive to a wide variety of game and nonhunted species. Other berries include raspberry, blueberry, marionberry, and blackberry. The common pawpaw has a rich, sweet fruit with a nutty banana flavor; it, too, is relished by many species of wildlife. Chickasaw plum grows like a thicket of small trees that provide excellent cover for quail, grouse, turkey, and other game birds. Deer and turkey seek out its sweet red fruit in late summer and eat it until it is gone. Buttonbush is a large woody shrub that grows to be between three and ten feet tall. Its seed is readily eaten by waterfowl. Lespedeza bicolor is a large leguminous shrub reaching heights of eight to ten feet. It can be planted to provide excellent cover for deer, game birds, and small game. The longer you wait to plant hard- and soft-mast trees, shrubs, and bushes, the longer you and the wildlife will have to wait to reap the benefits.

For much more detail on all types of traditional food plot plantings, fruits, and nuts, visit www.deerdoctor.com and check out *The Shooter's Bible Guide to Planting Food Plots*. This full-color book has 208 pages jam-packed with helpful planting suggestions, tips, seed resources, a glossary, and much more.

Mast is often categorized as either soft or hard. Hard mast consists of hard-shelled seeds that have a relatively long shelf life and are typically high in fat, carbohydrates, and protein. These characteristics make them a food source that is both high in energy content and available well into the winter months. For many areas throughout New England, the Midwest, and Northeast, hard mast is a key food source for survival during the winter months when other sources of nutrition are most limited. Some examples of hard mast include chestnuts, acorns, hazelnuts, almonds, pecans, hickory nuts, and walnuts. Table 1 provides a list of numerous Ohio hard-mast producers and wildlife that consume them.

Acorns from all types of oak trees are considered hard mast. Photo Credit: Depositphotos.

Soft mast is fleshy, perishable fruit that is often high in sugar, vitamins, and carbohydrates. It is usually not available in great quantities in winter months. Soft mast is a crucial energy source. During drought years, soft mast may be a critical source of moisture for some wildlife and their young. Some examples of soft mast include apples, pears, plums, peaches, black cherries, persimmons, pawpaws, and blackberries.

Whenever I plant any types of trees, particularly my nut or fruit trees, I always protect them by using Plantra® Grow Tubes. They will not only protect the trees but they will also help them to grow more quickly and healthier. This sidebar is meant to provide you with more information about these very valuable devices that can be used not only for trees but also for shrubs, vines, and even garden plants!

Plantra® Grow Tubes:

What are they—Plantra grow tubes act like mini greenhouses for trees, shrubs, vines and garden plants. They are translucent to sunlight and are uniquely designed to provide both greenhouse benefits and physical protection. This potent combination grows deciduous (broadleaf) seedlings fast, healthy and balanced from roots to shoots.

Tube wall construction, open diameter, and sunlight optimizing properties of each Plantra tube design are a function of its intended purpose. Some Plantra grow tubes are built for wild land, urban and nursery tree establishment while others are intended to quickly grow agricultural plants such as grapevines, orchard trees and blueberry bushes. Plantra grow tubes are ready for the job the day you plant and are UV resistant to last for years in the field until the seedlings are well on their way.

Tube heights for wild land, urban and nursery plantings range from 6ft down to 2ft tall tubes. Taller grow tube heights offer the most benefits. For example, 5ft grow tubes are the bare minimum to provide any deer browse protection and it takes a 6ft tube height to thoroughly stop deer browse damage. Shorter tube lengths (2ft to 4ft) should only be used on dwarf varieties which require lower branching patterns as these heights only protect against damage from smaller animals including mice, voles, and rabbits and also from weed sprays and some equipment damage like string trimmers and mowers. The manufacturer suggests using a taller grow tube for semi-dwarf and full-sized trees.

Why they work—Plantra grow tubes were born from the traditional "tree tube" (sometimes called "tree shelter") concept which today, still remains narrowly focused on providing physical protection for small seedlings. Physical protection is indeed important but Plantra didn't stop there and instead made the leap to invent the "grow tube" by combining the physical protection of tree tubes and tree shelters with sunlight optimizing greenhouse benefits. Combining sophisticated light-diffusing construction with spectrally selective pigments Plantra grow tubes are translucent to specific wavelengths of light plants need and delivers sunlight the way plants can best use it. This potent combination creates a growth maximizing microclimate inside a rugged, protective tube necessary to help young seedlings to older trees and plants survive and grow rapidly.

Why you should use them—Plantra grow tubes helps to eliminate threats to seedlings and sapling trees. One of the biggest threats to young tree survival is the chewing and gnawing that many animals do to a plant or young tree. All too often it kills the seedling or tree. The vast majority of wild planted trees by growers suffer the fate of being either being eaten by deer or having their stems stripped of bark by buck rubs and/or girdled by a host of rodents including, rabbits, mice and voles. Plantra has a range of tube sizes and heights matched to specific seedlings, plants and trees that make the job of successful establishment a reality.

Another serious threat to seedling survival is desiccating wind. Plantra's superior greenhouse microclimate helps retains leaf moisture, reduces water stress and eliminates other negative impacts that stop the growth of unprotected seedlings. Using Plantra grow tubes means your trees will survive and grow quickly and all but eliminate the wasted time and cost to replant. To find out more detailed information, Plantra® Grow Tubes, DVD demos, tree guards and all the other Plantra® products visit www.plantra.com

Chapter Twenty-Six

The Ten Top Fall Food Plots for Northern Areas

How to plant a variety of productive and nutritious food plots has unquestionably become the most sought-after information by hunters across North America over the past couple of decades. It is virtually impossible to find an outdoorsman who doesn't know about the benefits of planting food plots.

With that said, not every hunter who plants food plots or is thinking about planting a few plots wants to become a land steward or get involved with a detailed deer and food plot management program. The fact is, countless hunters simply want to plant food plots to attract deer when they want to see them the most, during the daylight hours of hunting season.

Therefore, this chapter is intended to provide time-tested advice and guidelines to help anyone who wants to plant winter-hardy food plots to draw deer to the lands they own or lease from late October through January. Each plant covered will withstand

It is virtually impossible to hold deer, particularly mature bucks, on your land 100 percent of the time. This is true whether you own one or a thousand or more acres Photo Credit: CanStock Photos.

Photo Credit: Fiduccia Enterprises.

cold winter climates even in northern areas throughout the country. No matter if you have one acre or one thousand acres, to plant the seeds I recommend here will enhance your chances of drawing deer to your land during the daylight hours of hunting season.

Reality Check

Before going any further, let me make a few points about planting food plots and dispel the myth that by planting food plots hunters can hold deer on their lands. The hard truth is that actually holding or keeping a mature buck on a piece of property for an indefinite period of time, whether the land is five acres or five hundred acres, boils down to one basic statement: It can't be done! It is sensible to believe, however, that it is possible to include plantings appealing enough to attract does and bucks more consistently to your land and entice them to remain there for longer periods of time. This is particularly true if the seeds planted can't be found on properties bordering or within easy travel distance from your land.

There are some hunters who would like to plant food plots but have heard claims that it is akin to baiting for deer. Most times, the people who make such claims either don't own or lease hunting property or their property isn't favorable for planting food plots. It has also been my experience that people who claim hunting over a food plot is baiting are the same ones who have often hunted deer over a cornfield, apple orchard, grain field, stand of acorns, or field of alfalfa. Enough said? If you have a desire to plant a food plot, plant it and then decide for yourself if it is similar to hunting over bait.

Cool-Season versus Winter-Hardy

While the common term cool-season plantings accurately describes plants that can withstand some degree of temporary cold weather, many of these plants will not tolerate frigid temperatures. Additionally, many cool-season plantings will die or go dormant after a few hard frosts. So when I use the terms cold-season or winter-hardy to define plants, they are plantings that will survive and flourish in low winter temperatures of 0° to 10° F. Winter-hardy plantings remain attractive to deer long after killing frosts occur, and they are eaten by deer into the late fall and winter months. They are the best choices for northern climates and the wisest choices for hunters who want to see and bag deer heading to their plots during the daylight hours of the entire hunting season.

This dandy buck was killed in a winter-hardy plot of purple top turnips. Photo Credit: Fiduccia Enterprises.

The seeds I discuss in this chapter emphasize one or more of my favorite winter-hardy plantings in each species group, such as clovers and other legumes, brassicas, small grains, grasses, herbs, forbs, and other plant types. They are guaranteed to extend the growing season well into December and January. I have had extensive experience planting these winter-hardy seeds for many years, and they have repeatedly succeeded in drawing deer to my land during hunting season. What makes them even more appealing choices is that a majority of them are among the easiest seeds to grow. They will definitely help you achieve your goal to draw deer into your lands. So here they are.

The Brassicas

Brassicas are among the species I always recommend as winter-hardy plantings. In fact, they could be classified as extreme winter-hardy plantings. Brassicas are high in protein, and deer find them digestible. When fertilized properly, the crude protein content of brassicas can range from 15 to 30 percent in the leaves and from 8 to 15 or more percent in the roots. The leaves provide more than 90 percent digestibility. Well-maintained brassica plots are productive plantings that can produce six or more tons of forage per acre.

This volume of production makes brassicas a top choice for plantings, particularly on small acreage food plots, which is why they are commonly considered a favorite resilient planting among those who plant food plots. Unlike other forage crops that become fibrous when they mature, the fiber content of brassica leaves doesn't increase with age. This means that brassica leaves remain digestible to deer throughout their growing season. Additionally, deer tend not to eat brassicas in their early stages of growth, as the leaves tend to taste bitter. This is one reason brassicas are rarely bothered by deer during the summer months. Once the plants reach maturity in late fall, however, the starch in the leaves converts into sugar, which makes them sweeter and more palatable. The amount of time required for brassica plants to reach maturity depends mostly on the species and variety of types planted.

Kale is an excellent winter-hardy brassica. However, it must be planted early because it grows slowly, taking 110 to 150 days to reach maturity. Photo Credit: Fiduccia Enterprises.

Most of the cold-tolerant plantings should be seeded between sixty and ninety days prior to the first expected killing frost. Forage kale and a couple of other varieties of winter-hardy plants are slow growers and therefore need extra time to grow to maturity. They can be planted a little earlier than suggested in order for them to provide the best growth, nutrition, and the maximum amount of forage.

Plants within the brassica family that are used to attract deer include forage rape, forage kale, a variety of turnips—such as appin, barkant and purple top—and canola rapeseed. The lesser-known but equally attractive group of brassicas includes ground-hog radish, rutabaga, swede, mustard, cabbage, and cauliflower. All the brassicas make excellent food plot plantings. Their only downside is that they should not be planted in the same plot for more than two consecutive years to avoid insect and root disease problems. Therefore, when planting brassicas, the plan must include some forethought about new locations to plant them every two years. Even though brassicas have to be rotated, they are definitely worth planting.

Major-Plus Swede: This plant, also known as the rutabaga, is by far my favorite brassica. Major-plus swede is a highly digestible, later-maturing swede noted for high yields and excellent disease resistance. Major-plus leaves are high in energy and low in fiber, and its high leaf yield makes it a preferred food by deer. It is characterized by a white fleshy bulb and bronze skin color. Deer will heartily graze the leaves, stems, roots, and bulbs at different times during the growing season. A plot of swede will look like a minefield after deer begin eating the bulbs in late fall and into January. I recommend planting swede as a stand-alone crop not mixed with any other seed.

Swede's tiny seeds can be top-seeded and they germinate quickly. It is one of the easiest seeds to grow successfully. For best results, when rain is predicted fertilize the plants after they reach a few inches high with Triple-19. Photo Credit: Fiduccia Enterprises.

Major-Plus Swede Recap

- **Seeding Rates:** As a stand-alone crop, broadcast the tiny seeds at one to two pounds per acre prior to an expected rainfall.
- **pH Level:** Requires pH levels of 6.0 to 6.5.
- **Planting Time:** In the North, plant in mid-May to mid-June.
- **Maturity:** About 120 days.
- **Depth of Seed:** Plant one quarter of an inch below the surface. Swede can be top-sowed successfully but only in a well-prepared plot. The seed must also be compacted to make good soil-to-seed contact. For best top-sown seeding results, plant prior to an expected rainfall.
- **Fertilizer:** At planting, fertilize with three-hundred to four hundred pounds per acre of T 19-19-19. Six weeks later, finish off with one hundred to one-hundred fifty pounds of 34-0-0 (ammonium sulfate). Try to fertilize when rainfall is predicted within forty-eight to seventy-two hours.
- **Companion Mixes:** Does well planted alone, which is how I recommend planting this seed. Swede can be mixed with other brassicas, clovers, wheat, and chicory, but I recommend that only in large plots of one acre or more.
- **Crude Protein Levels:** Tops provide from 15 to 30 percent protein levels. Roots have 8 to 15 percent protein levels.
- **Overgrazing:** Is generally not an issue after thirty days.
- **Extends Grazing Season:** From October through January, but by November plots will look like they were dug up with spade shovels! Deer will dig up the swede bulbs even under several inches of snow.
- **Temperatures:** Tops will survive in extremely cold temperatures between 15° and 20° F. Bulbs will survive in temperatures 10° colder than the leaves.
- **Avoid:** Don't plant in places with a high rate of sulfur in the soil. Does not do well in wet or inadequately drained soils.
- **Avoid:** Do not plant in the same food plot for more than two consecutive years.

There is no doubt that swede will attract deer during the hunting season. Deer will begin eating the leaves after the first few hard frosts of late October or early November and consume the bulbs from November through December. Photo Credit: Fiduccia Enterprises.

Forage rape is a fast-growing plant that provides a high yield. It is a winter-hardy planting that is still viable from November through January. Photo Credit: Fiduccia Enterprises.

Forage Rape: This brassica, like swede, is exceptionally winter hardy. Its leafy greens will draw deer to food plots throughout most of the United States and Canada. During my thirty years of planting food plots, I have found forage rape to be among the easiest seeds to plant and grow—fast to germinate and easy to maintain. Deer will browse the rape leaves during the summer, but they don't eat the plant aggressively until forage rape undergoes a few hard frosts in late fall.

There are a few different types of rape seed, the most popular being dwarf essex rape, but I plant an improved variety called bonar rape. Bonar is a late-maturing forage rape that was specially bred for improved palatability and a higher stem-to-leaf ratio. It is high yielding and can provide quality winter feed. Note that bonar has been used extensively in New Zealand, where it has consistently outperformed other forage rape brassicas.

Forage rape is one of many winter-hardy plantings that can extend a deer's grazing season well into November and, most times, through December. When buying forage rape, be careful not to confuse it with oil-seed rape, more commonly called canola rapeseed. There is rarely a season that I do not plant forage rape in one or more food plots.

To give rape the best start possible, it should be planted early. In the North, plant forage rape anytime after the Fourth of July. I try to plant it when I know the forecast calls for rain within the next few days. Rape will be ready to browse by deer within thirty to sixty days after it has established itself. For best results, plant rape in a plot that has good soil drainage. While forage rape will tolerate lower pH levels of 5.3 to 5.9, it prefers a pH level higher than that.

Before planting, wait until the weeds emerge, and when they reach about two

Although forage rape can be planted as late as August, I generally plant it earlier, usually early July. Photo Credit: Fiduccia Enterprises.

inches in height, use an herbicide that kills both grass and broadleaf weeds. Be careful to follow all instructions exactly when using any herbicide. After spraying to kill weeds, wait to plant the plot at least seven to ten days. Disk the soil lightly, while being careful not to turn it under any deeper than a half inch or so in order to break up the compacted surface. This will significantly limit new weed growth.

Rape seed is tiny, and like all tiny seed plants, it can be successfully top sown but only on a well-prepared soil bed. I prefer planting rape on lightly tilled soil one fourth to one half inch deep. To assure good soil-to-seed contact, I use a compactor to firm up the plot. I often use a simple three-point hitch harrow attached to the back of my Arctic Cat ATV. A harrow will level furrows or ridges and finish off the ground evenly.

Forage rape can be broadcasted at rates between five to ten pounds per acre. Be sure not to use more seed than is recommended. Planting too much is among the biggest causes of growing spindly food plots. In fact, sometimes overseeding can cause complete plot failure. This is true of all types of food plot plantings. To achieve the best results, fertilize forage rape directly after planting it with three hundred to four hundred pounds per acre of T-19, or 19-19-19. About two weeks later, add about one hundred pounds per acre of 34-0-0. The fertilizer will help the rape attain maximum crude protein levels between 15 to 30 percent. I have had excellent success by planting forage rape as a stand-alone crop not mixed with other seeds. Over the past twenty-five years that I have planted forage rape, I have found that deer find it digestible, and they will enthusiastically seek it out, especially from late October through December. This is the prime time of year when hunters want to attract and keep deer returning to their hunting lands. You will be amazed at how many deer will visit your forage rape plot during hunting season. One last interesting note about planting brassicas is that all brassica plots seem to draw deer in during daylight hours of the hunting season. I think it is because brassicas are so palatable and nutritious even in the coldest of weather. In foul winter weather, deer actively seek out brassicas to provide them not only with nourishment, but also the energy they require during the winter months.

Forage Rape Recap

- **Seeding Rates:** As a stand-alone crop, broadcast forage rape seed prior to an expected rainfall at six to ten pounds per acre.

- **pH Level:** Will tolerate low pH, 5.3 to 5.9, but prefers soil with a pH between 6.0 and 6.5.
- **Planting Time:** To ensure this plant attracts deer late into the deer season, plant it no earlier than late June in the North. I plant my forage rape in late June to make sure it will receive sufficient rainfall. It can also be planted in July, but if you do, plan it to match a predicted rainfall.
- **Maturity:** Thirty to ninety days.
- **Depth of Seed:** Plant no deeper than one quarter of an inch below the surface in a conventionally prepared seedbed. It can be successfully top seeded.
- **Fertilizer:** Planted alone, fertilize with 300 pounds of T-19 (19-19-19) and 100 pounds of ammonium sulfate (34-0-0) at planting.
- **Companion Mixes:** Does well alone but can be mixed with other brassicas, small grains, and clovers. Only mix it with other seeds in plots that are one acre or larger.
- **Overgrazing:** When planting dwarf varieties, limit grazing for at least sixty to ninety days.
- **Extends Grazing Season:** Deer browse the leaves lightly in summer, but they heartily feed on them from October through December.
- **Caution:** Rape needs good soil drainage. Forage rape should be planted in at least a half-acre plot to avoid deer eating all of it before the end of November.
- **Avoid:** Don't plant in the same food plot for more than two years in a row.

Winter-Hardy Clovers

It has been my experience that while some food plotters realize there are several clovers that can tolerate cooler temperatures, not many realize that some clovers are winter-hardy and, as such, can tolerate frigid temperatures of 0° to 10° F for several days. The winter-hardy clovers will definitely be attractive to deer in winter temperatures above that. There are many

This buck fell victim to visiting a plot of Kopu clover on a sunny late November day. Note the leafless trees in the background. Photo Credit: www.Wildlifeperfect.com.

clovers and legumes that are rated as winter-hardy (WH), very winter hardy (VWH), and extremely winter-hardy (EWH) plantings. The extremely winter-hardy plants can withstand prolonged temperatures of 5° F with no snow cover. When they are covered with snow, they will survive in subzero temperatures!

These winter-hardy clovers include alsike clover (WH), jumbo ladino (VWH), Alice white clover (VWH), persist brand red clover (VWH), sanfoin (VWH), marathon red clover (VWH), kura clover (EWH), fixation balansa clover (EWH), and the birdsfoot trefoils: certified norcen birdsfoot (VWH), Bruce birdsfoot (WH), and bull birdsfoot (EWH).

You can find a listing of the best clovers, legumes, and other suitable plant species in my book *The Shooter's Bible Guide to Planting Food Plots* on my website, www.woodsnwater.tv. The winter-hardy season plantings are diverse enough to double as both warm season and winter season plantings. Winter tolerant means they can endure temperatures below 5° to 10° F for extended periods of time. Freeze out will normally occur after prolonged temperatures of 0° to 5° F. While any of the above clovers will definitely fit the bill for you as winter-hardy plantings, I'm only including two of my favorites here.

Extreme Winter-Hardy Clover

Fixation Balansa Clover: This clover is rated as extremely winter-hardy. It is a small-seeded, cold-season, annual legume that is palatable and produces exceptional quantities of nitrogen. Fixation balansa is a later-maturing variety, which makes it an excellent forage crop for deer and other wildlife. As an added bonus, it is an excellent bee attractant to help pollinate other plantings and trees.

With the correct management of mowing and fertilizing, balansa can return for several years after a single seeding. It is so winter hardy that it has withstood temperatures as low as 5° F. A dense stand of balansa clover does a superior job of suppressing

Fixation Balsana is a massive clover. Flowers vary from white to pink. It is very attractive to bees, but more importantly, it is a very winter-hardy clover that can withstand temperatures as low as 5 degrees F. The leaf margins are commonly serrated. Photo Credit: OUTSIDEPRIDE.COM.

spring weed growth by shading the soil and out-competing weeds for water and nutrients. It increases the water-holding capacity of soil, has a thick organic growth, and has an impressive root system, thus erosion and runoff are greatly diminished.

Balansa is large leafed and dense, and deer find it highly palatable. Balansa flowers vary from white to pink. When planting fixation balansa clover, plant it at one fourth inch depth on a well-prepared soil bed. Make sure the seed has good seed-to-soil contact. Balansa clover will reseed itself if it is allowed to bloom. Cut it prior to blooming if you don't want it to reseed.

Like all clovers, balansa requires an inoculant. In fact, fixation balansa clover's inoculant, called Trifolium Special #2, is relatively rare. Therefore, I recommend trying to buy it pre-inoculated or from a seller who has the Trifolium Special #2 on hand to sell.

Fixation Balansa Clover Recap

- **Seeding Rates:** Planted as a stand-alone plot using five to eight pounds per acre in a prepared seedbed.
- **Inoculate:** Use Trifolium Special #2.
- **pH Level:** Maintain levels between 6.0 to 6.8.
- **Planting Time:** Can be planted as early as the first of May. I plant it no later than early June.
- **Depth of Seed:** Plant one quarter of an inch deep and compact to get good seed-to-soil contact.
- **Fertilizer:** Use 300 pounds per acre of T-19-19-19.
- **Companion Mixes:** Does well planted alone. Can be planted in a mix with small grains.
- **Overgrazing:** Once established, resistant to heavy grazing pressure.
- **Extends Grazing Season:** From October to late December and beyond.
- **Caution:** Make sure it is inoculated before planting.
- **Avoid:** Planting later than mid-July.
- **Note:** Fixation balansa clover is among the hardiest of the extremely winter-hardy clovers.

Alice White Clover: Alice white clover is an outstanding white clover cultivar known for its large leaf, vigorous and tall growth, and extreme winter hardiness. It is highly palatable and performs well under heavy grazing by deer and other wildlife. It is also an excellent source of nitrogen. Alice white clover is aggressive enough to compete against grasses, but a well-prepared plot for Alice requires good seed-to-soil contact, which is vital to having a successful stand. It is advisable to treat a plot with herbicide to kill weeds and grass prior to planting Alice white clover. Buy this clover pre-inoculated. White clover can be used as new seedlings or to overseed existing plots of clovers. White clover can be planted in the spring or fall, but I like to plant Alice in June. If planted in the fall, allow at least eight weeks before a killing frost. Almost all white clovers grow best in well-drained, fertile, loamy or clay soils with pH levels of 6.0 to 7.0. Adequate levels of calcium, phosphorus, and potash are also important, so fertilize the plot with three hundred to four hundred pounds per acre of T-19-19-19. Once it has been fertilized, the clover will become dense and leafy.

During the spring and summer, if the deer are not keeping your Alice white clover plot grazed, which is highly unlikely, it is important to keep the plot mowed during maximum growing periods. Try to maintain Alice clover at a height of three to nine inches. Cutting a plot of Alice short in the fall allows vigorous regrowth of the clover. I generally mow it in mid-September.

Alice White Clover Recap

- **Seeding Rates:** In a stand-alone plot, seed at two to four pounds per acre. When mixed, use 1 to 3 pounds per acre. I plant Alice as a stand-alone clover plot.
- **Inoculate:** Available pre-inoculated.
- **pH Level:** Likes pH levels of 6.0 to 7.0.
- **Planting Time:** Can be planted in early spring. I plant Alice in late May or early June.
- **Depth of Seed:** Plant no deeper than one quarter of an inch under the soil prior to a rainfall.
- **Fertilizer:** Use 300 to 400 pounds of T-19 at planting.
- **Companion Mixes:** Best used as a mix with grains and grasses.
- **Protein Levels:** Good.
- **Pliability:** Very high.
- **Overgrazing:** Generally not an issue once established.
- **Extends Grazing Season:** Well into winter.

The Small Grains

I grow most grains other than corn. I originally stopped planting corn because it was so expensive. As of this writing, oil prices have dropped from their $145 high to

Winter triticale is a hybrid grain of fall rye and winter wheat. Photo Credit: Depositphotos.

as low as $44 a barrel, which makes corn more affordable. However, I have had such success with grain sorghum, also known as Milo, that I have decided to stick with it.

The small grains include both winter and summer varieties. While I do plant an occasional summer variety, I regularly plant winter varieties. The winter types of grains that are available include corn, grain sorghum, grain rye (Secale cereale), triticale, wheat, barley, oats, and buckwheat.

Winter Triticale: This is my favorite small grain, which is a cross between fall rye and winter wheat. It is much leafier than rye and has better feed value, although rye will produce more tonnage than triticale. Winter triticale is an ideal winter-hardy grain that I never miss planting. Its protein levels range between 15 to 25 percent, which makes it terrific forage for deer, turkey, pheasants, and geese. Many wildlife managers rate triticale higher as a wildlife food plot grain than wheat or rye. It can be planted earlier than wheat—generally in mid- to late August or September in the North. In some cases, it could even be planted as late as October 1, and deer would still be able to graze it by mid-October or early November. I usually plant my winter triticale during the last week of August. There are a lot of triticale varieties to choose from, and some were created particularly for fall and winter production. They are the wisest choice for those managers looking to increase the winter hardy offerings. I use Tritigold-22. Triticale is sold as both grain and forage varieties.

Winter Triticale Recap

- **Seeding Rates:** Broadcast alone at 100 pounds per acre. With legumes half that amount. With clover and other grains about twnety-five pounds per acre.
- **pH Level:** Likes pH levels of 6.0 to 6.5.
- **Planting Time:** Last week of August or by the first week of September.
- **Depth of Seed:** Plant one-half to three-quarters of an inch deep in a well-prepared plot that is compacted well to prevent turkeys and birds from eating the seed. For best soil-to-seed contact, plant just prior to a rainfall.

- **Fertilizer:** At planting, use 300 to 400 pounds of T 19-19-19 and one hundred pounds of 46-0-0 in late fall.
- **Companion Mixes:** Does well planted alone. Can also be mixed with other grains or legumes.
- **Crude Protein Levels:** From fifteen to 30 percent.
- **Overgrazing:** Generally not an issue after thirty days.
- **Extends Grazing Season:** From October through December.
- **Temperatures:** Withstands late winter frigid temperatures.
- **Caution:** Use winter forage varieties for deer.
- **Avoid:** Don't plant in acidic soils.

Triticale:

As some of you who have read my other books know, I am an enthusiastic *Star Trek* fan, also known as a Trekker. Therefore, whenever I can make a *Star Trek* reference when I write—or on our television show—I shamelessly include it. So for those of you who are dyed-in-the-wool Trekkers, here is a bit of *Star Trek* trivia that relates to the hybrid grain of rye and wheat known as Triticale.

In an episode on the original *Star Trek* series, the USS *Enterprise* receives a top-priority order to safeguard a shipment of Quadro-Triticale grain on Deep Space Station K-7, where the Klingons are on shore leave. Captain Kirk is aggravated to be asked to protect a shipment of grain that is destined for the famine-struck Sherman's Planet. Kirk is further annoyed by Federation Undersecretary of Agriculture Nilz Baris and even more by his is vexatious assistant, Arne Darvin, who advises Kirk that Starfleet Command is worried the Klingons may try to embezzle the triticale grain.

Additional complications develop when a space trader named Cyrano Jones gives Communications Officer Uhura a purring ball of fur known as a Tribble. Totally enchanted by the creature, Uhura takes it back to the *Enterprise*. Lieutenant Commander Dr. McCoy quickly discovers that Tribbles are born pregnant. Soon there are more Tribbles than can be counted, and because the more they eat, the more they multiply, their population levels expand exponentially. Before the crew knows what is happening, the ship is overrun by the furry creatures. When Kirk goes to inspect the status of the grain, he finally discovers why the Tribbles are multiplying so quickly—the creatures ate all the Quadro-Triticale. The bins where the precious grain was stored are bare and contain countless dead Tribbles.

It's discovered that the triticale grain was poisoned by the Undersecretary's assistant, Darvin, who is actually a Klingon who had been facially altered. His true identity is uncovered when Captain Kirk discovers that Tribbles loathe Klingons and Klingons despise Tribbles. The Tribbles squeal loudly whenever they are in close proximity to a Klingon. The episode ends with the Klingons leaving the space station. Chief Engineer Scotty rids the ship of all the deceased Tribbles by beaming them onto the Klingon ship and explaining to Kirk, "They'll be no tribble at all!" However, the precious cargo of Quadro-Triticale grain is gone and has to be replenished for the starving inhabitants of Sherman's Planet.

Our son Peter at the fourteenth Annual 2015 Official Star Trek convention in Las Vegas. Creation Entertainment owns and operates many other very popular convention events including; Stargate, Supernatural, The Vampire Diaries, Xena, The Twilight Saga, the Walking Dead, The Originals, and others. If you're a Star Trek fan, join the fun and become part of the family of friends from all over the world in Las Vegas for the 2016 fiftieth year celebration of Star Trek. It promises to be the biggest Star Trek event ever! Visit ww.Creationent. com to get more information.

Rye (Secalecereale) should not be confused with ryegrass. Our food plots are never complete without adding this small grain bunchgrass into our mix of food plots. Photo Credit: Fiduccia Enterprises.

Winter Rye (*Secale cereale*): This top-shelf cold-season grain is among the best winter-hardy deer attractants of all the small grains. Winter rye grain is not ryegrass. It is a cereal rye and the most well liked of the small grains among food plot managers. It is even more tolerant of cold temperatures than winter wheat. Rye reaches heights of two to five feet tall. Deer eat the seed heads and the leaves. Rye is also nutritious, provides 10 to 25 percent protein levels, and is easy to plant and grow. I have never experienced a crop failure when using rye. For a winter plot, plant rye the same time as triticale—the last week of August or by the first week of September. I generally prefer late August if the weather is cooperative. If you plant rye alone, use about 100 to 120 pounds per acre. In mixed plots, use about half that amount. I have discovered that rye will often reseed itself when mowed. There are countless varieties of cereal rye to choose from. The best ones to buy are the forage varieties, such as winter king, wintermore, and Wintergrazer-70.

Winter rye thrives on well-drained, loamy soils but is tolerant of both heavy clays and dry, sandy soils. It can also withstand drought better than other cereal grains, in part because of its prolific root system. Winter rye can also grow in low-fertility soils where other cereal grains may fail. Optimum soil pH for winter rye is 5.0 to 7.0, but pH in the range of 4.5 to 8.0 can be tolerated.

Rye is an attractive food plot, particularly in fall and winter. If you have never planted cereal rye, give it a try. You'll be pleasantly surprised by how easy it is to plant, how well it grows, how trouble-free it is, how much the deer like it, and how long it will last into the cold winter months. Rye is one of our must-plant food plots on our land.

Winter Rye Recap

- **Seeding Rates:** Broadcast alone at 1½ bushels per acre (about eighty to eighty-five pounds). When drilled or planted in a mix, use half that amount. It is best planted prior to an expected rainfall.
- **pH Level:** Tolerates acidic soil but prefers pH levels when they are about 5.5 to 6.5.
- **Planting Time:** As a winter crop, plant the last week of August or first week of September.
- **Depth of Seed:** Plant one quarter to three-quarters of an inch deep on a well-prepared seedbed. Compact thoroughly to avoid having turkey and other birds eating the seed.
- **Fertilizer:** At planting use 300 to 400 pounds of T-19-19-19.
- **Companion Mixes:** Does well planted alone. Secale cereale (rye) can also be mixed with a variety of clovers, other legumes, peas, wheat, and chicory on large plots of two acres or more.
- **Extends Grazing Season:** Deer eat rye October through January.
- **Temperatures:** Extremely winter hardy and will withstand late-season winter temperatures.
- **Avoid:** Don't confuse rye grain with perennial ryegrass.

Winter Rye is another easy plant to grow. It will provide an excellent winter-hardy crop for deer to forage on. Photo Credit: Frigid Forage.

Forage Chicory: This herbaceous cool-season plant is a highly nutritious perennial that is part of the sunflower family. Forage chicory is a low-growing rosette plant with broad leaves in the winter that are similar to dandelions. In spring, it rapidly produces large numbers of leaves from the crown. Properly maintained chicory plots can last for several years. Chicory should be grazed or mowed prior to bolting, or flowering, as deer will lose interest in the plant after because it loses its palatability.

Chicory is quick to seed, and because it has a deep taproot, it is drought tolerant. Forage chicory will withstand heavy grazing pressure, which makes it a good choice in areas with high deer densities. It is one of the finest forages for extracting nutrients from the soil and transferring them to deer, which helps provide heavier body weights and larger antlers. Its protein levels range from about 10 to 30 percent!

There are several types of chicory, including oasis and forage feast. The brand I plant is called six point chicory. It is a hardy, nutrient-rich taproot herb widely adapted in the

Chicory is one cold-season crop you don't want to forget to include in your winter-hardy plantings. It will draw deer like a magnet throughout the entire deer season from October to December. Photo Credit: Fiduccia Enterprises.

United States. Six point chicory is digestible, palatable, and provides high feed value to grazing wildlife. I use six point because it has been bred to be winter hardy with a good resistance to bolting, which makes it an excellent companion in perennial mixtures for summer and fall forage feed. However, I plant it as a stand-alone crop.

Chicory should be sown into a fully cultivated seedbed after weeds have been killed with an herbicide. Plant at a depth of three-eighths to one-half inch deep. Chicory responds well to nitrogen and likes a pH level of 5.6 to 6.2, which will result in optimal growth. It can grow well on a wide range of soil types, including sandy soil and silt loams, but in southern areas, chicory prefers well-drained soils. It grows best on high-fertility soils with moderate to good drainage. The best time to plant chicory is around mid-spring to take advantage of warming conditions during establishment. Chicory can also be sown effectively in the late summer or early fall, but it needs at least six weeks before the first frost arrives. I prefer to plant it in mid-May to mid-June.

Chicory is a terrific plant to extend the grazing season well into late December. Over the years, I have noted deer are attracted to chicory all year long but eat it most heartily from late October through December. Once you discover how easy it is to grow and how attractive it is to deer, chicory will quickly become one of your favorite and most successful winter-hardy plantings.

Forage Chicory Recap

- **Seeding Rates:** Broadcast at six to eight pounds per acre prior to an expected rainfall when possible.
- **pH Level:** Levels of 5.6 to 6.2.
- **Planting Time:** In the North, chicory can be planted from early May to early August.
- **Maturity:** Thirty to sixty days.
- **Digestibility:** Extremely high—about 95 percent!
- **Depth of Seed:** Plant three-eighths to one-half inch below the surface.

- **Fertilizer:** At planting use 300 to 400 pounds of T-19-19-19.
- **Companion Mixes:** I suggest planting chicory as a stand-alone food plot. However, it does well when mixed with other brassicas, clovers, and small grains.
- **Crude Protein Levels:** From 10 to 30 percent.
- **Overgrazing:** Generally not an issue after thirty days.
- **Extends Grazing Season:** Deer eat chicory intently from October through January.
- **Temperatures:** Withstands winter temperatures well.
- **Avoid:** Do not allow flower stems to exceed ten inches in height.

Small Burnett: This plant is a perennial forb. I use a brand called delar small burnett. It is an evergreen herbaceous flowering plant that remains green well into winter and will not freeze out easily, which makes it an excellent winter-hardy planting for all wildlife, including whitetail deer, which relish it. It is an enduring plant that can live for long periods of time. It does well in open areas but will grow in areas that are somewhat shaded, too. Small burnett is adaptable to most parts of the United States and some areas of Canada. It is a favorite seed used by many experienced food plot managers as part of their wildlife food plots, especially in northern areas. It does best when planted in upland well-drained soils and needs at least ten inches of rainfall per year. Small burnett prefers pH levels between 6.0 and 7.0 but will tolerate a wide variety from 4.6 to 7.5.

As a stand-alone crop, small burnett can be seeded into a well-prepared soil bed about one fourth to one half of an inch deep at fifteen to twenty pounds per acre. When mixed with other seeds, use about five pounds per acre. I have successfully planted it in May at a depth of one fourth of an inch using a cultipacker. As with a majority of my plantings, I seed it when I expect a rainfall. Delar small burnett germinates quickly with its flowers blooming as early as May. Small burnett could be planted as a mix with grains, such as rye, wheat, barley, or triticale, or with winter-hardy clovers, such as jumbo ladino, Alice white clover, or marathon red clover. I have planted small burnett with the clovers mentioned above and with chicory. Fertilize small burnett with two hundred to three hundred

Small Burnett is another winter-hardy forb that deer love to eat. Like chicory it will provide excellent forage throughout the deer season. Photo Credit: Frigid Forage.

pounds of T-19 at planting. Delar small burnett grows from twelve to eighteen inches tall. What also makes small burnett intriguing to plant as a food plot, at least to me, is that it is literally a food plot for deer and people. As a Ferengi of *Star Trek* would say, *hu*-mans can eat small burnett, too! The leaves have a pleasant flavor that tastes like a cucumber and can be used in cold drinks and salads.

Small burnett is one of the first plants deer and wildlife will feed on in early spring, and it is definitely one of the best seeds to use as a top-notch deer attractor. Deer like the foliage because of its cucumber-like flavor. Deer, elk, and turkey will dig through the snow to get to small burnett because, even then, it still maintains a high level of palatable forage for deer and other wildlife. In fact, all wildlife benefits from a food plot of delar small burnett.

Small Burnett Recap

- **Seeding Rates:** Broadcast at fifteen to twenty pounds per acre prior to a rainfall when practical.
- **pH Level:** Likes a pH level between 6.0 and 7.0.
- **Planting Time:** In the North it can be planted from April to May.
- **Germination:** Can be slow in some areas, but generally it germinates quickly.
- **Depth of Seed:** Plant one quarter to one half inch below the surface.
- **Fertilizer:** At planting 300 to 400 pounds of T 19-19-19.
- **Companion Mixes:** Can be planted alone or mixed with grains, clovers, and chicory.
- **Overgrazing:** Can be susceptible to overgrazing in areas of high deer densities.
- **Extends Grazing Season:** From late October into December.
- **Temperatures:** Withstands very cold temperatures.
- **Caution:** Requires mowing in late summer for best production.
- **Avoid:** Top seeding.
- **Cultivated Plants**

Sugar Beets: Beets are cultivated tubers that provide a leafy, palatable, nutritious food source for deer and other wildlife. Sugar beets, especially, are to deer as candy is to children. Once deer discover what sugar beets are, they will consume them enthusiastically. Deer benefit twice from sugar beets by eating the leaves and the root. Sugar beets have exceptional winter hardiness, which provides deer with high sugar and protein contents. They also provide high digestibility, and deer benefit substantially from the beet mineral intake.

Deer will start to feed on the tops of sugar beets regularly starting in September. They will have dug up the bulbs as late as December on our land. Photo Credit: Ronald Groskopf of www.bucklunch.com.

Sugar beets have helped tremendously to draw deer into my food plots from late October through January, which makes them one of the ultimate plantings for hunting season. Deer will paw them up even when the sugar beet plots are covered by several inches of snow until they have eaten every last beet. Once there have been several hard frosts, deer will enthusiastically and relentlessly visit sugar beet crops at all hours of the day and night.

Sugar beets are a top-notch choice for deer managers who want to assure themselves of seeing deer in their food plots during daylight hours from late October to January. Some managers swear that sugar beets provide the highest digestibility of any forage— up to 98 percent! Their sugar content can range as high as 20 percent, and their protein content is between 12 to 15 percent. Those figures are hard for an overwhelming number of food plot plants to even match, never mind come close to beating.

It is crucial to make sure that your intended sugar beets plot is weed-free prior to planting the seeds to guard against crop failure. Plant in April or May in the North when an expected rainfall is coming, and fertilize them at planting. Sugar beets must be rotated every year. It is not recommended to plant them in the same plot two years in a row.

I have said this in many other writings, but I state it once again here. When it comes to buying sugar beets, your best choice will be to buy them from a company called BuckLunch (www.bucklunch.com). By far, they have the most reliable product. More importantly, if you have questions, you can actually talk to a human being by calling or emailing Ronald Groskopf at Ronald.Groskopf@beetseed.com. Ron is pleasant to deal with and is a storehouse of knowledge when it comes to anything related to planting sugar beets.

Sugar Beet Recap

- **Seeding Rates:** Broadcast alone at six to eight pounds per acre.
- **Maturity:** Short growing season of ninety to one hundred days.
- **pH Level:** Prefers pH levels of 6.5 to 7.5.

- **Planting Time:** Plant in early spring.
- **Depth of Seed:** Sow ½ to 1½ inches deep in a well-prepared plot. Compact the plot to attain the best soil-to-seed contact. Plant preferably prior to a predicted rainfall.
- **Fertilizer:** At planting use 400 pounds of T-19-19-19 and 25 pounds of manganese sulfate if necessary.
- **Companion Mixes:** Plant alone.
- **Crude Protein Levels:** From 12 to 15 percent.
- **Sugar Content:** About 20 percent.
- **Digestibility:** Near 98 percent!
- **Overgrazing:** Generally not an issue after thirty days.
- **Extends Grazing Season:** Well into December and later.
- **Temperatures:** Withstands extreme late-winter temperatures.
- **Caution:** Plant no more than one year in the same plot, then rotate sugar beets to other plots for three consecutive years following.
- **Avoid:** Do not plant in soils of pure clay.

If you want to attract deer to during hunting season, you must plant sugar beets. As my friend Ron Groskopf emphatically assures me—"Whitetail deer love sugar beets!" Visit www.bucklunch.com for more information. Photo Credit: Fiduccia Enterprises.

Fescue and Other Grasses

Bariane Tall Fescue: There are many grasses that can be planted, but the only two I have found to be truly attractive to deer are bariane tall fescue and Timothy grass. Bariane is classified as having excellent winter hardiness, and Timothy is classified as a perennial cold-hardy bunchgrass. Both are highly adapted to northern climates.

Timothy is among the most palatable grasses for deer and will attract them throughout the spring and summer and into late fall. Bariane tall fescue, however, is categorized as having made the ideal grass to include in this chapter because of its hardiness.

Bariane tall fescue, a popular late-maturing, endophyte-free fescue, is also soft-leafed, which makes it an excellent component when planted with alfalfa or other clover or legume mixtures for grazing deer and other wildlife. Moreover, bariane has superior tolerance when intensively grazed.

Bariane is also a digestible variety with high palatability to deer. Tall fescues are adaptable species and grow well in dry or wet conditions, so they are a good choice for wetlands. Tall fescues are also persistent, and they typically grow early in the spring.

Be careful if you buy older types of tall fescues; they are not as palatable to deer because of their rough leaves and woody texture. Barenbrug's tall fescue, however, has newer, much softer-leafed varieties that are high yielding with significantly improved palatability and digestibility. Many fescue varieties contain a harmful fungus called endophyte that makes the plant less palatable. All barenbrug forage varieties are either endophyte-free, endophyte friendly, or have a beneficial endophyte that does not harm domestic or wild animals. So, if you have been thinking about planting a grass as part of your food plot program, why not plant yet another winter-hardy plant that will be sure to help draw deer to your property?

Bariane Tall Fescue Recap

- **Seeding Rates:** Broadcast alone at twenty to twenty-five pounds per acre or in a mix at four to ten pounds per acre.
- **pH Level:** Prefers pH levels of 6.0 to 6.5.
- **Planting Time:** Plant in spring or in fall.
- **Depth of Seed:** Plant one quarter of an inch deep in a well-prepared plot that is well compacted for best soil-to-seed contact just prior to a rainfall if possible.
- **Establishment:** Timothy and bariane are easy to start.
- **Fertilizer:** At planting use 300 to 400 pounds of T-19-19-19.
- **Companion Mixes:** Plant with winter-hardy clovers or other legumes.
- **Palatability:** High.
- **Overgrazing:** Generally not an issue after spring green up.
- **Extends Grazing Season:** From summer to early winter or longer.
- **Temperatures:** Has excellent winter hardiness.

Food Plot Consulting

For more than twenty years, I have been a professional wildlife food plot consultant. During that time, I have visited innumerable properties throughout the Northeast and evaluated lands to help clients develop sound food plot management plans. During an on-site visit, I share my experience in a down-to-earth, easy to understand manner. Whether a property owner is a first-time food plotter or a seasoned veteran, the insights provided help take their food plot management plans to the next level.

The advice shared with clients is guaranteed to save them time, frustration, and money. A sound food plot plan is a prerequisite to improving anyone's hunting success and developing a more appealing piece of property for deer and other wildlife to utilize.

As a food plotter, nothing is more irritating to deal with than working hard to plant a piece of land only to end up having less success with the plantings than expected or, worse yet, to have them fail entirely.

What an On-Site Evaluation Includes

Of course, evaluations vary from property to property. However, they cover all aspects of potential seed plantings, hard and soft mast trees, shrubs, and improvement of naturally occurring vegetation. An on-site evaluation should cover the following points to improve your hunting strategy.

- **Where to Plant Food Plots:** Like most successful farming practices, food plots grow best in areas that have historically provided flourishing vegetation growth.
- **Creating a Refuge:** A refuge or sanctuary is a key element for keeping deer using a property on a consistent basis. In fact, several families of does, yearlings, and fawns will eventually use a sanctuary as their primary bedding area. This is only true, however, if a refuge is created and used exactly as the dictionary defines the word. Any size property can dedicate sufficient acreage to create a successful large or small sanctuary.
- **Is it Possible to Hold Deer on a Property?:** The realistic and frank answer to the question is NO. With that said, however, the advice provided from years of proven tactics will encourage deer, particularly adult bucks, to use any given piece of property much more often. The visit will also include information about creating buck and doe beds, using low-impact hunting tactics, creating water holes, specific tactics to attract deer from surrounding properties, defining pinch points, using inside corners, and other strategies for attracting deer.
- **Creating Instant Deer Cover:** A primary way to create instant cover that also provides an ongoing source of food is through hinge-cutting. I also cover improving the overall health and production of natural vegetation, including bushes, berries, oak trees, forbs, hard and soft mast, browse, and even weeds. Did you know that deer eat many different types of weeds—or that poison sumac and poison ivy are preferred food sources for deer?
- **Reducing Predator Populations:** Lastly, I provide a simple but extremely effective tactic to significantly reduce coyote and bear predation of deer on a piece of hunting land without ever having to lift a firearm or set a trap.

If you would like to enhance your food plot management plans by scheduling an on-site visit, email me at peter@fiduccia.com.

Chapter Twenty-Seven

Field Dressing: Step-By-Step

To ensure the most flavorful tasting game meat, it is essential for a hunter to know how to quickly and effectively field dress harvested game, thereby assuring the animal will go from the field to the table, in *prime* eating condition. The tips and instructions in this DIY section will help you eliminate "gamey" tasting meat from the animals you shoot. There should be no doubt that knowing how to properly field dress deer and other big game animals is *the* most important element for quality, terrific-tasting, game meat.

Before the advent of the most helpful field-dressing tool: the "Butt-Out," one of the most crucial steps in the field dressing process was removing the anal tract and bladder. The key task at hand is to do this without puncturing either and thereby causing unwanted spillage within the body cavity. Leaky fluids and materials from a deer's anal tract and bladder can ruin the taste of game meat or, worse yet, contaminate the meat.

Cutting around and removing the anal canal on deer is, however, an unavoidable and necessary step when field dressing. With Hunter's Specialties Butt Out® big game field dressing tool, hunters can quickly and easily remove the anal alimentary canal on deer and deer-sized game.

STEP # 1
Turn the deer over on its back on as flat a surface as possible. The head, however, should be slightly higher than the rest of the body, so that gravity will help slide the entrails out of the body cavity more easily when they are cut free.

Photo Credit: CPI.

STEP # 2

If you use a Butt-Out tool, the next step is to remove the anal tract. Insert the Butt-Out all the way into the deer's anal cavity and push it into the anal tract as far as you can (all the way to the end of the tool's handle). Next, slowly turn the tool until you feel it "catch." This is typically not more than eight to ten turns. Then, slowly and steadily pull the tool out. It will remove about a ten-inch section of the deer's intestine to the

Photo Credit: Hunter's Specialties.

outside of the body cavity. Almost the entire section will be filled with deer pellets (dung). Where the pellets end the anal tract will appear white. This is where you can cut off the intestine and lay it aside. Now the rest of the field dressing process will be accomplished much more quickly and effectively.

STEP # 3

Make a shallow two- to three-inch long cut on the side of the penis (or the udder if it is a doe). Separate the external reproductive organs of a buck from the abdominal wall. If it is a doe, remove the udder. Milk sours quickly in the udder, causing a foul smell and can give the meat a very disagreeable taste. Check the local game laws before removing the genitals. Some states require that they remain attached to the carcass. If they can be

Photo Credit: CPI.

removed, however, carefully cut them free of the skin and let them hang over the back of the anus. It is important not to cut them free of the viscera at this point.

STEP #4

Straddle the deer while you are facing its head. Pinch a piece of skin in the belly section and pull it up and away from the body. Insert the tip of the knife blade and make a very shallow slit into the muscle and skin which will prevent accidently puncturing the intestines. Make the cut just long enough to insert your first two fingers.

Photo Credit: CPI.

Form a "V" with your with your index and first fingers and *very carefully* continue to slit a thin layer of abdomen muscle and skin all the way up to the sternum of the rib cage. As you make this cut, the intestines and stomach will begin to push out from the body cavity but will not fall entirely free as they are still attached by connective tissue.

STEP #5

If you are *not* going to mount the deer's head, the next step is to make a cut through the rib cage. While straddling the deer, slightly bend your knees and face the head and with the knife blade facing *up* position it under the breastbone. Place both your hands over each other and around the handle of the knife for leverage. With both hands, cut through the cartilage in the center of the breastbone and continue cutting

Photo Credit: CPI.

up through the neck. *If you intend to mount the deer's head stop at the brisket line and skip steps 5 and 6.*

STEP #6

Once the neck is open, free the windpipe and esophagus by cutting the connective tissue. Grasp them firmly and pull them down toward the body cavity while continuing to cut any connective tissues as you proceed.

Photo Credit: CPI.

STEP # 7

If you *are* going to mount the deer's head you will have to tie off the gullet (throat) and then push it forward as far as possible and cut it free from the windpipe. Also cut around the diaphragm and remove the connective tissue of the lungs and other organs. Then *carefully* reach up as far as you can into the throat area—as high as your arms will take you—to sever the esophagus and trachea. Be aware of where your knife blade is, as most knife accidents occur during this step where you can't see what you're cutting.

STEP # 8

If you haven't already removed the rectum with a Butt-Out tool, it is at this point you will have to address that job. Some prefer to remove the rectal tract and urethra by slicing between the hams or split the pelvic bone. Others remove the anal tract first by placing the point of a knife to the side of the rectum and make a cut that completely encircles the rectum. Position the tip of the blade into the pelvic area and cut around the entire anus. Free the rectum and urethra by loosening the connective tissue with the tip of the knife blade. To prevent any leakage from the anal tract or the urethra, tie it off with a stout piece of string. The next step is the

Photo Credit: CPI.

tricky part of the whole process. Push the tied-off rectum and urethra under the pelvic bone and into the body cavity. If you choose to, you may opt to split the pelvic bone which makes removing the rectum and urethra easier—but it requires using a stout knife or small axe.

Step # 9

Grasp one side of the rib cage firmly with one hand and pull it open. Cut all remaining connective tissue along the diaphragm free from the rib opening down to the backbone. Stay as close to the rib cage as possible. Be careful not to puncture the stomach, intestines, or any other internal matter. Now repeat the same thing on the other side so both cuts meet over the backbone.

Photo Credit: CPI.

Reach up and grasp the windpipe and esophagus and pull them down and away from the body cavity. Detach the heart and liver. Now all innards should be free of any connective tissue allowing you to scoop out all remaining entrails onto the ground along with as much blood as possible from the body cavity.

STEP # 10

Once all the entrails have been eviscerated from the deer's body cavity, it is important to cool the cavity as quickly as possible. Prop the body cavity open with a stick or a very handy tool made by Outdoor Edge called Rib-Cage Spreader.

If at all possible, wash out the body cavity with water or snow. Remove as much dirt, debris, excess blood, etc., as possible. Hanging the deer right away will also greatly

Photo Credit: CPI.

enhance the cooling process. If hanging it isn't possible—turn it over — open cavity down and let any remaining blood or fluids drain away.

DID YOU KNOW?

- There is no real benefit in cutting a deer's throat to "bleed-it-out."
- Using a small knife with a three- to five-inch blade is the ideal size knife to use when field dressing a deer.
- Cooling the deer as soon as possible will help retain the overall flavor of the meat.
- To "age" deer meat properly, it must be placed in a refrigerated cooler with the temperature consistently ranging between 38 and 42 degrees Fahrenheit. Hanging it in a tree to "age" for days or even longer periods of time only causes the meat to decay over time and makes it much *less* flavorful and tender.

Chapter Twenty-Eight

Skinning a Deer Made Easy

Once you have properly field dressed your deer, the next step to better tasting venison is to quickly remove the deer's hide in order to cool down the meat. This do-it-yourself tip will demonstrate how to skin a deer using nothing more than a sharp knife, sharpening steel, small saw, gambrel, and deer hoist. These tools are all that are needed to make this task go smoothly and help provide you with better tasting wild game.

SKINNING TIP # 1

Peel the deer's skin (and hide) over the hind leg to reveal the large tendon located at the back of the leg. Carefully slit any connective tissue between the bone and the large tendon. Next, place the end of the gambrel between the leg bone and the tendon (see photo). Now hoist the carcass to a height at which it is comfortable to work.

Photo Credit: CPI.

SKINNING TIP # 2

With the knife blade turned away from the carcass, cut the hide along the inner side of each leg. Turn the knife blade back toward the meat and begin skinning the hide around the leg (see photo). Pull hard on the hide with your hands once you reach the outside of each leg.

Photo Credit: CPI.

SKINNING TIP # 3

With a firm grip, pull the remaining hide down the outside of *each* leg until the skinned part reaches the deer's tail. Separate the tail as close to the deer's rump as possible, being careful not to cut into the meat. The tail should remain inside or attached to the hide. Continue skinning the hide along the deer's back by pulling the hide in a downward motion with your hand. Slice it free as close to the meat as possible.

Photo Credit: CPI.

SKINNING TIP # 4

Once you reach the middle of the deer's back, grip the hide with both hands and continue to pull it down. Use the tip of your knife blade only when you need to free the hide in places where it hangs up, while being extra careful not to slice into or cut off pieces of meat still attached to the hide. Also, be careful not to cut holes in the hide while using the tip of the knife blade. With your hands, continue to peel the hide down the deer's back and around the rib cage until the hide reaches the front shoulders.

Photo Credit: CPI.

SKINNING TIP # 5

At this point, cut along the inside of each of the front legs with your knife and peel the hide off the front legs. With a stout knife or butcher saw, remove the front legs just above the first joint, located slightly above the hooves of the deer.

SKINNING TIP # 6

Keep pulling, cutting, and peeling the hide as far down the deer's neck as possible. Once you have pulled the hide to the lowest point on the neck, cut the deer's head free of the body with a saw. Once the hide is removed from the deer, spread it out on a clean, flat surface with the hair facing down. Scrape off any remaining pieces of fat, tallow, meat and blood. The hide is now ready to be salted, if it is going to be preserved.

Photo Credit: CPI.

Photo Credit: CPI.

DID YOU KNOW?

- It is much easier to skin a deer or other game animal while the animal's hide is still warm.
- To make the job of skinning go more quickly, hang the deer by a pulley so you can raise or lower it to eye level without straining. This will also prevent you from getting a stiff back and/or neck. I highly recommend a deer pulley made by Buster Greenway of E-Z Kut Ratchet Pruner.
- To prevent the hair of the deer's hide getting on the meat, cut through the skin from the inside out. By skinning the hide in this manner, your knife will slip *between* the hairs instead of *slicing* them in half and getting them all over the meat. It will also prevent your knife from dulling as quickly.
- To avoid accidently removing useable pieces of meat, use as sharp a knife as possible while skinning the hide from the deer. Remember to touch the knife blade up repeatedly (with a steel) as you trim the hide from the deer.

QUARTERING A DEER IN SEVEN EASY STEPS

In today's economy, it is practical to try and save the costs (approximately $100) of taking your deer to a professional butcher to have it processed. With a little patience and information, you can easily quarter your deer at home—even though it may seem like a daunting task at first. The reality to make this "job" a convenient and fun project, simply requires understanding basic deer anatomy and the portions of the deer you will be working with.

Many folks believe that quartering a deer at home involves a lot of expensive butchering tools, takes a lot of time, and requires a large working area. But in reality, all the tools that are necessary to get the job done quickly and easily are a *quality* knife, sharpening steel, and a small saw. With a little know-how, anyone can remove a deer's forequarters and hindquarters, tenderloins, ribs, and backstrap at home by following these simple step-by-step directions.

STEP # 1

Begin by using a sharp hunting or butchering knife and push the front leg away from the deer's skinned carcass. Place the knife with the sharp edge *down* and cut the connective meat and tissue free from between the leg and the rib cage. Continue cutting through this section until you reach the shoulder. The process becomes much easier if someone holds the carcass securely while you cut it. If you don't have help available, another option is to tie the opposite leg to an anchor point to help steady the carcass.

Photo Credit: CPI.

STEP # 2

At the point where the front leg reaches the shoulder, remove it by cutting between the shoulder blade and the back. Repeat steps one and two on the opposite front leg. Once both legs are off, remove the layer of brisket meat that is located over the deer's ribs.

Photo Credit: CPI.

STEP # 3

Now, cut the meat at the base of the neck, which will enable you to cut the backstrap free. With your knife blade facing *down* and the tip of blade pressed closely to the bone, guide the knife slowly down toward the rump of the deer. Be extra careful not to cut into the backstrap in order to avoid leaving any of its prime meat behind. Once you have reached the rump area you can cut off the backstrap.

Photo Credit: CPI.

STEP # 4

Next, cut one of the hind legs off to expose the ball-and-socket joint. Separate the joint by *forcefully* pushing the leg backward until the joint pops apart. Now cut through the joint. Carefully work your knife around the tailbone and pelvis area until the leg becomes totally free. Repeat this step on the opposite rear leg.

Photo Credit: CPI.

STEP # 5

After trimming away the flank meat below the last rib, you can begin to cut the tenderloins from the inside of the deer's body cavity.

Photo Credit: CPI.

STEP # 6

To remove the ribs, simply saw along the backbone of the deer. Cut around the base of the neck and then snap off the backbone. Set aside the neck and head. Carefully bone-out as much useable meat from the neck as possible. It makes terrific chopped meat or can be used for sausage.

STEP # 7

To enhance the taste and tenderness of the ribs, carefully trim away all the gristle and fat at the bottom of the rib sections. If you want to make the ribs into short ribs—saw them in half. If you prefer not to eat the ribs, don't disregard them! Instead, bone the meat from the ribs and grind it into sausage or burger meat.

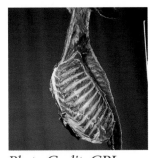

Photo Credit: CPI.

Photo Credit: CPI.

DID YOU KNOW?

- Flank meat is often used to make jerky. The flank cut can also be ground up and used as burger meat.

- By removing the tenderloins *before properly aging* your deer, you will prevent the tenderloins from turning black and dehydrating. Removing them before aging the meat will dramatically increase their flavor and tenderness.

- The primary cause of bad tasting game meat is caused from not removing as much of the "silver-skin" (the shiny, slimly looking connective tissue) and the tallow (fat) from the meat as possible. This is how venison becomes "gamey" tasting. Removing every piece of tallow is a time consuming process. It is well worth the extra effort, however, in order to get the best tasting wild game. Fat from domestic animals imparts a tasty flavor to the meat. That is definitely not the case with wild animals, particularly with antlered game. By removing as much silver skin and tallow as possible, you'll improve the overall flavor of your venison tenfold!

Chapter Twenty-Nine

Venison Table Fare

When the fruits of your tactics have paid off, it's time to enjoy savory venison. Here are several of (my wife) Kate's recipes. In addition to being my business partner since the mid-eighties, Kate has capitalized on both her cooking skills and the culinary cuisine we have enjoyed at various outfitters throughout North America.

Some of the recipes come from her many cookbooks; they are noted accordingly.

VENISON FILET WELLINGTON

Ingredients

2 to 3 pounds venison loin, well-trimmed
2 tablespoons clarified butter, room
    temperature
2 to 4 slices bacon
2 tablespoons butter
3 tablespoons olive oil
2 tablespoons chopped shallots
½ pound fresh white or straw mushrooms,
    finely chopped

1 egg, separated
2 tablespoons cold water
1 sheet frozen puff pastry, thawed per
    package directions
flour for rolling out pastry
1 cup shredded fresh spinach leaves
½ cup shredded Swiss cheese
Hunter's Sauce

Preparation

Heat oven to 325°F. Heat a large, heavy-bottomed skillet over medium-high heat. While the skillet is heating, rub the venison with clarified butter. Add the loin to the hot skillet and sear to a deep brown color on all sides. Transfer the loin to dish and set aside to cool to room temperature. Meanwhile, add bacon to same skillet and fry until cooked but not crisp. Set aside on paper towel-lined plate.

While the loin is cooling, prepare the filling. In a medium skillet, melt the two tablespoons of butter in the oil over medium heat. Add the shallots and sauté until golden, stirring constantly; most of the liquid evaporates. Set mushroom mixture aside to cool.

Beat the egg white lightly in a small bowl. In another small bowl, lightly beat the egg yolk and water. Set both bowls aside.

To prepare the shell, roll out pastry on a lightly floured surface to a rectangle one to two inches larger on all sides than the loin. Spread the cooled mushroom mixture over the pastry, leaving one inch clear around the edges. Layer the spinach, cheese and bacon in a thin trip over the center; the strip should be about as wide as the loin. Place the loin on top of the bacon. Brush the edges of the pastry with egg white; this will help hold the pastry shell together while it is baking. Wrap the pastry around the loin and crimp the edges very well to seal. Turn the pastry-wrapped loin over so the seam side is down. Place onto a baking sheet. Brush pastry with egg yolk mixture; this will provide a beautiful glaze to the Wellington.

Bake for 10 to 15 minutes, or until pastry is golden brown. The loin should have reached an internal temperature of 130°F. Remove from oven. Slice into individual portions and serve immediately with Hunter's Sauce. (excerpted from one of Kate's first book, *The Venison Cookbook*, available from Skyhorse Publishing and Amazon. com.)

VENISON FILET WITH MORELS

Every time I take any big game animals, especially a whitetail, I remove the tenderloin as quickly as possible. No matter how long I have been doing this, it never fails each time I begin to remove them, I'm already planning in my head how I will cook this choicest of all the cuts. One way to enhance tenderloin to its max is with this recipe!

Morel mushrooms are a wonderful delicacy that must be cleaned properly before eating. The simplest way is to slice them lengthwise, and dunk in heavily salted, heated water. There are all sorts of critters and dirt that can find a nice home in these delectable fungi. Jostle them around in the pot for about 5 minutes. Then drain on a paper towel. These mushrooms are best eaten fresh but can be dried for later use, too.

Ingredients

1 pound venison tenderloin, cut into one-half inch thick steaks
one-half cup flour
2 tablespoons pepper
½ pound butter (2 sticks)
2 tablespoons freshly chopped chives (or wild onion tops)

⅓ cup sherry
½ pound morel mushrooms, cleaned, rinsed and chopped
2 teaspoons flour
⅓ cup beef stock
salt and pepper to taste

Preparation

In a large Dutch oven, heat one stick of the butter until sizzling. Press the pepper into the loin steaks and then dip them into the flour. Sauté them in the butter until just browned on both sides. Do not overcook. Cook them until about medium-rare. Remove and keep warm.

Add in the remaining butter, chives, sherry, and mushrooms to the pan. Cook about 5-7 minutes until the mushrooms become tender. Mix the flour with the beef stock and stir to get out any lumps. Add this to the pan to thicken the sauce. Season with salt and pepper. Plate the venison steaks and pour the mushroom sauce over! Serves 4. (excerpted from Kate's best-selling title, *Cabin Cooking*, available from Skyhorse Publishing and Amazon.com.)

VENISON STEW WITH BARLEY

Since this stew is prepared in a skillet, make sure you have one that's large enough – at least 12 inches in diameter. The aroma while this stew is cooking will have you fighting back hungry ones until it's time to eat!

Serves: 4
Prep Time: 30 minutes
Cooking Time: 2 hours

Ingredients

½ pound pearl onions★

9 large fresh shiitake mushrooms, stems removed and discarded (½ to ¾ lb. white mushrooms may be substituted)

2 cups peeled, cubed butternut squash (1-inch cubes)

1 tablespoon canola oil

1 ¼ teaspoon crumbled dried thyme, divided

1 ½ lbs. boneless venison rump, cut into 1-inch cubes, all connective tissue removed

Seasoned pepper (such as McCormick's California Style Blend Garlic Pepper)

3 cups beef stock or canned unsalted beef broth

1 bay leaf

1 large clove garlic, minced

¾ cup pearl barley

Water as needed (approx. ¾ cup)

Chopped fresh parsley for garnish

Preparation

Heat large saucepan of water to boiling. Add pearl onions and boil for two to three minutes to loosen skins. Drain and cool slightly. Cut off root ends. Squeeze onions from stem end; the onions will slip out of their skins. Place onions in a large bowl.

Cut mushroom caps into halves (white mushrooms may be halved or left whole, depending on size). Add mushrooms, squash, oil, and 1 teaspoon of the thyme to the bowl with onions, stirring gently to coat vegetables. Heat large nonstick skillet over high heat. Add vegetables and sauté until browned. Use slotted spoon to return vegetables to bowl; set aside.

Sprinkle venison with seasoned pepper. Brown seasoned venison cubes in small batches and transfer to a plate. When all venison is browned, return to skillet. Add beef stock, bay leaf, garlic and remaining ¼ teaspoon thyme. Heat to boiling. Reduce heat, cover and simmer for 15 minutes. Stir in barley. Cover and simmer for 45 minutes. Stir vegetables into stew. Cover and simmer until vegetables and barley are tender, about 45 minutes longer; add water as needed during cooking to keep mixture moist. Remove bay leaf. Sprinkle stew with parsley and serve.

★You can use thawed frozen pearl onions in place of fresh if you'd like; it'll save you some time, as you won't need to boil and peel them. (excerpted from *The Venison Cookbook*, available from Skyhorse Publishing and Amazon.com.)

ASIAN VENISON LETTUCE WRAPS

Ingredients

1 ½ pounds ground venison
3 tablespoons sesame oil –
1 teaspoon garlic powder
1 cup water chestnuts (8 oz. can), minced
1 cup mushrooms, minced

¼ cup onions, minced
2 tablespoons hoisin sauce
¼ cup Kate's Asian Grill Sauce
Lettuce leaves
Chinese mustard

Preparation

Heat a large sauté pan over medium heat. Add 1 tablespoon sesame oil to warm slightly. Add in the ground venison and cook until it is no longer pink. While it is cooking, sprinkle with garlic powder. When the meat is browned, remove it from the pan. Do not drain. Let it cool slightly.

Combine the cooked venison, mushrooms, water chestnuts, and minced onions in a bowl. Return empty pan to medium heat. Add 2 tablespoons sesame oil and add in venison mixture. Season with hoisin sauce and Kate's Asian Grill sauce. Mix well to let all flavors blend together. Serve in lettuce leaves and top each portion with a bit of Chinese mustard.

BOURSIN STEAKHOUSE VENISON POCKETS

Ingredients
1 to 1 ½ pounds venison loin steak, thin,
¼ cup Kate's Gourmet Steakhouse Grill Sauce
1 medium onion, sliced
4 ounces Boursin cheese (herbed cream cheese)
2 large pita pockets, halved

Preparation
Place the Steakhouse Grill sauce and the venison steak in a zip-top bag and let marinate about 30 minutes.

Preheat the grill for about 20 minutes. The grill should be hot enough that you can hold your hand over it for only a few seconds.

Place the onions slices on the grill. To make sure the slices do not fall through the grates, place them in a hinged basket. Cook until they are browned on both sides. Place the steaks on the grill and cook for about 1-2 minutes each side, depending upon the thickness of the steak. Remove when it is medium rare. Cut into slices and set aside.

Spread Boursin cheese (or any soft herbed cheese) on the inside of each of the pita pockets. Place a slice of grilled onion and some steak sliced inside the pocket. Repeat for the remaining pockets. Place the assembled pita pockets on the grill and heat for about 30 seconds each side.

Serve immediately. Side accompaniments may include sour cream, salsa, guacamole, chopped black olives, or sliced jalapenos. (excerpted from Kate's *Grillin' N' Chili'n'* cookbook available from Skyhorse Publishing and Amazon.com.)

FAST AND EASY TERIYAKI JERKY

Prep Time: 15 minutes
Marinating Time: 8 to 12 hours
Drying Time:
    Oven: 4 to 6 hours (150 to 200 degrees with oven door slightly ajar)
    Electric Dehydrator: 5 hours (145 degrees)
Yield: 1 to 1 ½ pounds of dry jerky

Ingredients

5 pounds venison meat (preferably a sirloin or round cut)
2–8 ounce bottles teriyaki sauce
1–8 ounce bottle soy sauce
2 teaspoons black pepper

Preparation

Rinse meat thoroughly in cold water to remove any foreign matter (hair, blood, etc.). Trim all fat, tallow and silver skin completely from the meat. Slice meat into ¼ to ½ strips, across the grain.

Place all ingredients (except the meat) in a sturdy zip-top plastic bag. Close bag. Hold bag securely at the top, shake vigorously to mix ingredients well. Open bag, add meat and shake vigorously, until meat is well covered. Allow to marinade in refrigerator for 8 to 12 hours, turning bag frequently.

Drain meat well. Discard marinade. DO NOT REUSE! Blot the meat strips dry on paper towels.

Place meat on dehydrator trays or oven racks, making sure not to allow the strips of meat to touch.

Allow the strips to dry in the oven or in an electric dehydrator. When the jerky is done, it will crack but not break when bent.

(This and the following two recipes are excerpted from Kate's latest book, *The Jerky Bible*, available from Skyhorse Publishing and Amazon.com)

HIGH MOUNTAIN GROUND VENISON JERKY

I enjoyed the end-product the first time I tried making jerky with a jerky gun. For those who are new to making jerky and want to try a simple method to making consistent product, give this method a try.

Prep Time: 15 minutes;
Marinating Time: 32 hours
Cooking Time: Oven (150 degrees—4 to 5 hours)
   Electric Dehydrator (4 hours—145–155 degrees)
Yield: ¼ pound jerky strips

Ingredients
1 pound ground venison (no additional fat added)
¼ teaspoon nitrite
4 teaspoons Hi Mountain seasoning
¼ cup of water
Additional Item: Jerky gun

Preparation
Dissolve the nitrite and seasonings in the water. Place the ground venison in a mixing bowl. Pour the dissolved seasonings over the ground venison and mix well. Form the meat into a log. Refrigerate about 1 ½ days.

   Place the meat into the jerky gun. With uniform pressure, make strips of the jerky onto the dehydrator trays. Try to make them the same thickness and length. Give enough space in between the strips to allow air to circulate. After about 3 hours, turn the strips.

   After 4 hours, remove a few pieces and let them cool. Test them by bending the strips. If there is moisture present, let the meat cook a little longer. If the strips bend and do not break, they are done. If the strips bend and break in half, they have been overcooked.

   Once the strips are dried thoroughly, let them cool. Then store them in an airtight container or vacuum seal them in plastic bags for longer storage.

10-PT WHISKY JERKY

Prep Time: 15 minutes
Marinating Time: 24 to 48 hours, depending upon how strong of a marinade flavor you want
Drying Time: Oven (150 degrees—4 to 5 hours)
   Electric Dehydrator (4 hours—145–155 degrees)
Yield: ¼ pound jerky strips

Ingredients
1 pound of venison (moose, deer, elk, caribou) sirloin
⅛ cup Worcestershire sauce
⅛ cup soy sauce
1 teaspoon hickory liquid smoke
¼ teaspoon garlic powder
¼ teaspoon onion powder
¼ teaspoon black pepper
1 tablespoon honey
3–4 tablespoons TenPoint Whisky

Preparation
Use a cut of sirloin or loin that is slightly frozen. Try to keep the slices as uniform as possible to ensure similar cooking times. Cut the slices about 3/8-inch to ¼-inch thick. This will make slicing easier. Use a sharp knife or electric knife and cut thin strips against the grain of the meat, for more tender, yet brittle jerky. Or, if you prefer jerky that is more chewy, slice the meat with the grain.

   In a large zip-top plastic bag or nonporous bowl, combine all other ingredients and mix well.

   Place the meat strips in the bag with the marinade or in the bowl and mix well. Make sure all slices are covered with the liquid. Cover the bowl tightly or remove as much air from the plastic zip-top bag and seal closed. Let the meat soak in the marinade anywhere from 24 to 48 hours in the refrigerator. Turn the meat a few times to ensure that all surfaces are covered by the marinade.

   Preheat your dehydrator to145°F or your oven to about 150 to 170°F.

   Remove the meat slices from the marinade and throw the marinade away. Pat the slices dry.

Dehydrator: Place the slices on the trays with room in between to allow air to circulate. Leave the meat in the dehydrator for about 4 to 6 hours, turning once after 2 hours.

Oven: Lay the meat strips on an oven rack. Prop the oven door open slightly to allow moisture to escape. Cook for about 4 to 6 hours. Turn the strips once after about 2 hours.

After 4 hours, remove a few pieces and let them cool. Test them by bending the strips. If there is moisture present, let the meat cook a little longer. If the strips bend and do not break, it is done. If the strips bend and break in half, they have been overcooked.

Once the strips are dried thoroughly, let them cool. Then store them in an air-tight container or vacuum seal them in plastic bags for longer storage.

VENISON SCHNITZEL

Prep Time: 10 minutes
Cooking Time: 15 minutes
Serves: 3 to 4

Ingredients

1 pound venison cutlets, pounded to ¼-to ⅛-inch thick
¼ cup butter (½ stick)
½ to 1 cup sliced onions
1 teaspoon paprika
1 cup low-sodium chicken broth
½ cup sour cream

Preparation

In a sauté pan over medium-high heat, melt the butter. Add in the sliced onions and cook until lightly browned. While the onions are cooking, dredge one side of the cutlet(s) in seasoned flour. Once the onions are lightly browned, remove them from the pan and set aside in a bowl. Place the floured side of the cutlet(s) in the pan and cook a few minutes until lightly browned. Turn, then season with paprika, 1 cup low-sodium chicken broth and then the cooked onions. Turn the heat to low, cover, and let simmer about 10 minutes. Once done, remove the pan from heat. Put the sour cream in a heat resistant dish. Take a few tablespoons of the hot liquid from the pan and mix into the sour cream to temper it. (Increase the temperature of the sour cream so that it does not break apart when you add it into the pan.) Once the sour cream is tempered, stir it in to the pan and season it with salt and pepper, if desired.

Serve as is, or with hot buttered noodles or spatzle (German egg dumplings).

SUMMER AVOCADO VENISON BURGERS

Serves: 4
Prep Time: 15 minutes
Cooking Time: 8 minutes

Ingredients
1 pound ground venison
3 tablespoons grated onion
2 tablespoons chopped parsley
Worcestershire sauce, to taste
salt and freshly ground pepper, to taste
1 ripe avocado, peeled and pitted
2 tablespoons plain nonfat yogurt
1 teaspoon lemon juice
½ teaspoon lime juice
4 Kaiser rolls or hamburger buns, split
hinged grill basket
2 tablespoons canola oil

Preparation
Preheat the grill for about 20 minutes. The grill should be hot enough so that you can hold your hand over it for only a few seconds.

Combine the venison, onion, parsley, Worcestershire sauce, salt and pepper. Form into four patties.

In a small bowl, mash the avocado with the yogurt, lemon, and lime juice. Season with salt and pepper. Set aside.

Lightly oil the hinged grill basket and place the four burgers inside. Grill the burgers for about 3 to 4 minutes each side. Just before the burgers are done, lightly toast the rolls/buns on a cooler section of the grill.

Place each burger on the bottom half of each bun and top with the avocado mixture. To spice it up a bit, top with a splash of Tabasco or other hot sauce! Serve immediately. (excerpted from Kate's *Grillin' N' Chili'n'* cookbook available from Skyhorse Publishing and Amazon.com.)

THAI PITA BURGERS

Serves: 4 or 5
Prep Time: 15 minutes
Cooking Time: 10 minutes

Ingredients
1 pound ground venison
3 tablespoon, Asian peanut sauce
2 scallions, or green onions, finely chopped
1 teaspoon freshly grated ginger root
salt and pepper to taste
1 tablespoon canola oil
4 or 5 large pita halves

Preparation
Preheat the grill for about 20 minutes. The grill should be hot enough so that you can hold your hand over it for only a few seconds.

In a bowl, gently combine the venison, peanut sauce, scallions, and ginger root. Season with salt and pepper.

Shape in to 4 or 5 patties. Lightly brush the patties with oil. Place in a hinged grill basket and grill about 3 minutes per side.

Toast the pita halves on a cooler section of the grill and then place the burgers inside. Top each burger with a slice of fresh tomato.

GRILLED SAUSAGE WRAP

Serves: 4
Prep Time: 20 minutes
Cooking Time: 20–30 minutes

Ingredients
4 venison sausages
1 ¼ cup Italian dressing
1 eggplant, cut in lengthwise slices
1 zucchini, cut in lengthwise slices
2 red bell peppers, cut into wedges
1 red onion, cut into ½-inch slices
2 metal skewers
4 large tortillas, 12-inches
1 tomato, sliced

Preparation
Preheat the grill for about 20 minutes. The grill should be hot enough so that you can hold your hand over it for only a few seconds.

In a large bowl, combine one cup of the dressing, eggplant, zucchini, and red bell peppers. Mix to coat thoroughly. Thread the onion slices on the metal skewers. (This prevents the onion slices from coming apart when turning them.)

Place the sausages on the grill and cook to crisp the outside skin, about 3 to 5 minutes. Turn occasionally. Then move to a cooler section of the grill to continue cooking.

While the sausages are cooking on a cooler section of the grill, begin cooking the vegetables. In batches, remove the vegetables from the dressing and grill them until lightly browned on both sides. Brush the onion slices with some of the dressing before placing on the grill. Grill until slightly brown on each side. Set aside and keep warm.

When the venison sausages are almost done, heat up the tortillas on the grill. Place the tortilla on the grill and heat for about 15–30 seconds each side.

Slice the sausages lengthwise, place two halves in the middle of each tortilla, layer with some grilled vegetables and tomato slices. Drizzle with a little of the remaining Italian dressing (not the amount used for marinating) on the sausage and vegetables and roll up the tortilla. Serve warm.